THE NOBLE EXPERIMENT

True Stories & Hard Truths from My Time in the DEA

by

DAVE GADDIS

ISBN: 978-1-957883-01-4 Paperback
ISBN: 978-1-957883-04-5 eBook
Library of Congress Control Number: 2022907175

Editing by Jessica Balboni and Mysia Haight
Cover design by Dana Bree, StoneBear Design

StoneBear Publishing LLC - 06/2022
Milford, PA 18337

www.stonebearpublishing.com

DEDICATION

A few months ago, I attended back-to-back Celebration of Life events for Jerry Rinehart and Doug Driver, two much-beloved, recently passed DEA agents and longtime friends of mine. The moving presentations and the chosen speakers at both events reminded me, yet again, of the unwavering dedication DEA agents have when it comes to fulfilling their oath of office, a commitment each agent lives by since the very first day they're sworn into duty. Jerry, who'd joined the DEA in 1970, was a kind and generous man. A born mentor, he was always willing to give his time to educate other agents on every aspect of drug enforcement imaginable. His professional accomplishments were vast, and included many well-earned accolades, including a recognition from the US Attorney General for his work against the Medellin drug cartel (including the takedown of Pablo Escobar).

Doug, a North Carolina native, was an incredibly career-driven, devoted family man. Like Jerry, he worked tirelessly throughout his career on a wide range of cases, including the federal indictment and prosecution of Carlos Lehder, an infamous Medellin drug kingpin who owned the Bahamian island of Norman's Cay, and used it as a base through which to smuggle countless tons of cocaine into the US.

These two men represent, to me, everything I respect and hold most dear about my DEA family: loyalty, dedication, diligence, compassion, faith, and, perhaps more than anything, decency of character and spirit. It is to these men and women to whom I dedicate this book: the unsung heroes we refer to as Heaven's Warriors, all of those DEA agents, past, present, and future, who share the common goal of working tirelessly to make this world a better and safer place.

On a more personal note, I also want to give my sincere gratitude and thanks to my fearless partners Alex Dominguez[1], Chris Feistl[2], AD Wright, Bill Baxley, Jim Rose, and Carlos Mitchem. I will cherish their friendship, trust, and loyalty to my grave, as I know they will carry mine.

To my daughters Talia Cristina and Laura Andrea: you are my pride and joy. It means so much for me to have you know more about what your dad did both before and after you came into my life and changed it for the better, forever. Every single day, you two inspire me to be my best, and I will love you, and be there for you, always.

I also dearly love—and am indebted to—my incredible stepdaughter Alisa, her husband Ronny, and my grandchildren Aubrey and Silas. I am so much richer with all of you in my life.

To my mother Laura, my father David, and my sister Shari: you taught me the true meaning and value of hard work, honesty, and compassion for others in need. I owe everything to you, not just my accomplishments, but who I am as a person, colleague, son, brother, parent, and friend.

TESTIMONIALS

"A genuinely crafted story and chronicle by an actual trench warrior. Dave Gaddis gives the reader a rare view behind the curtain that only a legit pro can do. Great mix of white-knuckle and serious prose and thought. Dale!"

—**Alex Dominguez**, DEA Special Agent (Ret.)

* * *

"A well written and captivating story by one of DEA's finest. Dave takes the reader on a thrilling journey, providing a behind the scenes look into operations most never get to see."

Chris Feistl, DEA Special Agent (Ret.) and lead character in NARCOS Colombia

* * *

"An outstanding read. Having known Dave Gaddis for nearly four decades and serving as his partner in the early stages of our careers, I can state with clarity that Dave was exceptionally good at the tasks he carried out for the DEA. Smart, imaginative, innovative, sometimes funny, and steadfastly dedicated to the mission. This book was written by a man who was driven to go after and target those responsible for pushing poison on the countless victims left in their wake. While serving as a sobering reminder of the personal and professional life of a true DEA warrior; Dave also highlights the sometimes glamorous and the far too often daily tedious tasks undertaken by DEA agents around the globe. The Noble Experiment assertively sums up the character of the author for Dave has always been the right man, at the right place, at the right time."

AD Wright, DEA Special Agent-in-Charge, Miami (Ret.)

"Dave Gaddis is a true American hero, who gave it all to make America a better place, bring some of the most dangerous international drug traffickers to justice and to mentor and guide future DEA leaders. What an honor to have worked with Dave on the front lines and a blessing to call him a friend!"

Carlos L. Mitchem, DEA Regional Director-Southern Cone, South America

* * *

Prior to writing a memoir about his long career in DEA, Dave Gaddis realized that almost every tale had been told.

"Hundreds of books documenting the DEA experience have already been written... How would mine differ?" he asked a friend.

In The Noble Experiment, he manages to make each story stand out. Whether it's one of his first raids in Miami or a visit to the DEA psychologist, the anecdotes hold this book together as not just another memoir, but an insightful glimpse into the life of a counter-drug agent. And for the newcomer, there's plenty of booze, bang-bang and testosterone too.

Malcolm Beith, Author & Investigative Journalist

* * *

"Dave Gaddis' "The Noble Experiment: True Stories and Hard Truths From My Time In The DEA" is a sweeping, clear-eyed story of his 25 years as a DEA special- agent, a career that spanned Miami, Central America, Colombia and Mexico. Gaddis' friendly, casual writing provides a first look at his life as an agent on the job. But it also carries an urgent message: Forty-years of the much-ballyhooed U.S. war on drugs, has been largely a failure. Gaddis offers a compelling firsthand look

inside the global drug trade from corrupt government officials in Latin America to the insatiable appetite for drugs in the U.S. to interagency rivalry that at times was an obstacle in the fight against well-armed, well-funded narcos. The Noble Experiment is an essential, thought-provoking read that comes at a critical time as drug addiction in the U.S. and drug violence in Latin America and Mexico leave a trail of destruction across North America."

Alfredo Corchado, Mexico Border Correspondent for *The Dallas Morning News* and author of *Midnight in Mexico*.

FOREWORD
by
LEE STAPLETON

Imagine being a federal agent for mere months and already getting into a shoot-out and killing a terrible, murderous creature.

In January 1987, I had been an Assistant United States Attorney (AUSA) in the Southern District of Florida for five years. I was assigned to the Narcotics Section – that's where the action was. South Florida was the epicenter of narcotics trafficking – Miami was the capital of Dopeland.

DEA Group 4, Miami Field Division was the cocaine lab group. It kept on top of coke labs, chemicals, chemists and cooks. I was the AUSA assigned to the group – if an agent needed legal advice, a search warrant or an indictment, they came to me.

DEA Special Agent Dave Gaddis was assigned to Group 4. We became friends quickly, going to a University of Miami football game with a bunch of friends not long after he arrived in Miami. Dave was and is a supremely likable person. Tall, handsome, red-haired with a distinctive Southern accent, he radiated good cheer and competence at the same time. He is also a smart and funny guy. His partner, A.D. Wright, a former college football player and a new agent, had an infectious laugh and was a big, teddy bear of a guy.

In mid-January 1987, I had drafted a search warrant for the agents of Group 4. It was an unusual situation. Cooking coke is a smelly business (literally!), so coke labs were usually in isolated areas. This lab was in Miami Lakes in a lovely residential neighborhood – nice houses, manicured lawns – suburbia.

On January 21, 1987, the agents went to execute the warrant. During the middle of the afternoon that day, I received a call informing me that there had been a shooting when the agents went to execute the search warrant and telling me only that an agent was on his way to get me and bring me to the scene. The blue light was flashing and siren was wailing as we sped up from downtown Miami to Miami Lakes. Most of the trip was in the left-hand shoulder lane so we could bypass rush hour traffic – a white-knuckle ride.

When I arrived at the house, there were federal agents everywhere. I saw Dave sitting on the curb, covered in blood. I went over to him and once I realized that Dave was not hurt, I sat next to him on the curb. The bad guy had shot A.D. in the eye and Dave had shot and killed the bad guy. I held Dave's hand and we sat on the curb without saying much. Soon both of our hands were covered with A.D. Wright's blood.

Sometimes when I try to explain what it was like to someone who was not part of that time and place I realize that it is almost impossible. When I look back, some of the events that occurred seem surreal, even though I was there.

Dave has found words to describe those adrenalin fueled, go-go days. He has written a book that explains the landscape of federal drug enforcement through the work that he did with DEA. He had an impressive career, spending time in Central and South America, including time in both Mexico and Colombia, and he ultimately rose to "boss" level. He speaks Spanish fluently, with a Southern drawl. He left DEA at the top of his career and went on to have a great second act doing global investigations with his own company. In the book, Dave lays bare the smarts and bravery of DEA agents, but he does not sugar coat the problems they confront – turf wars with other agencies and prosecutors and sometimes flawed policy.

Dave provides thoughtful observations addressing current narcotics policy and enforcement and offers well-reasoned suggestions to address issues with respect to that policy. You may be surprised at some of his insights and conclusions.

"The Noble Experiment" is a riveting read. Dave puts into words and explains a fascinating time that was often stranger than fiction. His words are true.

Lee Stapleton, an Assistant United States Attorney for the Southern District of Florida from 1984 to 2000, served as the Chief of Narcotics and, as the Chief Assistant United States Attorney for the largest U.S. Attorney's Office in the country. She is now a shareholder with Carlton Fields in Miami, Florida.

TABLE OF CONTENTS

Table of Contents

PREFACE

One particularly dreary afternoon in early 2021, I decided to ring up Coleman, an old friend of mine from the DEA. After our usual pandemic-haze-induced, "Is this all really happening?" banter, I told him I'd started a book about some of our most memorable experiences together on the job. As usual, Coleman didn't miss a beat: "Well hell, Dave, ya might as well—everyone else is!" I laughed, and had to agree: at this point, it seems as if hundreds of books documenting the DEA experience have already been written. And that gave me pause: How would mine differ, especially when it's so easy to assume that there's nothing new to add, and every tale has already been told? But I soon realized: that's a terribly erroneous assumption. Take it from someone who knows: When it comes to our DEA and the stories and experiences therein, there really is no limit.

To clarify, when I say "our DEA," what I mean is that each and every Special Agent independently owns their experiences in the specific period during which they worked. In other words, while we may all technically have the same job description, our experiences differ dramatically in several critical ways: someone, for instance, may be headquartered in a tiny town, but face equal or even more formidable dangers then I did, despite the fact that I was almost always working in the most exotic and treacherous of locales. Every agent's experience within the DEA is different, collectively, it's "our" DEA. For me, I always refer to "my DEA" as being one long, exciting, surreal, perpetual playdate. I loved my job; I loved going to work every single day; I loved doing so for more than twenty-five years. When it was over, I missed it, terribly. But I also knew—and I think I always knew—that the life of an agent could never work for anyone well into the growing old stage of life, no matter how young their spirit. When I retired in 2011, I knew it was the right time. And I've never looked back.

To my great surprise, writing this book brought back so many of those feelings of youthful energy and excitement—emotions I hadn't felt in years. It also brought about a real sense of gratitude: How lucky was I to even have these memories in the first place? The simple act of retelling some of the stories would sometimes spark such an adrenaline high, I probably could have skipped the double cups of coffee (but didn't). And caffeine is a poor substitute, anyway: the adrenaline produced by the field work of a DEA Special Agent is rivaled only by the work of combat soldiers, special operations forces operatives, and intelligence officers working directly with our enemies on the front lines. A DEA agent is, ultimately, made up of four equal parts: cop, prosecutor, spy, and diplomat. They must excel at collecting intelligence, then be able to build enough evidence needed to successfully prosecute a case, and only then can they set about tackling the daunting challenge of hunting down (and capturing) their targets (without losing their own life in the process). It's an incredibly rare person who can succeed (let alone excel) at wrapping all of those esoteric skills into one powerful trifecta of talent, the kind of talent that truly sets them apart, and puts them in a league of their own.

While there were, of course, the occasional times I took a lesser, punk-level trafficker off the street (and happily so), for the most part I spent the entirety of my DEA career pursuing narcos at the absolute highest level: the legends, the kind of men they make movies about, the Kingpin traffickers. Powerful as they all were, they were also each unique in their own ways. Some, like Joaquin 'Chapo' Guzman Loera and Ismael Zambada Garcia, never made it past grade school, while others were surprisingly erudite and well-educated. But there was one thing that they all had in common, every single one of them: greed. Greed for money, greed for power, greed for control more than anything. Of course, with money comes power, and with power comes control. Every single one of those greedy bastards was filled with the insatiable desire to control the world around them, and, with the insane amounts of money that dealing drugs provided, they did. Some wielded their tyranny over relatively little worlds, places like la Tuna Badiraguato, Sinaloa Mexico, El Valle de Garrapatas (The Valley of Ticks), Cauca Colombia. Others oversaw worlds spanning as many as three or four continents, allowing them to simultaneously wreak havoc, infiltrate global banking institutions, and corrupt countless government officials on a global scale.

If I could explain the heart and intent behind this book, it would be with these three quotes:

"The ultimate measure of a man is not where he stands in moments of comfort and convenience, but where he stands at times of challenge and controversy."
— Martin Luther King, Jr.

"Whether it be true or not that every man has his peculiar ambition, I can say that I have no other ambition so great as that of being truly esteemed of my fellow men, by rendering myself worthy of their esteem. How far I shall succeed in gratifying this ambition, is yet to be developed."
— Abraham Lincoln

"Greater love hath no man than this, that a man lay down his life for his friends."
— New Testament, John 15:13

Of course, the stories in this book hardly represent all of my adventures and memories from my time in the DEA—in truth, they barely scratch the surface. Some stories can't be repeated because they contain strictly classified material, some because of enforcement-related concerns protecting tactics, methods, and techniques and some, to be honest, I just don't want to tell at all. My good friend and former Director General of the Colombian National Police, Jorge Castro-Castro once told me that the best stories any narc has to tell are the ones that are never written. But, no matter how dedicated, skilled, or determined those in the DEA may be, the reality is that they cannot fight this battle alone. After reading this book, I hope you'll agree that everyone— whether civilian, senator, parent, or teacher—must work together in order to enable real, lasting change.

Lastly, as much as I loved writing this book, in the end I realized that I wasn't just writing it for me. Certainly, I do want these stories to serve a kind of purpose, a glimpse into the life and world of a DEA agent, the cause we all devote our lives to, and the very real drug war that rages on to this day. But perhaps more than anything else, my sincere hope is that the book provides you with even the briefest of escapes, and that you enjoy reading these stories even half as much as I enjoyed reliving them.

CHAPTER 1

SWORDS DRAWN

"I'm hit! Dave, I've been hit!" These six words roll through my memory like it occurred yesterday, but it was January 21, 1987. I was a rookie DEA agent based in Miami, Florida, with only seven months of "wet feet," working as an "extra" on other more experienced investigator's case surveillances.

That's what every rookie agent did for the first year: whatever you were told by senior agents! There were days when I drove the Supervisor's OGV (official government vehicle) to a detail shop to get his "ride" cleaned up. But most days during those first six months, I worked as an agent assisting a number of senior agents who had done the exact same thing when they first joined DEA. I loved every minute of it and dedicated myself to learn from these experienced agents to form my own style and workmanship. As I look back forty years later, it worked!

Here's some background. I had finished a few years as an Intake & Assistant Probation Officer for the juvenile justice system in Madison County, Alabama—a job I used as the required "criminal justice experience" while studying at the University of Alabama-Huntsville for a BA in Criminal Justice. This was a stepping stone to my long-desired career in the DEA. I wanted to offer some service to my country while enjoying the excitement of policing and investigative work like I had seen in television shows such as *Hill Street Blues, Starsky & Hutch, Hawaii Five-O, Columbo, The Rockford Files*, and *Shaft*. (As a kid, I had watched them all.)

At twenty-four years old, I arrived at my first assignment as a DEA Special Agent in the middle of a "Colombian Cowboys" cocaine war throughout South Florida, and Miami was Ground Zero. The majority of agents who worked in the Miami Division Office actually bought their houses and lived their off-duty lives in neighboring Broward County. Towns like Pembroke Pines, Jacaranda, and Coral Springs were the favorite spots for DEA agents to seek sanctuary from the violence and bustle of a Latino-infused Dade County. However, I was an exception to that rule. I didn't endure two years of background investigations, followed by nineteen weeks of training at the DEA Academy in Quantico, Virginia, only to disappear from the battle fronts in the 1980s' drug wars on weekends and holidays. I was in this job one hundred percent! So, I moved into an apartment in Kendall, a suburb southwest of Miami that had the hustle and bustle of many cultures, including the drug culture that DEA was built to take down. This was the beginning of a great adventure. From eating Ropa Vieja with Mariquitas and Bistec Milanesa to sipping on the Café Cubano, I felt like I had died and gone to heaven! Why? Because each day brought me something new to experience, new to learn, and new to accomplish.

Upon arrival to the Miami office, I was immediately informed that my assignment would be in Enforcement Group 4: the Clandestine Laboratory Investigations or "Clan Lab" Unit, under Supervisor John Andrejko. This was a lucky break—John was the best in the business and mentored me through the first four years of my schooling as a DEA agent. John was an old school yet law enforcement progressive New York and Miami veteran who had always kept himself in superb physical condition. His claim to fame was running 10 K under forty minutes, but he was also capable of doing forty pull-ups on any given day. His twenty-one-inch biceps earned him his nickname: "Johnny Arms." Let's just say, I really looked up to the guy. Back in the 80s, a DEA Miami Supervisor was like a high school guidance counselor or team coach; he or she spent more time teaching and mentoring their "students" than they spent with their own families. In the same way an Alpha wolf protects his pack, a DEA Group Supervisor protects and organizes his enforcement group. "JA" was the best drug enforcement tutor at that time, and I was lucky to have him as mine.

In one of my first cases with DEA Miami Enforcement Group 4, we had identified a chemical supply store in Broward County that had sold the ingredients needed to convert cocaine base to cocaine hydrochloride—the flaky, white powdered stuff that millions of Americans were paying a hundred bucks or more per gram to snort up their noses. This is what we in the drug enforcement industry call "a lead," and man, was I excited about it! We found a suspect with a criminal background, buying suspicious chemicals with cash only, and taking them directly to a luxury house in the upscale suburban neighborhood of North Miami Lakes. We suspected we had a clan lab that was converting base to hydrochloride.

For weeks, Group 4 had scheduled surveillances on the suspect's movements. We had identified him by the name he used when introducing himself to the chemical providers: Sammy Garcia. A Cuban who spoke limited English, Sammy was a confident man who did not take many precautions while running around and spent most of his time inside his North Miami Lakes home, which he shared with his paramour and her grandchildren. Sammy knew that having young children coming in and out of his home would only help camouflage his criminal lifestyle in a swanky Miami Lakes community. However, he was an easy surveillance target. What's more, the house was located in the Miami Lakes Country Club, a plush community just northwest of the downtown Miami skyline, a place where you would never expect to find a dangerous clan lab with explosive, corrosive chemicals that could take out an entire neighborhood with a single spark.

Being a Wednesday (hump day), we had two non-enforcement events planned for later that day: first, a softball practice for a few of us playing in a league of our own, and of course, after the practice we'd go to Ma-Grundy's Bar & Grill, just around the corner from the office. Ma-Grundy's was a dark, dirty dive bar where many of the Miami agents visited on a regular basis. Large pitcher of draft beer for $3.75—man, those were the days! (What? You're surprised DEA agents drank midweek? How do you think we got to the next day?!) After-hours drinking was medicine to tolerate the long hours and filthy dirtbags we had to arrest and incarcerate. Playing softball was an unusual event for us, but pulling the group together and strategizing our case work at Ma-Grundy's was routine.

Before our recreation on this Wednesday afternoon and evening, Group 4 had work to finish. We had surveilled Sammy several times back and forth to the chemical supply store and knew he was "cooking" something illegal. Yet, due to our playful activities later that day, we decided to take the shortcut of paying Sammy a visit at his house and doing a "knock & talk." A knock & talk is the simple technique of walking up to the front door of a suspect's house, or perhaps waiting for them to leave in their car, and blocking them in their driveway to initiate a discussion and simply asking them to allow you (and your agent colleagues) to enter and search their house.

The knock & talk was perfectly legal and a successful investigative technique, especially with the foreign suspects due to their lack of knowledge of US laws and their familiarity with the practices of foreign security forces, who would regularly violate anyone's civil rights to get done what they wanted. Later in my career overseas, I learned that Latin American police would not only stretch the law, but also break it to make their cases. Latin America's police in general, and of course there were exceptions, often practiced the mantra of "the ends justify the means," and their public understood this practice and acquiesced to those norms. Latino drug traffickers in Miami were no different. By doing a knock & talk at Sammy's place, we could avoid spending the three-day process of preparing a formal affidavit, meeting with federal prosecutors who would inevitably "massage" the affidavit for days on end, and then spend unnecessary time seeking out a federal magistrate to approve and sign off on a search warrant. The knock & talk was skipping all that judicial bureaucracy and getting right to the job we wanted to do and get done as quickly as possible. Or so we thought...

You see, I was full of shortcuts. As an impetuous rookie agent with a motivation to succeed, at that time I also thought that the ends justified the means. Back in those days, a special agent could legally use those shortcuts, and for a much smaller group of agents, pass over to the illegal matrix, and do so without anyone knowing about it. Such improper investigative practice had occasionally been exposed in DEA, and in those cases, our Office of Professional Responsibility, or Internal Affairs, came down hard on the violators. From time to time, this happened around DEA worldwide. The practice of stretching rules shouldn't be confused with corruption. Stealing dope or money and manipulating people to do so is corruption and 99.9 percent of agents would never cross that line. But taking a legal investigative "detour" to take down a drug trafficker every now and then was something I would definitely do.

Here I was a twenty-four-year-old kid with a gun, badge, and credentials, not to mention an overload of testosterone, to be a DEA agent in Miami—the gateway to Latin America and the Caribbean. I thought I could do just about anything I wanted! But that's where Johnny Arms kept me in line. JA walked the walk, and he knew when I was leaning towards a stray path from doing my job "by the book," which probably saved my career, even my life. Equally, my senior partner, Ken Peterson, was always there to keep me in check. Kenny was an experienced DEA criminal investigator, having worked in the field for more than twenty years by the time I met him. The physical antithesis of Johnny Arms, Kenny never exercised, drank beer on a regular basis, and would pull strings to get the best informants by his side. Kenny never crossed the line, but was a strategic genius and loved bending the rules if possible and if legal. And therein, I learned much from him too.

A typical DEA Miami enforcement group was made up of ten to fifteen Special Agents—or as we are technically categorized, Criminal Investigators—with a supervisor in charge of the group and supported by one or two administrative assistants. On that fateful day in 1987, we agents split up and covered three or four locations that we had identified as potential drug stash sites. Myself, my partner and "brother in blue" AD Wright, and Senior Agent Juan Vitieri (not his real name) were assigned to the Miami Lakes Country Club house for added surveillance. After several hours of no exterior activity, however, a knock & talk entry seemed appropriate and was approved by JA.

A native of Jacksonville, Florida, Adolphus "AD" Wright was a large, powerful man and a relatively quiet guy. Before joining DEA, he had no law enforcement experience, and from the beginning, DEA trained him correctly. He generally expressed himself with pointed, well-thought-out comments but also had a great sense of humor. AD would notice things that never occurred to me, but when he commented about a particularity of life, I found it hilarious.

Here's a classic example of AD's humor. Once I had an undercover meeting in South Lauderdale to buy four kilos of coke from a New Yorker named Rocky. AD covered the meeting from afar while I went to Rocky's house to discuss when, where, and how he would deliver the merchandise for an agreed upon price of $14,000 per kilo. When I finished the meeting and hopped into my red Corvette, I went around the corner and met AD, who swiftly kicked me out of the driver's seat, saying, "Switch seats; I want the wheel now." Anytime a GS-9 could drive a car like that, it was something special. I selected the Corvette over a collection of Mercedes and BMWs that DEA Miami kept in surplus for undercover assignments.

Rocky had a Corvette and was a "rough around the edges" kind of guy, so I thought the 1987 Corvette would impress him more than the other expensive classy vehicles. AD and I grabbed a quick lunch and headed back to our office so we could do the paperwork that documented the UC meeting. AD was cruising at an enjoyable fifty-five mph, listening to some smooth progressive jazz tunes. When on Dade County's highway 826 Palmetto Expressway, Rocky passed us in his own Corvette and looked at us, smiling and waving like a long-lost friend. He then sped away, weaving in and out of traffic like a NASCAR racer. As Rocky disappeared in the heavy traffic, AD quietly commented, "You think he's aware that for the next ten years, he'll be having sex with himself in prison?" This vision became reality after Rocky delivered the coke, and we gladly handed him over to the US Marshals. Convicted of possession and intent to sale over five kilos of cocaine, Rocky was sentenced to "Club Fed" for many years.

Senior Agent Vitieri was quite different from AD. Juan, a New Yorker who regularly spoke the lingo of 1960's law enforcement culture—peppered with phrases like "get bent," "find a gig" (case), and "clean your Rosco" (handgun)—was a man of high intelligence. He constantly gravitated to historical conspiracy cases and never worked undercover while I was in Enforcement Group 4. His historical conspiracy investigations also permitted a more stable nine-to-five schedule, as opposed to the crazy hours the younger agents worked pursuing active targets and getting our hands on guns, dope, and money. Juan had almost twenty years on the job and didn't feel like taking chances of any sort that might dampen his happy retirement plan. He occasionally went out on late-night casework, but didn't have the propensity to chase after killer narcos. Juan V was not the guy you wanted with you when you had to kick down a door or be in a firefight. Simply said, he didn't have the "edge."

At two o'clock on that fateful afternoon, the three of us met at a strip shopping center where we grabbed a sandwich and discussed a plan for the knock & talk and how to convince Sammy, if he was still there, to let us in the house and then do a quick search of our relatively unknown suspect's premises. There was even a brief discussion of not wearing our bulletproof vests underneath our DEA raid jackets, so as not to alarm Sammy or the other occupants, which might prevent them from acquiescing to our request of search their property. In the end, we agreed that if it got back to JA that we had not used our vests and jackets, he would kick our asses (and he could!), so we put them on in the parking lot before heading to Sammy's. This routine of dressing for a raid in a public place (supermarket parking lots, a hotel site, behind restaurants, and the like) always solicited yells of support from whomever; folks would shout messages like "Give 'em hell!" and "Watch your ass, officers!" from their cars or while just passing by. Although slightly embarrassing, I honestly got a kick out of it!

We set up on Sammy's house to determine if he was there. There were no movements, no activity at all, so we decided to advance on the house. When we pulled into Sammy's Miami Lakes Country Club driveway, it was a typical South Florida January day—sunny in the low 70's, with lovely low humidity. A great day to wear a bulletproof vest! As the only half-assed Spanish speaker (I'd learned basic Spanish growing up next door to a family whose parents were originally from Brownsville, Texas—their kids, Rudy and Yolanda, are my dear friends to this day—and later studying it in college), I was the guy who rang the doorbell and met Sammy as he opened it, wearing nothing but a pair of long sweatpants. He wasn't wearing shoes, slippers, not even socks, and was shirtless. An unassuming fat man with absolutely no muscular build, he seemed weak and amenable to do whatever we asked. However, I did notice one odd characteristic: his black, deadpan eyes. When I first looked at Sammy, I felt that I was looking into the eyes of a shark. I will never forget that moment.

In my broken Spanish, I told Sammy that we were DEA, we had information that something was improperly going on in his residence, and we wanted him to allow us to enter and search the premises for any illegal activity. Sammy immediately stepped aside and said, "Si, pase adelante." So, we came on in. The décor was contemporary but actually tasteful. It looked much like many other narco's houses I had already seen and searched during warranted raids. As I mentioned earlier, I initially believed Sammy thought that allowing us in the house was just something he had to do, in the same way he would have had to do it in his native Cuba under Castro's oppressive Communist regime. Little did I know: Sammy had other deviant and dangerous thoughts going through his mind.

Sammy led us into the living room. It was a clean house and the room appeared in typical Latino drug trafficker décor: mirrored walls, lots of porcelain and crystal statues, and expensive white leather furniture with white throw pillows sitting on an expensive white upgraded tile floor—everything in the room was white. He asked what we wanted to see. "Que quieren ver?" It was an easy question, but I didn't quite understand him and replied, "Que?" He had asked a simple question, "What do you want to see?" and I answered, "What?" Supposedly having encountered gringo speakers before, Sammy rolled his eyes and slowly pronounced each word in Spanish, "Que....quieren.... ver?" I understood him now and responded in broken Spanish, "Quimicas, tienes quimicas aqui?" ("Chemicals, do you have chemicals here?") Sammy didn't flinch or even blink. We knew that, somewhere in his house, he had those precursor chemicals used to make cocaine; at least, they were there a few hours ago when we surveilled him carrying them inside.

Thinking that the illicit chemicals would be located inside of the garage because of the pungent odor they naturally emit, I immediately peeled from our trio and entered the garage where I discovered something I'd never seen before: a Santeria shrine. Santeria is a pagan belief in voodoo magic, originated in West Africa and practiced by many drug traffickers from Latin America and the Caribbean, especially Haiti, Cuba, and parts of the South American coastline. I've since also learned that a white environment is significant to a practicing "Santero," or priest of voodoo.

Sammy's shrine featured a life-sized and eerily life-like statue of a man bleeding from the head and torso, whom I later learned was San Lazaro. This mannequin was surrounded by hundreds of lighted candles and an assortment of offerings at its feet. These offerings included liquors, various fruits and sweet breads, and even a recently sacrificed decapitated chicken, which its severed head laid lifeless in a bowl of its own blood. In our training, we had heard of Santeria, and I knew this practice went hand-in-hand with trafficker violence, especially against law enforcement. At that moment, I thought silently, "Oh shit, this guy's a santero—he invited us into this hell hole not to cooperate but to kill us! He will want vengeance for our intrusion!"

As I looked around and saw the chemicals just about everywhere (the garage was being used as his supply closet for the cocaine and a synthetic THC clandestine lab), I heard AD yell, "Dave, he's running!" I darted from the garage and back into the living room where I saw AD standing at the end of a hallway that connected the living area with bedrooms and a bathroom at the rear of the house. As I ran towards AD, Juan V sprinted past me in the opposite direction and ran out the front door, without saying a word.

Left on our own, AD and I set up covered positions on each side of the corners of the hallway that led to a bedroom Sammy had run into, slamming the door behind him. AD quickly told me that Sammy had asked to go to the bathroom to pee. As Sammy was leading AD and Juan V around the living room, he turned to AD and while grabbing his crotch, stated in broken English, "Go to bat-room?" But instead of walking straight into the bathroom, Sammy bolted right and ran into a bedroom, where he clearly had his firearms and ammo.

As I glanced down the hallway, AD said, "He's in there but we don't know who else is!" We looked at each other and AD commanded, "C'mon, Sammy, there's nothing to do in there. Come out here and talk to us." I repeated AD's statement in the best Spanish I knew but probably said something like, "Hey fuck-o, get your fat ass out here take it like a man!" AD made a couple more commands, but we heard nothing for what seemed like a couple of minutes until the door slowly creaked open with no sight of Sammy. Then we saw a pistol barrel slowly sticking out from around the edge of the door frame near the floor. Sammy was positioning for a fight.

I can't speak for AD, but I could hear my heart beating…tha-bump, tha-bump, tha-bump…and thought it would pop out of my chest! AD was on the left side of the hallway; I was on the right—not the ideal position for a right-handed shooter. To stay covered, I would have to fire my pistol—a government-issued Smith & Wesson .357 Magnum model 65, loaded with +P hollow point ammunition—with my non-preferred left hand. AD was also right-handed, so he had better control of his shots. From his position, AD took an "Israeli peek"—that is, a quick glance from around the corner to focus on your target—and observed Sammy lying on the ground in a prone position, with only one eye and his pistol barrel visible. AD shouted "Gun!" and I knew we were in some shit!

At that time, we heard three shots from Sammy...bop, bop, bop!...followed by the splintering sounds as his bullets whizzed by our heads and penetrated the wall behind us. With this "weak" left hand grip of my .357, I returned fire with one shot. Yep, there we were in the country's most violent city, ground zero of America's drug wars, with a damn government issued six-shooter revolver! Hell, the shooters at the O.K. Corral in Tombstone, Arizona, over a hundred years back had better fire power than AD and I. We could and should have brought our Remington 870 pump action 12-gauge shotguns to the door—but on a knock & talk, the goal is to make the suspect feel comfortable so they agree to the search. So, we left our shotguns in the OGV, and that was a big mistake.

Honestly, I did not even look to where I was shooting—I just wanted that dickhead to know I had bullets too! No, that was NOT part of our training, but it seemed like the natural thing to do at the time. There are some things the best training in the world does not prepare you for—like your heart beating out of your chest while sweat pours down your face and into your eyes and dampens your hands to the point of struggling to maintain a tight grip on your firearm or reloading it. Or having all of your natural physical senses shut down so you concentrate on one thing and one thing only: stopping the mortal threat that is intending to kill you!

We didn't know it at the time, but Sammy was an experienced gun fighter and a serial murderer—an enforcer for drug gangs in both Cuba and in Miami that had tortured and killed opposition drug traffickers for many years. Sammy had arrived in the USA in 1980 during the infamous Mariel Boatlift—a mass emigration of Cubans. At the time, President Jimmy Carter agreed to accept all Cuban dissidents who wanted to live in our country, and in turn, Fidel Castro exploited Carter's good nature by expelling thousands of prisoners and mental patients—some with a propensity to commit violent crimes.

By lying flat on his belly around the corner of a door frame, Sammy knew he would have adequate cover while steadying his shots with his elbows supported by the floor. Being an experienced fighter, he waited to get his next shot. AD, having once peeked around the corner, decided to do a second Israeli peek to focus on Sammy's position. When he did, Sammy fired a round directly at AD's head, and he missed. That's a good thing, right? No, not good at all. The bullet first hit the hallway wall just left of AD and then ricocheted, hitting AD and passing through his right eyeball, instantly ripping his eye from its socket and spraying human tissue from his head. Shit, he no longer owned that eye! The impact of the bullet passing through his skull knocked AD down and momentarily left him there, lifeless.

As I said, when in a gunfight all of your bodily senses pull together and focus on the single threat you are faced with. Eyesight becomes keen, hearing shuts out background noises, and the sense of smell becomes enhanced. This is nature's way of optimizing your ability to survive. I saw everything in slow motion, heard nothing of my and AD's yelling, and smelled the gun powder floating throughout the hallway. Even though AD was standing next to me when he was shot, I was intensely focused on Sammy and did not realize what had happened until he yelled, "I'm hit! Dave, I've been hit!" Reluctantly, I took my view off Sammy and looked to my left, seeing AD lying on the ground in a pool of his blood located in the middle of the hallway and in direct line of fire from Sammy. AD was stunned from his critical injury, barely mustering his consciousness and looking down at the floor, trying to regain the loss of eyesight in his remaining eye. At that very moment, I felt the weight of the world on my shoulders. "Is my partner, my DEA brother, going to die? Is Sammy going to kill us both? Where in the hell is Juan V?"

I reached down to grab AD and pull him towards me, but in doing so I opened myself into the direct line of fire—and Sammy shot twice at me. By the grace of God, neither bullet found its target, but I felt the heat of one pass by my head, which caused me to instinctively pull back behind the wall's corner where I had cover. I felt somewhat safe behind the wall, so why would I want to leave my cover?! Realizing that he was in grave danger of being finished off by Sammy, and already critically injured, AD dragged himself backwards across the hallway and into another bedroom. AD's blood trail was unmistakable, and Sammy could easily see it from his position down the hallway. I knew AD had survived, at least for now, and said to myself, "Okay, I'm forced to fire at this murderous bastard with my weak hand; he has all of the tactical advantage, so let's change the plan."

Knowing that AD was alive and again in a safer covered position, I had to change mine in order to gain cover while using my strong hand to fire upon Sammy and save my life, and perhaps AD's life as well. At that point, I decided to back up about eight feet to another corner of the hallway, which allowed me to take cover and use of my right (strong) hand to fire my weapon. As I was thinking, "Okay, Sammy, as soon as you appear from that hallway, I'm going to blast your ass," it felt like ten minutes went by, but it was actually seconds. In an instant, I saw Sammy exiting the hallway and running towards AD's position, rapidly firing his pistol. Sammy wanted to finish off AD, and then take me out.

The Mossad, Israel's National Intelligence Agency, teaches that in combat the opponent should not be a human target but rather an immaterial force to be stopped at whatever cost. The key is to not think of the human side and not act on emotion. The Mossad is one hundred percent correct. In a firefight, you don't think: you only react and rely on your training. When I realized what Sammy was doing, and the three of us were never more than fifteen feet apart throughout the fight, my simple instinct was to stop him. He became that inanimate object, and I instinctively fired three shots into Sammy's left torso, which spun him around directly towards me. Sammy fired two more rounds that landed in the wall exactly two inches to the left of my head, spraying paint and dry board all over my face and into my eyes.

AD, being a strong twenty-three-year-old former Florida State football player with muscles on top of his muscles, had somehow regained vision from his one eye adequate to defend himself and retarget Sammy. As Sammy was pointing his gun at me and firing away, AD fired twice, hitting Sammy in the right torso and causing him to immediately collapse to the floor. An autopsy later revealed that AD's shots entered through the right side of Sammy's torso, passing through both lungs and exiting his fat left chest. That was five direct hits in the torso with .357 Magnum +P ammo, and he was still fighting—fighting as if he didn't think he could die. For those of you not familiar with ammunition, the .357 Magnum +P hollow point is a very powerful round. Upon impact, this bullet smashes into its target at 1,450 feet per second and expands in the shape of a mushroom so that it rips apart all tissue, organs, and bone in which it comes into contact. This handgun with that particular ammunition would kill a bull. Sammy was fucked!

But Sammy's body spun back towards AD, and he shot AD directly in his chest, near his heart, knocking AD back a step. I saw this occur in slow motion—another effect of trauma and related stress. In fact, a sense of slow motion happens to nearly everyone enduring their FIRST human killing experience. In subsequent shootings, as I later found, I was not impacted in this way and more aware of my surroundings. What I saw next happened in extreme slow motion.

When Sammy fell to the floor, his feet were closest to me and his head in the opposite direction. He held his Walter PPK .380 handgun in his right hand and an empty magazine in his left that he had already emptied at us. Although fatally wounded and on the brink of death, Sammy was still lifting his pistol and pointing it towards AD to finish him off. I had two more bullets in my new yet already outdated DEA-issued revolver, so I took my time, stretched my neck to the right then to the left, and aimed, focusing on stopping Sammy once and for all. In an act that can best be described as how actor Danny Glover's character in *Lethal Weapon* aimed and fired at the bad guy who was speeding a car towards him, I took a deep breath and released, slowly rotated my head in a circular motion to loosen my neck muscles, took another deep breath, partially exhaled and aimed at Sammy's head, firing two shots about five seconds apart. As it turns out, I missed his head both times. For some reason, I shot low and hit Sammy in the lower abdomen. Due to our juxtaposed positions, however, those two +P hollow point lead bullets traveled up through his lower torso and stopped close to his collar bone, ripping up every organ and bone in its path. That did it: finally, Sammy was gone from Earth and working his way into Hell to meet Lucifer himself!

Through extensive investigation, we later discovered that Sammy had claimed self-conversion into a Santeria god and felt that he was completely invisible to police officers. In fact, during the post-shooting investigation and search of the house, a Metro Dade Homicide Detective with expertise in Santeria discovered a steel cross embedded in a circle wrapped in barbs that represents a spiritual defensive tool to defeat law enforcement. It was discovered hanging on the rear of the house's front door. In this firefight, Sammy thought he was immune from death, invisible to us, and that made him an extremely dangerous opponent to me and AD. It's not as easy to defeat an enemy who believes they can't die. But by the grace of our Almighty Father, we won and he lost this battle.

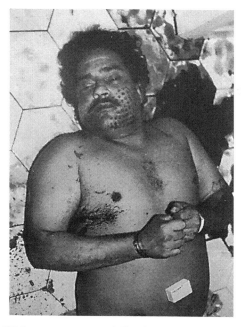

In January 1987 Sammy Garcia (alias) attempted to kill DEA Special Agents AD Wright and partner Dave Gaddis in Miami Lakes. It didn't go the way Sammy thought it would.

Now, the entire house was full of smoke and odor of gun powder. Sammy's live-in lady friend and two young girls, each about the age of four or five, were running around the house hysterically, having returned from the front yard where Juan V had run. Eventually, even Juan V returned to the house. By that time, however, I had seated AD in one of those elegant pure white leather chairs in the living room, which was quickly turning bright red from the bleeding, and asked him to stay calm, knowing he was already experiencing symptoms of shock. With AD seated and trying to emotionally absorb his critical wounds, I ripped his DEA raid jacket open and saw an amazing thing: the bullet that Sammy had shot at AD's chest was stuck exactly in the center of his vest. Soaked in blood from the eye wound, that bullet was embedded directly over AD's heart! I looked at AD and said, "Partner, what a great decision to wear our bulletproof Kevlar vests, right?" AD didn't answer; he remained quiet, focusing the energy he still possessed on staying alive.

DEA Special Agent AD Wright's bulletproof vest.
Note the bullet stuck in the center of the vest (circled),
which stopped a shot directly into his chest.

At that time, a Miami Lakes Country Club neighbor who worked as a medical doctor ran in to the house and took over triage efforts to save AD. Months later, DEA Miami awarded this fine doctor the highest recognition for a civilian in support to DEA. Juan V had radioed other agents through DEA's communications base, and they were beginning to arrive like fighter jets landing on a carrier. That's the thing about DEA agents, and law enforcement officers overall: they run into the crisis with gusto and not away from it. Although I can't remember all those agents and police officers who rapidly showed up, I appreciated every one of them. As someone who was personally on hand in a homicide case, I didn't need to be in that house, and my agents and cops made sure that I was removed from the immediate scene. They all did their part and handled what was needed.

A Miami US Assistant Attorney, Lee Stapleton also arrived almost instantaneously and offered me moral support. In those days, the DEA and US Attorneys were more than professional colleagues; we were friends. Lee supported Enforcement Group 4 and felt as much a sister to us as she was our federal prosecutor. Metro Dade Police arrived and homicide detectives were splitting responsibilities to interview and conduct their investigation. A helicopter ambulance flew in and landed in the street in front of Sammy's house to pick up AD. While he was being rolled on a gurney from the house to the chopper for transportation to the Bascom Palmer Eye Institute in Miami, everyone at that scene began to clap and cheer, so AD would know they had his back. AD lifted up his hand with a "thumbs up" sign those cheering him on and to the TV cameras and press that had arrived. There was an explosion of applause, even from the media, to support AD and the myriad of federal agents on the scene.

I was transported to the Metro Dade police precinct and gave a full statement as to what occurred. I inadvertently gave an incomplete statement because I had mentally blocked out many details due to post-traumatic stress. Four or five days passed before I actually remembered everything that had occurred that afternoon, and this is the first time I am sharing all the details with anyone.

DEA Supervisor Pat Shea—a former football offensive guard for the UNC Tarheels and US Marine who had the strength of an oak tree—was assigned to care for me and get me through that day's activities before returning me to my wife late that night. (Although JA had our backs, he was legitimately way too busy processing the homicide scene and sorting through the plethora of criminal charges to look after his traumatized agents.) First, Pat carried me to the Metro Dade Police precinct, where I met with detectives in the homicide division and provided my statement, which of course was clarified days later due to my initial memory failure from traumatic stress. From there, Pat and I went to the hospital, where AD was having emergency surgery to save his life. When we entered the waiting room, there were dozens of DEA agents on the scene, serving as security while providing AD's family with not only comfort but also a sense of discipline and order.

AD had just finished surgery and the surgeons told his wife that he would survive but had lost his eye. AD's wife was also a DEA Special Agent and had been privy to the second-by-second reporting of this incident. As soon as she saw me, she jumped up and ran in to my arms and began to cry. She said nothing, only wept. I told her that AD was the strongest man I knew and that he would be okay. The truth is that neither of us knew how he would come back from this trauma. It was a powerful moment to realize we had survived an extremely dangerous event, but AD was not out of the woods yet.

Fortunately, AD hadn't lost his sense of humor. Several days later, I was in his intensive care hospital room when Johnny Arms and his boss, Charles Lutz, walked in. The Miami Assistant Special Agent-in-Charge, Lutz was frequently (and discreetly) referred to as "The Iceman" by agents due to his calm and steely demeanor. A quiet type, Lutz only commented when he had something to say. At the end of their visit, Lutz asked AD if there was anything more that DEA could do for him or his family. Without hesitation, and with a big fat patch over his right eye and gauze around his head, AD looked up and in a perfect impersonation of then President Ronald Reagan, said, "Well, you can get Ronnie over here to say hi." Lutz's mouth gaped open with a stunned reaction to AD's expressing humor in such a difficult time. The Iceman looked at us as both JA and I busted up laughing. Lutz even cracked a smile, which he rarely did, and said he'd do what he could. While at that moment, even as he made us laugh, AD never smiled. I knew deep in my heart that he was worried about his lost eye and the potential impact that would have on the only career he had ever wanted and adored.

After the hospital visit on the day of the shooting, Pat drove me to Mike's—a 1970's cop bar. It offered the dark and peaceful ambience that Pat knew I needed to wind down the night before heading home after one hell of a day. I have never been a hard liquor drinker, but on that night, I had the two stiffest drinks I could order. I was grateful to be alive in this moment! From Mike's Bar, Pat drove me home. Shortly after midnight, I opened my front door to meet my wife, who was waiting for me. Donna had heard of our shooting from both DEA agents and the local media outlets. We embraced, deeply thankful that we were still a couple and she not a widow. Then, we went to bed. At three in the morning, Donna rolled over and placed her hand on my chest to simply check if I was okay. She immediately sat up and exclaimed, "Dave, your heart is beating out of your chest!" Abruptly awoken from a sound sleep, I got up and checked my pulse, which read 180 beats per minute. Apparently, my body was not yet over this experience.

One week later, I mistakenly thought my head was around this experience and volunteered to support another warranted raid that Enforcement Group 4 was conducting in the Southwest Miami district. The target site for the raid was another narco's house—this time, surrounded by a four-foot block wall with an eight-foot metal security fence, like those prisons use. The double-door gate was also metal walled. With keen awareness from years of experience supervising agents who had been involved in shootings, JA recognized the need for me to take a backseat role on this raid, and any future ones for the next couple of months. JA was thinking of my mental health, and for that, I will always be grateful. As it turns out, he was right.

I was placed on the perimeter with my Remington 870 12-gauge pump action shotgun and assigned only to call for reinforcements and cover fire for the entry agents. To accomplish this small yet important task, I had to drive up to the front of the fenced and gated yard, exit my official government vehicle, hold point on the fence while observing the other agents, including JA, execute the search warrant, make a hostile entry, and arrest the scumbags who were poisoning communities throughout Miami.

As the operation began and we advanced forward to the target in our vehicles, I stopped at the fence as assigned. I exited my OGV, and quickly advanced to the outer perimeter fence with my shotgun. My mind was racing, even swirling, and that's when

I froze. My shooting with Sammy came back in a flash: in my head, I was back inside that Miami Lakes house. Ready to fire my weapon, I was ducking as low as I could kneel down along that four-foot block wall on the fence line in an effort to not be shot at again. Although I watched JA and the rest of our team bust down the door and clear the house with multiple defendants inside it, my mind was not there—it was back with Sammy. Had an emergency occurred, such as another shooting, an injury, or even an explosion, I'm not certain I would have reacted as needed. Most likely, I would have failed my team.

The following week, I participated in a DEA mandatory psychologist appointment to discuss the shooting's effects on me. For more than one hour, I sat with the doctor performing my best undercover yet. Since 1986, any DEA agent involved in a fatal shooting is required to visit a psychologist at least once after the incident. This allows the agent to get any issues off his chest while the Doc can assess whether or not further examinations are necessary due to PTSD, or Post Traumatic Stress Disorder. By the way, what a shitty term that is. It's not a disorder; it's an *experience*, and calling it a disorder further discourages the individual from acknowledging the associated physical and mental aftershocks, which is the first step in getting assistance to a path of normalcy. I prefer the term Post Traumatic Stress Experience, or PTSE.

In my best undercover capacity, I never told the Doc of my "freezing" on the subsequent raid. Instead, I told him that I was fine, no problems. I lied because I didn't want anyone to tell me I couldn't get back out on the street and do my job.

I want to tell this part of my story to encourage others in law enforcement who experience a traumatic shooting to always seek professional outreach and be honest with whomever is trying to help. Killing another human, even one who wants you dead, is not normal and it doesn't feel normal. So, take it from me, self-reflection and acting on it is the quickest and most effective way to get back to the person who existed before the traumatic event. A "whole" law enforcement officer is one who is there for not only their team but also their family and friends.

I said that AD was a strong man; well, let me tell you how strong. He had a wonderful team of ophthalmologists who replaced his lost eye with a prosthetic. Within months of returning to work, AD retrained his eyesight so that he could qualify on the fifty-yard Qualification Training Course using only his left eye and became one of the most proficient shooters in DEA. AD moved forward as an undercover agent and never looked back; he was responsible for making some of the best DEA cases in South Florida. Fast forward from 1987 to 2013: AD Wright is the Special Agent-in-Charge of the Miami Division Office, the boss of all bosses and in my opinion an American Hero. That's how strong!

Months after my first traumatic kill, I was talking with my mom and dad, who came to visit us from Huntsville, Alabama. Dad, a retired US Army Special Forces combat veteran with two tours in Vietnam, told me that before this shooting, he worried about me every day. "Now, Dave, I'm not worried about you at all," Dad declared. "I know you can handle yourself."

CHAPTER 2

LA FAMILIA

I've never been that big on proverbs, but there's one I first heard many years ago that's always stayed with me: "A happy united family is but an earlier Heaven." Looking back on my childhood, I realize how lucky I am to be able to say I know that proverb to be true.

Born into a military family, I spent the majority of my childhood as a nomad of sorts, traveling from place to place as a result of my father's oft-changing deployments. While my dad was routinely off in faraway spots on behalf of the US Army Special Forces, my mother was always with us, wholly devoted to caring for me and my sister, selflessly tending to all of our (many) needs. We were very close, and I always felt secure in the solid structure and safety of my little family unit. However loving, though, both of my parents were quite traditional in their disciplinary approach (and neither spared the belt if we strayed into evil's lane), so my sister and I were raised to obey all of the classic manner-related rules: Never interrupt anyone in conversation, always say "Yes, sir" and "No, ma'am" to adults, and, most importantly, always respect and follow the Ten Commandments. But, regardless of whether or not our father was home, there was always an abundance of love.

I have so many fond memories of our time together in those early days: backyard games of Duck, Duck, Goose or Tug of War, played not just with our parents but with a great many of the neighborhood kids as well. And as a family, we ventured out whenever we could, taking the occasional trip to the North Carolina beaches of Surf City and Topsail Island, getaways we all cherished. When my father eventually took a job teaching an ROTC program at Alabama A&T University, we bought a farm and promptly went all out, raising chickens, cattle, goats, and even a horse. It's clear to me now that it was this idyllic time in our family life that has always drawn me back to the kind of serene lifestyle one can only find on a farm. I'm grateful for so many things, and my happy childhood is at the top of that list.

In high school I was a disciplined and successful athlete, focused primarily on football, wrestling, and track and field. My best friends, Craig, Jeff, John, Mark, and David (if my name had been Jesus, we could have formed a gang and called ourselves "The Disciples") would be up as early as I was, and together we'd spend our days tossing around whatever ball we could get our hands on until well past dark. This daily bonding—for so many, such an integral and influential aspect of sports—kept us quite close for many years.

After high school, a prestigious school in Colorado (the US Air Force Academy Preparatory School) offered me a position on their football team, and I jumped at the chance to play linebacker for the Huskies. After a year I was offered a coveted appointment to the US Air Force Academy but decided not to accept it, for reasons I could never have anticipated: to my horror, during that one, fleeting year, I had lost perfect vision in both eyes. Suddenly, I went from being a young, virile athlete who viewed himself as being essentially unbreakable to being not just sight-challenged, but faced with the fact that because of that, I'd never be able to qualify for pilot training. And without pilot training, my still-young, impetuous, naive self then pondered, why else would I want to be in the Air Force at all? So, begrudgingly, I headed back to the East Coast and decided to follow a different yet not altogether dissimilar path: one in law enforcement.

Once home, I enrolled at North Carolina State University (home of the well-known Wolfpack), declared Criminal Justice as my major (with Spanish as my minor), and "walked on" for a one-year stint as a defensive end for their football squad. After that first year (1981), and with nary a scholarship in sight, it seemed like the smartest thing to do was to hang up my cleats once and for all and rejoin my family, who'd recently relocated to Huntsville, Alabama. That following year I enrolled in the University of Alabama in Huntsville, and the next three years virtually flew by as I earned my degree in Criminal Justice. Unfortunately, during that time my eyesight grew progressively worse, and every year I was forced to get a new pair of glasses just to accommodate my rapidly-degrading vision.

In 1984, after months of living in fear of just how bad things might get, I heard of a new procedure that had been invented in Russia called Radial Keratotomy. The word in the medical community was that RK, as it became known, could transform poor—even terribly poor—vision into an astounding 20/20 in just a few weeks' time. Incredibly, I found a Huntsville-based surgeon who practiced it, and didn't hesitate to give him the green light (and the green bills) to cut into not one but both of my eyes. Even as a young man I knew I got lucky: it worked, and within a month I had 20/15 vision in *both* eyes and was able to see everything around me with near flawless sight for the first time in almost four years. Given my longtime desire to work in federal law enforcement, this was, for me, a total game changer.

In retrospect, I can see that my awe and respect for my father and his own selfless service to his country is what must have driven me so passionately down the path I chose. In my heart, I knew that I wanted to do something equally important, to be equally of service, and to my mind, there was (and is) nothing more patriotic than devoting one's life to a career in law enforcement or to serve as a soldier.

Of course, as any police officer or soldier will tell you, neither career path is a lucrative one. Thinking strategically, I thought that, given my college degree, I might pursue work in the Federal Government, in which law enforcement pays substantially more than they do at the municipal and state levels. I sent applications to every Fed alphabet agency in existence, and they all showed interest (with the sole exception of the CIA, which sent me a very polite letter, essentially saying that because I wasn't fluent in at least one foreign language, I was more or less useless to them). Without any hesitation, I picked the FBI and the DEA as my two top choices. The FBI acted first—deeming me ready to be hired—and promptly flew me to the Emery Medical Center in Atlanta, Georgia, for a physical examination. This was the final bit of vetting before the official background investigation and, of course, the RK I'd had done two years ago was the one and only red flag. (At the time, RK was an immediate disqualifier for FBI applicants, as there hadn't yet been enough research done on possible long-term effects to one's vision.) Still, when I got the official word that I'd been disqualified, it was a real kick in the stomach. But I didn't stay despondent for long: not long after that setback, the DEA called and offered me a Special Agent position.

They didn't share that same concern over the specialized RK eye exam, and I was thrilled, to say the least (not to mention relieved). In truth, the DEA had been at the top of my wish list for two reasons: one, because of the unparalleled street action that came with the job, and two, because their hiring processes were much faster than those of the FBI, and I needed to start my federal career as soon as possible. When I did take the DEA's required physical exam, it didn't include that complicated ophthalmology examination. I wasn't even asked about it, in fact, and I knew better than to bring it up voluntarily. And so, in January of 1986, it became official. I was going to join the DEA, and at the tender age of twenty-four, I was truly off and running.

Champing at the bit to start my new life, I reported to the DEA Atlanta Georgia Field Division on February 18, 1986, where I was sworn in by Special Agent in Charge Ron Caffrey. After graduating from the DEA Academy that June, I left Atlanta for Miami to embark on what would ultimately become my own journey of adventure and discovery, or *The Noble Experiment: True Stories & Hard Truths from My Time in the DEA*. To my surprise, one of the very first things I noticed was how openly supportive my new colleagues were of each other's families. It was my first exposure to what family meant to the DEA (which, I also learned, was actually a family unto itself), and I immediately loved being a part of it.

Of course, strong as my own familial bonds may have seemed, being in the DEA is hard on every marriage. And mine was no exception.

While still in college I met Donna, a lovely young co-ed and Delta Zeta sorority sister. After a two-year courtship, we were married at the Redstone Arsenal Chapel in Huntsville, Alabama. We both graduated soon after and immediately focused on maintaining our jobs, the kinds new graduates typically qualify for: namely, the ones that barely cover the bills. I worked full-time with the Madison County·Juvenile Justice and Detention Center and, tasked with the unenviable third shift (eleven p.m. to seven a.m.), it was hardly an ideal situation, let alone for a newlywed. My days were packed. After I got off work in the early morning, I raced off to attend class at the university. Once classes wrapped, I'd hustle to the university library to bury myself in my studies before finally dragging myself home for a five-hour power nap (all I could squeeze in before the alarm rang, which was my cue to get up and ready for work and start all over again). I was so damn busy, and it was such a sleepless blur, that nearly everything about that period in our lives remains foggy. I literally can't even remember exactly when (or even if!) Donna was working, but she must have been, because at eleven thousand dollars per year we could never have survived on my paltry salary alone. Our collective bills consisted of pretty much only two things: rent and groceries. But, as with so many other newlyweds in love, even with no money left to spare, we always made the most of our time together, which was mainly spent walking, jogging, and caring for the two ferocious Yorkies we'd adopted.

When the DEA offered me a job (a career, really), Donna knew that it was my dream come true and, to her credit, selflessly volunteered to leave her entire family behind in Huntsville to relocate with me. What made that gesture even more admirable was the fact that neither of us had the slightest clue where we'd even be sent. As it turned out, that place would be Miami, Florida. We'd imagined the worst, but we'd lucked out once again.

And so it was that in a swelteringly hot July of 1986, Donna and I drove our two cars from Alabama to Miami, our feisty little Yorkie twosome in tow. We were both so young, energetic, and eager to get there that we barely made any stops along the way. At one low point, we found ourselves caught up in a particularly nasty storm on Interstate 75, the kind of storm that makes it almost impossible to see more than forty feet in front of you. Unexpectedly, I lost track of Donna, leaving her alone and struggling to navigate her car through far more perilous driving conditions than she'd ever experienced. In those days, of course, there were no cell phones, and no way for her to contact me. Scared and lost, she had no choice but to do her best to try and get through it in one piece. When the skies finally cleared and she was able to catch up with me, she signaled for me to pull over, and I saw the panic in her gestures and expression. We quickly found a safe spot on the Interstate shoulder, and I walked over to Donna, who was furiously lowering her window. Before she got it even halfway down, she gave me a hard look and calmly said: "Dave, if you *ever* leave me in the lurch like that again, I'm telling you, I will turn right around and go straight back home!" I knew I'd screwed up—royally—and I apologized, sincerely assuring her that I'd never, ever let something like that happen again. And I never did.

When we finally arrived in Miami—two tired twenty-four-year-olds without a clue—we felt like we'd just landed in a foreign country. We didn't know where we were going to live, or how we were going to navigate our way through this intimidating, enormous new city. But we both kept our spirits up, and as soon as I went off to my first official day of work, Donna began looking for a job of her own. Ahead of her time, Donna had majored in Business Administration, with a minor in a field that was barely in its nascent stages back then: Information Management Systems. Hard to believe now, but when we graduated in 1984 and 1985, it was incredibly rare to come across a computer at all, let alone someone skilled in operating one. This gave Donna an advantage in her job search, and soon we were both earning an income, with Donna choosing to take a job with the University of Miami. After that we settled in quickly, finding a lovely little apartment in West Kendall (and eventually buying a little starter home off of Southwest 157th Street), befriending neighbors, and discovering our favorite local restaurants and shops. It truly felt to both of us like absolutely nothing could possibly go wrong. Ah, the blissful ignorance of youth.

As is the case with so many other couples, in the end it just came down to this: Donna and I simply married too young. We were a great team for seven years, but at some point, we began to grow apart, each of us heading in different directions as our marriage slowly weakened. Donna was excelling in her career, often meeting new, intimidatingly intelligent and highly educated people, while I was falling deeper and deeper into my never-ending chase for the countless dirty scoundrel narcos, which necessitated more and more time away spent internationally, far from Miami. And when I *was* home, it seemed like my mind was still on foreign ground. Finally, and with much sadness, Donna and I divorced in 1992 and went our separate and radically different ways: she to build an impressive career in academic alumni affairs, and I to traverse the seedy abyss of international drug trafficking.

After that—not including my training and my Snowcapper days—my career ultimately led me to make new home bases in nine (nine!) different places, four of them Latin American (thank God for that minor in Spanish). I fell in love and remarried during my first overseas assignment in Costa Rica, and my lovely, brilliant daughters, Talia and Laura, were born in Costa

Rica and Mexico, respectively. Both spent a significant portion of their childhoods overseas, and both are fluent Spanish speakers (and far more skilled than their father). Talia and Laura always seemed to have the innate ability to seamlessly assimilate into their environment no matter how new or exotic, regardless of how American or Latino the culture. To this day, I remain impressed by their adaptability and their strength of character (not to mention grateful for it). However, being the child of a DEA Agent in Latin America—or *anywhere*—is hardly what you'd call an easy path. There were all those moves, of course, and again, I was always impressed with how they persevered. But leaving friends is hard, not least for young girls. And my daughters had to say goodbye far too many times. But to their credit, they still managed to keep (and cherish) a great many of those friendships. My girls are incredibly loyal, steadfast, kind, and truly special.

And boy, do they have some good stories to tell. One time, while we were navigating my DEA Level V car (a fully-armored vehicle with heavy Kevlar coating) around the hectic streets of Bogota, both of the girls were (understandably) complaining about not being able to roll down their bulletproof windows. Over and over, I'd hear, "Dad, it's so stuffy back here! We're DYING!" Naturally, and like so many dads before me, I busted out my not-so-secret diversionary weapon: ice cream. Ice cream worked every single time (and I got to reap the benefits, as well). Pro tip for anyone traveling to Latin America, especially La Michoacana, in Mexico: There's just something about the ice cream there (perhaps it's the fresh cream they use, or the way they shave the ice?) that makes it stand out from any other. It's ambrosia.

Another time, in 2004, two of my Colombian bodyguards were bringing Talia back to our apartment from school when they stopped at an intersection. Glancing up, Talia instantly recognized the home of a friend who'd called in sick that day and, thoughtful as always, thought she might check on him. Somehow, Talia found a way to depress the lock function (which was supposed to have been fully blocked), which, in turn, immediately swung open the Level V's heavy, armored door. Talia immediately jumped out and took off, racing up toward her friend's front door.

(Incidentally, these two bodyguards were a hilarious-looking pair, and I took to referring to them as Laurel and Hardy, based on their radically opposite body types. I eventually gave the "Hardy" of the duo the nickname "Jelly," an homage to the character from the movie *"Analyze This!"* with Billy Crystal and Robert De Niro).

Later that afternoon, when I was filled in by the Laurel of the twosome, I found out that as Talia ran down the street in Bogota, Jelly had run as fast as he could right on after her, with his Uzi submachine gun bouncing off his formidable gut and a Beretta 9MM semi-automatic pistol nearly sliding out of his tenuously-belted pants all the while. As you can imagine, all the transfixed, confused Colombian bystanders gave Talia and Jelly a wide berth while looking on in shock and amusement, until Jelly at last caught up with Talia on her friend's porch. The neighbors must have thought it was a kidnapping attempt in effect! And I have no doubt that this particular workday was not among Jelly's favorites. Nearly having a heart attack while trying to chase down an agent's little girl on the backstreets of Colombia is not exactly what any bodyguard signs up for. To his credit, he never, ever complained. And I probably still owe him some ice cream.

Then there was the day I found out that both of my daughters, then away from our home in Mexico City on a school ski trip to the US Rocky Mountains, were trapped in a blizzard and couldn't get to the Denver airport. Due to the (literal) mountain of snow, the entire group—students, teachers, and chaperones alike—had found themselves stranded at the resort, with the bleak outlook of at least a week's wait ahead of them if not more.

In the DEA, we always pride ourselves on looking out not just for each other but also for each other's families, so I didn't hesitate to ask a few of my DEA Colorado-based friends to check up on them, which, of course, they immediately did. And when the weather sufficiently cleared, a few of them even took it upon themselves to serve as personal chaperones home, going so far as to escort my girls (as well as their entire group) not just to the airport but all the way to the actual departure gate. Even the top agent present, Jeff Sweetin (then the Special Agent in Charge for DEA Denver), made a point of going to the gate so he could personally greet all of the students and their chaperones, some of whom were so overcome with relief and appreciation that they literally hugged him, tears in their eyes. (Even speaking as a DEA Agent, I can only imagine the stress that must come with chaperoning children—let alone forty of them—in foreign territory, under crisis conditions. I think I'd choose battling cartels.)

Now, as any dad will tell you, it's not often that you impress your kids (and even less often that they *acknowledge* it), so when it happens, you cherish it. On this day, the girls felt like little superstars. Apparently, top cop Sweetin had walked up to a teacher, flashed his badge, and said something to the effect of, "I need to talk to the Gaddis girls." Very dramatic! The stunned teacher (who was probably still reeling from being stranded in the Rockies with forty teenagers) pointed them out, and stepped back. As everyone else watched, rapt, Sweetin walked over to

Laura and Talia and then his authoritative demeanor softened: "Girls," he said, "I've known your dad so many years, and met him so long ago, that it was back when I had *hair*." Always sharp, Talia shot right back with: "Well, don't feel too bad. He doesn't have any either." Everyone laughed, the mood of the group officially went from anxious to relaxed, and, at last, everyone felt safe in the knowledge that they were going to be okay. The DEA has a knack for that—providing not just protection but actual comfort as well.

When my girls finally got back safely to Mexico City and I nearly crushed them both with my hugs, Laura asked, "Dad, are you important or something?" I savored the moment, then calmly responded: "Yes, honey. I am, in fact, so important that cops will be checking on you for the rest of your life, so remember that!" Typical dad move: Show off a bit to your kids when you get the chance *and* make an attempt to keep them in line at the same time. It's a good thing for them I never sent Agent Sweetin on any of their dates.

One quick sidenote: Almost two decades after that storm and not long after I retired, I got a call from Agent Sweetin. In a rare display of open concern and show of emotion, he explained that his daughter-in law-and grandchildren were in desperate need of a place to stay after hurricane Michael had decimated the Marine Corps Camp LeJune in North Carolina. The "kids" had made a hotel reservation in Charlotte, and Jeff was asking if he could leave my phone number with his daughter-in-law in case of further emergency. At the time, Jeff's son was in the military and deployed abroad, and it wasn't a stretch for me to imagine how terrible and helpless both Jeff and his son must have felt, being far away and unable to help. But as fate would have it, I'd recently moved and was selling my former home on Lake Wylie, not too far from Camp LeJune. I didn't give it a second thought. Immediately, I called the realtor, cancelled all scheduled viewings, and made sure that Jeff's family knew that they were welcome in that home for as long as they needed it. Again, it was hardly a selfless, incredible act on my part; it was simply the DEA way.

Both of my kids are now university graduates busy making their own way through this crazy world. It's a joy watching them as adults, knowing just how much they have to offer. I was a proud father back when they were busy outrunning bodyguards, and I'm a proud father now. And as a parent, I hope I've made my own parents proud in turn.

Now I find myself in a very different (and far less dangerous) phase of my life. I'm still enjoying every possible minute of life, thanks in no small part to my daughters Talia, Laura, and Alisa, son-in-law Ronny, and grandchildren Aubrey and Silas. And make no mistake: I know that being able to look back with no real regrets *and* look forward with excitement and optimism is a true privilege. Those twenty-five years with the DEA gave me a sense of purpose that I think will always be with me, not to mention pride in my work, lifelong work friends (extended family, really), discipline, and the chance, even, to try an entirely new venture post-DEA twice over: first, as a Security Risk Management Consultant, a role I've loved now for ten straight years, and second, as an author. Sure, it took me thirty-five years of fighting in the drug war and watching it wreak havoc, followed by countless months watching a pandemic do the same, but I finally realized that it was time to share some of my stories that still amaze me even to this day.

Most importantly, though, this book has given me a chance to reflect on what really matters the most to me: my family, a word that can mean so many different things to so many different people. Looking back on my own childhood, adulthood, friends, adventures, jobs, achievements, and even mistakes, one thing has become very clear. In the end, they have all carried me through one wonderful, exciting, incredible existence—and my adventures aren't over yet. And for all of it, for every last little crossroad, every last little challenge, every last little blessing, I am eternally grateful.

CHAPTER 3

THE AGENCY

The US's endless war against drug trafficking has seen a hundred years of successes, and a hundred years of failures. The sheer volume of illegal drug (and money) seizures alone, combined with the DEA's ceaseless efforts to disrupt and dismantle every targeted drug trafficking organization, is undeniably impressive. Still, it always seems like not enough progress is being made. For all the seizures and arrests and wins, the collective reach and strength of the cartels has only grown over time. Far worse, though, is the indisputable fact that the only thing that's grown even more rapidly than the number of criminals is our own nation's ongoing lust and demand for illegal drugs. And it's that constant craving that fuels the fire, keeps the criminals in business, and makes every single day for the DEA an overwhelming and uphill battle.

Ever since President Nixon created the Drug Enforcement Administration in 1973 with a single stroke of his pen, the DEA has evolved into one of the most well-regarded and trusted law enforcement agencies in the world. Its development also brought about a newfound, much-needed sense of cohesion and unity (trying to explain it, of course, is far more complicated). Originally, the FBN (Federal Bureau of Narcotics) had shared narcotics investigative responsibilities with the Bureau of Prohibition/Bureau of Drug Abuse and the Food & Drug

Administration. Each of these agencies had their own group of agents, all working under a single command called the Bureau of Narcotics and Dangerous Drugs (BNDD), which, in turn, brought together narcotics enforcement agents from both bureaus *as well as* US Customs officers. When the DEA was formed, all narcotics enforcement agents then officially worked together for the US Department of Justice. And if all of that is incredibly confusing to understand, imagine having to navigate the actual inner workings of this reporting structure on a daily basis.

Now, with twenty-one US-based field divisions and nearly a hundred offices abroad in sixty-one foreign countries, the reach of the DEA quite literally spans the globe. A good number of the investigative cases are co-managed by domestic investigators and their international counterparts, and often include the additional efforts of local and/or state investigators (all of whom are either deputized to work alongside the agents—referred to as DEA Task Force Officers—or have a close and carefully built relationship with them). Investigators also frequently work with various trusted intelligence analysts and headquarter-funded intelligence coordination centers, in order to connect the dots with investigations being conducted by the foreign-based DEA agents and their own host nation law enforcement and security force counterparts. It's a vast, complex, and incredibly well-organized machine, with all the moving parts doing their best to work together as seamlessly as possible. Of course, as with so many other law enforcement organizations and efforts, communication is key. But there is another element that is equally critical, and often overlooked: the simple yet absolutely vital act of careful planning. And lots of it. In fact, every single DEA case varies wildly in both scope and size, but they always share one common, crucial denominator: The Operations Plan.

When I first joined the DEA in 1986, I was a young, inexperienced agent trying to find his place, both professionally and personally, in Miami. Every day—sometimes, every hour—I was introduced to something new, and it seemed that all of them were of equal importance. But I quickly found myself immersed in the details and minutiae of what was clearly going to become my eternal life jacket: the OPS plan. This, I soon learned, was every agent's "bible," heavily relied upon for defining and fulfilling case goals with as little risk to life or limb as possible. Regardless of the case's significance or level of urgency—vehicular surveillance, controlled delivery of drugs and/or money, raid and arrests of suspects—the OPS plan was *always* where we began.

My 3 Amigos (Left-Right).
DEA Special Agents Alex Dominguez, AD Wright and Chris Feistl

To successfully develop an OPS plan, a lead agent must first complete a form that all DEA tactical operations are then planned around. Taking the proper amount of time to prepare is absolutely critical, with the final amount varying in length depending on the complexity of the case, the size of the locations, the number of people targeted, and the potential risk to agents (based on the targeted organization's history of violence). Every last DEA operation is considered to be potentially dangerous, but the level of danger is measured in calculable risk. The primary role of the OPS plan is to weigh that risk and assess the chances for a successful operation.

The form itself is incredibly lengthy and requires a strict attention to detail, necessitating inclusion of all manner of minutiae about the background of the case, including highly specific facts about the suspects (not to mention, all of their associates, vehicles, locales, businesses, assets, and locations they most frequent). A typical OPS plan includes a plethora of possible factors: uniformed police officers, a local SWAT team, K9 crews for search and crowd control, decoy vehicles. We always use the three S's—surprise, speed, and simplicity—in our planning. Sometimes, amazingly, the OPS plan ends up being the most challenging part of the entire endeavor.

But agents are reminded of its importance literally every single day—in fact, I still remember one case in particular that had me thanking God for its very existence. In the early aughts, one of my agents was conducting a vehicle surveillance in Puerto Rico, investigating one of the many local drug gangs, all of which were made up of violent, reckless, and murderous criminals. While the agent was sitting in his OGV with his eye on an apartment building well-known as an oft-used location for drug-trafficking by a particular gang, one of its members snuck up behind the agent, took out his gun, and attempted to shoot him in the back of the head. Luckily, the agent had just glanced in his side mirror, and spotted the aspiring executioner approaching. Acting immediately, he had *just* enough time to grab his Smith & Wesson 870 pump action 12-gauge shotgun, roll out of the car, and shoot the bastard right in the stomach—at the exact time *he* was being shot at. Incredibly, the agent sustained a bullet injury through his thigh but still managed to neutralize the perpetrator (who survived, but was forced to celebrate his recovery by immediately facing attempted murder charges).

Another cocaine load taken off the U.S. streets in a DEA Miami Enforcement Group 4 case - bagged and tagged!

If not for the OPS plan, no one—not the DEA, the FBI, or the state or municipal police—would have had any idea where this had happened, let alone who might have been responsible if the agent hadn't survived. But because there existed an OPS plan detailing the four W's (what, when, where, why), the agent and his colleagues received immediate, desperately needed backup. And the gang member himself faced immediate, desperately needed justice.

To this day, the DEA works closely with every single federal agency in the alphabet, along with military, intelligence, and law enforcement. Some of those relationships are smoother and stronger than others, but the rule of thumb is always the same: cooperate and deconflict. But the question still remains: which agency should be the axle on the wheel? Who, at the end of the day, should be controlling the spokes?

A highly-decorated and respected former US Army General once told me that, at the end of the day, the approach of "One Team, One Fight" is the best—and the only—path to ultimate success in the world of international drug enforcement. And he was right: what was once the only agency ever created in order to combat the ever-growing dangers of illegal drugs in America is now only a spoke on the wheel to accomplishing that task. In the end, there will always be strength in numbers, and there will always be strength in unity. And that is exactly the way it should be.

CHAPTER 4

BAHAMA MAMAS

About six months after the shooting with Sammy, I was driving to work down the Florida Turnpike on a seemingly typical Monday morning. For those of you not familiar with it, the Turnpike is a north–south traffic artery just west of Dade County, one with far less traffic than other roads. I then lived on the south side of Dade County, and the Turnpike offered me the quickest route to my office: most days, I'd just jump on Highway 836 (also known as the Dolphin Expressway), which then led me directly to the DEA's Miami office within the Koger Executive Center. The only actual toll highway in Dade County at the time, the Turnpike did indeed have less traffic, but it also had an infuriating toll booth where all that traffic continuously backed up. So, depending on the time of day, I could either get myself to work in seamless fashion, or find myself buried in a sea of bumper-to-bumper traffic, angrily staring down a line of cars stretching a quarter-mile long.

On that particular morning, as I was headed northbound in my OGV (Official Government Vehicle), I suddenly realized I'd left an investigative report at my house. Worse, this wasn't something I could just pick up later: this was a surveillance report covering a recent operation, a draft I'd worked on diligently all weekend long, and it was due to be turned in that day. While most people probably wouldn't realize it, report-writing is actually one of the most critical aspects of the job, because those very reports are what prosecutors, judges, and defense attorneys will all eventually rely upon once a case gets to trial. And while most DEA agents find writing them to be an arduous and endlessly boring task, the reports themselves still need to be grammatically flawless, factually precise, and reflect only the exact points the agent is describing as being part of his or her truthful testimonial. Making sure each fact is included *and* also entirely accurate is imperative, as any competent prosecutor can-and will revisit those facts in the courtroom during the course of the agent's testimony. No agent would ever want to find themselves in a position where they couldn't swear truth to their own report's details and facts, and, to wit, there's an old DEA adage about the important role these reports play: "If it ain't written down, it didn't happen."

In fact, two issues defense attorneys often raise during a trial are whether the agent took complete and wholly accurate notes during the operation and, also, exactly how much time passed between the completion of the operation and the subsequent drafting of the actual report. Anything less than a perfect report presents the defense attorney with an opportunity for rebuttal, and if any of the facts are proved wrong, then the entire report might as well be wrong (along with the agent in charge). Thus, all it really takes is the mistaken inclusion of one miniscule factual error in one short report, and a guilty client could very well wind up going free as a result. If—God forbid—no notes are taken on site at all, and an agent only gets around to writing their report weeks later, the defense attorney would inevitably, immediately assert that because so much time had passed, and the agent's memory of the facts could thus be challenged, the value of the report itself is permanently tainted. Time and again, it's through these small yet powerful assertions that the criminal defense attorneys wisely attempt to get their clients "off the hook," and the DEA's policies and practices exist in order to prevent such maneuvers. For this reason, DEA policy requires that all reports be written within forty-eight hours of the official end of the enforcement actions being described.

On this particular Monday—the day of the deadline—I knew full well that I was due to submit my finalized surveillance report. Naturally, Murphy's Law intervened: I realized that I'd instead, of course, left the draft sitting out in plain sight right atop my kitchen table, next to a half-consumed bagel and a (now probably ice-cold) cup of coffee. Still, in a half-hearted attempt to prove myself wrong, I glanced over to the passenger seat to my briefcase, reached over to flick open the latches, and BAM!, promptly rear-ended the car idling in front of me at the dreaded Turnpike's toll booth. Immediately, my heart sank. Trust me: if there are two things you don't want happening to you right before the start of your DEA workweek, it's to piss off your direct supervisor or to damage the US government-owned vehicle said supervisor has entrusted into your care. And I'd just managed to pull off both at the same time.

The amount of paperwork that has to be done as the result of an OGV accident is absolutely brutal. In terms of sheer volume, it's equally as daunting as any report concerning theft or, even, the loss of a DEA firearm. In retrospect, I recognize that any potential liabilities resulting from operating a government vehicle could in fact be just as serious as any related to, say, gun possession. But in my mind, I had better things to do that day than to anchor myself to a rigid, steel-case work desk in order to write an accident report. Shortly after I begrudgingly sat down and began to focus on the task at hand, the Associate Special Agent in Charge, Sam Bilbrough, marched into our office space and, barely hiding his grimace and an undeniably stern look, walked directly over to my desk. Sam had always been supportive of me, and had also been outspoken about how impressed he was with the way my Enforcement Group 4 partner, A.D., and I had handled the shooting at Sammy's house on that recent, infamous day. However, supportive as he may have been, Sam was also the lead manager of all OGVs in the Miami Office.

"So, I heard you royally fucked up my car?" Lacking an appropriate and immediate response, I was momentarily speechless, and assumed I was screwed. "No, sir!" I finally said. "It was actually the Turnpike toll booth's fault...but I'll take the blame." Sam, a tall, dignified, older fellow (at the time probably around sixty, a good thirty-five years older than I) with a real talent for handling any and all administrative affairs with a straightforward approach, said, "Well, you know what they say around here: today's hero is tomorrow's zero. And it's gonna cost ya.... but I actually have a job that may put some extra money in your pocket, if you want it."

I just sat there, dumbfounded. Was I being fired, and was Sam actually offering me work, and probably just out of pity? Was I about to lose my entire career and life's work as a result of a simple traffic accident?

"We've got a new interdiction program happening now, in the Bahamas," I heard Sam say, "and I'm gonna send you over there for a couple of months. You'll get a daily per diem, and you'll save a ton of money, trust me. How's that sound?"

I continued to look at Sam in shock, busily trying to process how this had gone from total disaster to total jackpot in less than a minute. Two months in the eternally sunny, eternally beautiful Bahamas, with an added paycheck, to boot? I didn't have to think twice. Within that very same week, I bid farewell to the tollbooth and boarded a plane to Paradise.

Operation BAT (Bahamas and Turks Caicos) used the Blackhawk and Dolphin Helos to capture drug smugglers in the Caribbean

Thus, began BAT ("Operation Bahamas"), the reason for my brief but amazing time on the islands of Turks and Caicos. In short, BAT was a drug smuggling interdiction program, initiated by the DEA Miami Division in response to the National Drug Control Strategy set forth by Vice President George H.W. Bush in the mid-1980s. After the unveiling of Norman's Cay (one of the smaller of the Bahamian islands) as the primary cocaine smuggling hub of Colombian trafficker Carlos Lehder, the United States decided to set up several programs designed to block the rapidly growing free-flow of cocaine then pouring into Miami, and Operation BAT was one of the first. The DEA's Miami Field Division began to send agents over to the Bahamas on a rotating basis, with steadfast support from both the US Coast Guard and Army Aviation groups. Both groups were of critical importance, flying helicopters around the Bahamian and Turks and Caicos Islands in order to help us search for and capture potential drug smugglers within those regions. BAT was, in fact, specifically designed to disrupt the Colombian traffickers' various routes, forcing them to choose replacement routes that were—

unbeknownst to them—far more ideal for us to efficiently and successfully seize the cocaine and make our arrests. Ultimately, the strategy both worked and didn't work at the same time.

While BAT did succeed in blocking many of the smugglers (by essentially destroying their reliance upon long-preferred trafficking routes), it also prompted the major drug cartels of Colombia and Mexico to enter into transnational drug smuggling accords, resulting in Mexico's eventual dominance of the majority of cocaine smuggling into the United States. To our surprise, the very success of Miami's drug enforcement efforts had also led to a nearly instantaneous collapse of the drug enforcement authorities along the US southern border. In other words, we'd swatted down a fly only to watch, aghast, as that fly then morphed into a monster. Of course, hindsight is indeed 20/20, but back in the mid-1980s DEA Miami simply did what they deemed the most effective way of derailing all of those persistent Colombian traffickers so intent on using the Caribbean as their own private international expressways. Essentially, their consistent, flagrant use of these islands allowed them to easily continue to pour their poisonous narcotics directly into the United States of America. Worse, the US seemed to be welcoming that poison with open arms.

After I got settled in the Bahamas, I headed to my BAT orientation, which took place at the US Embassy in Nassau. Once there, I was immediately introduced to two incredible investigators from the Nassau office: Bill Ledwith and John Gartland. Bill and John were recognized as highly professional and outstanding agents, both of them uniquely experienced criminal investigators with superior knowledge of conspiracy law. During this particular time in their careers, they also had BAT and an entire air force backing them up, so they were really loving life. I also met Pat Shea that same day, who became a dear and lifelong friend of mine. Pat was the same supervisor who'd cared for me on the day (and night) of Sammy's shooting back in Miami Lakes, a kindness I'll never forget or take for granted. After the Sammy shooting, Pat had been transferred from the Miami office to Nassau on a permanent change of station (a new assignment, basically) and was there to help Supervisory Agent Ledwith manage OP BAT. It turned out Pat was a perfect fit for the job: a former US Marine who'd fought in Vietnam before joining the DEA, he'd already spent much of his career fighting to take down many infamous drug traffickers in New York, including Nicki Barnes, Frank Lucas, and several members of the East Harlem Purple Gang. Pat's scope of responsibilities included not only overseeing the DEA's role within the OP BAT program, but also serving as head liaison between the DEA and the US Army and Coast Guard aviation resources. It was an immensely challenging job, and Pat Shea was more than up for the challenge. As for my other two new colleagues, Bill Ledwith had come from a stint as a Massachusetts State Trooper and was thriving in his fast-blossoming career in the DEA, as was John Gartland. Years later, both John and Bill became Senior Executive Service members, and each of them ultimately had an immense and lasting influence on a great many successes within the DEA.

During my tenure in OP BAT, I took part in daily aerial patrols, focusing primarily on the zones both the DEA Nassau and Miami intelligence had revealed to be the main hotspots for smuggling activities. These activities included the smuggling of aircrafts and other vessels, many of which we frequently stopped and searched—searches that almost always led to subsequent drug seizures and drug-related arrests. On the occasions we didn't do either, we'd still wind up with enormously invaluable intel just by collecting any and all information on the individuals present, particularly when they had no justifiable reason or explanation for being there. DEA Miami intelligence also focused on drug traffickers running smuggling operations within the Caribbean, of which there were a great many. Operation BAT members—armed as they were with the triple helix capabilities of helicopters, firearms, and Bahamian Strike Force officers— served as the enforcement arm of those endeavors. During those memorable sixty or so Bahama-based days, we helped seize countless boats and planes that were either in the midst of transporting cocaine, or had just finished doing so, leaving fresh traces of cocaine residue (our evidence) behind.

In addition to the Nassau OP BAT office, there was one other, smaller deployment location tucked away on Georgetown, a quaint and quiet island located approximately a hundred and fifty miles southeast of Nassau. Had I been given a choice between the two (which, of course, I wasn't), I would've picked Georgetown without hesitation, simply because of the sheer volume of drug trafficking action in that relatively small region. While so many of the DEA guys and gals based back in Nassau were distracted by the countless pristine beaches, five-star restaurants, and casinos, Georgetown was the antithesis of a tourist trap, offering no such perks. Whenever we were there, rather than indulging in haute cuisine or mindlessly gambling away our earnings, we passed our time fishing and lobstering out on the open water in a decrepit dingy we deemed our very own "USS Minnow," all of us more than content to be living in our rented, unfinished houses. On the rare occasion we did have a day off, a group of us from the DEA, Army, Coast Guard, or another agency would inevitably gravitate directly toward the Minnow. Better still, that little dinghy didn't just offer us some much-needed serenity and air; it also provided us with an endless supply of free (self-caught!) food. Thanks to the Minnow, my own efforts, and the bountiful waters of Georgetown, I saved a lot of money from my unused per diem and enjoyed every second of it, to boot. To this day, I recognize what a wonderful opportunity that was—not to mention, what a blast—and how it simultaneously served as a natural salve for all of the stress that came along with our jobs. But, no matter how soothing the waters or how blissful the temporary escape, work was always our main focus. As much as we loved the Minnow, we always had our priorities straight. Back to work we always went.

I took part in a great many OP BAT patrols, often with the aid of the spectacular Sikorsky UH-60 Black Hawk, a helicopter capable of housing a large group of us at any given time. Typically, we'd have at least a dozen of us on board: myself, another DEA agent, and perhaps ten or so Bahamian Strikeforce officers (all of whom were also deployed on interdiction efforts, and served as the DEA's only legal resource for making lawful arrests and drug seizures). The Strikeforce guys were real tough sons of bitches, each towering well over six feet and with solid, muscular builds that could put The Hulk himself to shame. Not unlike The Hulk, they rarely ever spoke and when they did, you couldn't understand a damn thing they said anyway.

Our outings were almost always memorable for one reason or another. One afternoon, we spotted a gigantic hammerhead shark-spanning easily fifteen or sixteen feet-stealthily cruising roughly twenty feet or so below the water. High up in the Black Hawk, the Army Warrant Officer pilots were enjoying following this massive beast around, albeit from the safety of our perch about a hundred feet above sea level. Eventually, all of us became fixated on the hammerhead, studying him as he'd dart frenetically from left, to right, then back left again, and then into what seemed like a never-ending series of circles. At some point, the pilots joined in on the action and suddenly we, too, were making our own spinning maneuvers, testing all the physical limits of a seventy-million-dollar government aircraft in the process. After about ten minutes of this surreal little dance, I started to feel queasy. Closing my eyes in an effort to stop the spinning only made me feel more and more lightheaded and, to my horror, I realized that I was getting airsick. Of course, surrounded as I was by my motley crew of Lou Ferrigno look-alikes, I was determined not to come off as a wimp, so I kept quiet and just silently prayed it would pass. Of course, the more we continued to follow the hammerhead, the worse I got, and eventually I knew that it was just a matter of time before I'd be looking for a place to throw up as covertly as possible.

Some background on the Hawk: The UH-60 comes equipped with a door on one side, typically used to seat the mechanic so that he or she, with their elastic harnesses securely attached, can safely lean out and survey the tail for any mechanical problems. Or sometimes just better assist the pilots with certain tight, tricky landings. This "mech" seat, as we called it, was always preferred by those of us from the DEA for two reasons: it provided you with plenty of air, keeping you cool on eternally hot Caribbean days, and it was also just the best damn seat in the house. Whomever lucked into that seat had the best view of what was going on outside. The other seats, located in the back and sides of the fuselage, were far less ideal and always rife with stomach-turning odors coming from the diesel. On this sortie, thankfully, I was the lucky one. If I was going to be sick, this was the right seat to be in.

When I realized I couldn't hold back any longer, I chose to puke in an MRE ("Meals, Ready-to-Eat") bag. MREs were a critical part of our gear, relied upon in case we ever crashed and needed enough food to last a day or two before being rescued. With easy access to my lone plastic MRE pouch in my rucksack, I grabbed it and hastily ripped it open, dumping the bag's contents right back into the rucksack in the process. At this point, there was no turning back: as I felt the contents of my stomach working their way up toward my esophagus, I stretched the top of the pouch open as wide as possible and held it to my mouth. At the same time, I shot a fleeting glance back over to the Strikeforce guys, all of whom were busy pointing at me and laughing their asses off. Worse, my fellow DEA colleague was sitting silently nearby, shaking his head, clearly ashamed that his own counterpart couldn't keep it together. Let it be said: there is no compassion in war, and for one quick minute, this most definitely felt like war.

For those of you lucky enough to have avoided learning the hard way about the finer points of puking: it's always the first time, and perhaps also the second, when most of whatever it is you've eaten comes spewing out like water from an old, busted fire hydrant. Dreading the inevitable, I forcefully pinned the bag to my mouth and leaned slightly out the window, determined not to let anything leak back inside the aircraft. Unfortunately for everyone involved, things didn't exactly turn out as I'd hoped. When I did finally heave, it was followed by my worst nightmare: the tragic combination of the force from my puke, along with the exterior windage added by my leaning outside, caused the now fully barf-filled MRE pouch to literally fly out of my hands and directly back into the helo, where its unsavory contents somehow managed to smack every single one of the Strikeforce guys in the face. Assuming I was now in for a major ass-kicking,

I figured I might as well just go for it, and launched helplessly into my second and then third bout of retching-now without the added benefit of the bag-and then sat, spent, watching as every last bit of it flew back *yet again* in the exact same direction it had the first time. Any remaining smiles or cackles of laughter immediately stopped and, one by sickened one, the Strikeforce guys all began to puke themselves. Suddenly, we had a full-on vomit orgy on our hands, and for the next hour and a half we were forced to sit there in our communal puke until the Blackhawk at last made it back to shore. Immediately upon landing, and quite understandably, the aircraft pilots made it crystal clear to us that they wanted nothing to do with the mess. Fortunately, because the pukefest had been a US and Bahamian group effort, the Strikeforce called in their own cleaning crew, who mercifully took charge of the less than desirable mission. As for me, I went directly back to the relative serenity of the staff house, feeling surprisingly good.

On another, somewhat less nauseating mission, DEA Nassau had passed along some recent intelligence to us that a Bahamian citizen (and well-known cocaine smuggler) named Charlie Jones (a pen name) had been using speedboats in order to transport both cocaine and marijuana from one island to another island, one with the added bonus of a landing strip. Typically, Charlie's routine was to pick up the drugs while out on the open water, then deliver those drugs to the strip-equipped island for a transportation fee. Our contacts in Nassau provided us with the necessary grid points and we flew directly to the spot, hoping to find Charlie already there with his load.

When the Blackhawk dropped us (myself and two Strikeforce policemen) off at the sole pier on the island we didn't see Charlie, but we did see two "Bahama Mamas," both focused on intently cleaning sea turtles to prep for later sale in their village. It was unquestionably illegal to kill those turtles, but no one in this tiny village ever seemed to care. One of the Mamas quickly became belligerent with me and my Bahamian police brothers, livid with us for invading their "neutral" space. Both were intimidatingly large women and as they cleaned and prepped the turtles were simultaneously eating some of the raw meat, which looked far more like someone's intestines than any kind of culinary delicacy. But these women seemed to love it, going so far as to tell us: "This make you good lover, skinny man!" For my part, I told them that I'd gladly take their word for it, and passed on their invitation to indulge in a bite. We knew the women were sympathetic to Charlie and other dealers, which made perfect sense: it was, in fact, the revenue from the thriving drug trade that supported so many of the residents of this extremely poor island.

After our infiltration, the Blackhawk lifted and circled high in the sky further out of sight, just in case Charlie or another smuggler approached the pier. After about ten minutes of being on the receiving end of some lighthearted (yet impressively graphic) sexual harassment courtesy of the Bahama Mamas, I heard a voice blaring over the RF radio: "A speed vessel is approaching from the South at a high speed. It could be Charlie. Repeat: speed vessel approaching. Could be Charlie. Over." The voice belonged to one of our US Army pilots, one with years of experience dealing with maritime interdiction operations. The Strikeforce guys and I pulled swiftly away from the pier and hid ourselves within the nearby brush, waiting impatiently to see if the boat would stop at the pier.

About four unbearably long minutes passed before we saw the "go-fast" speed boat come into view. From where we were, we could see that the boat held only one passenger, and from our collective intel we could also see that the passenger appeared to match Charlie's description. Charlie himself was an interesting fellow to look at: though somewhat short in stature, he more than made up for it in sheer girth, likely weighing in at around two hundred and fifty pounds (most of it in his belly). He was a very dark-skinned man with impressively long dreadlocks and was sporting a typical Bahamian ensemble: sandals, shorts, and a tank top replete with the indelible image of a naked, rocket-riding white woman on the front.

As Charlie continued his approach and began to slow down, the Bahama Mamas began jumping up and down in unison, waving their arms high in the air and yelling repeatedly, "POLICE! The police are here!" The pier itself was about fifty yards long and, luckily for us, Charlie couldn't possibly hear them over the cacophony of the boat's engines. Emboldened, we made our move and ran out to the pier just as Charlie was docking and beginning to tie the boat down. When he looked around and finally saw us-now coming on fast and furious and only about twenty yards away-he spun back around, deftly untied the boat, and jumped back in. Impressively, he actually almost succeeded in taking off. But just as his hands touched the steering wheel, I jumped in head first and tackled him, hard. I'd like to take credit for some kind of superhuman speed, but the truth is I was able to reach the boat before the Strikeforce guys only because they were all carrying M16 submachine guns, while I had just my 9mm pistol, holstered. Trust me, you can run a whole lot faster without a Long Arm weighing you down.

It didn't take long for the Strikeforce guys to catch up to me—but by that point, the boat had already drifted at least ten feet from the pier with Charlie and I on board, wrestling and thrashing around furiously amidst heaps of fishing tackle and about four hundred pounds of tightly-packaged marijuana. Wrestling Charlie was no easy feat: the minute I'd finally get him in a full Nelson hold, the sheer force of his weight—along with that formidable belly of his—would pull me right back around like a flag waving on a pole. Charlie outweighed me by at least sixty pounds, and he was wisely using every bit—and pound—of that advantage. Finally, one particularly itchy-fingered Strikeforce cop shot his M16 into the air in order to get Charlie's attention, and it did exactly that. Unfortunately for everyone, it also captured the immediate attention of our pilots, both of whom were still flying high above us. From the radio, I heard: "Shit! Is that SOB shooting at us?!" Immediately I yelled at the cop to stop shooting up into the sky: we still had all our people up there. His face immediately dropped and, clearly ashamed, he apologized: "Sorry, mon!"

I next threw a tow rope over to the other Strikeforce cop, who pulled us rapidly back to the pier, at which point Charlie was finally, and officially, arrested. He was both handcuffed and blindfolded, per the Bahamian cops' custom (protocol until they got him to the actual jail). But Charlie had other plans: handcuffs be damned, he wanted to keep fighting: despite my firm hold, Charlie began trying to kick the same Strikeforce guy who'd cranked a round just minutes ago. Apparently, Charlie could see under the blindfold—at least well enough to try and kick that cop right in the balls. After Charlie's third attempt failed, Officer Itchy Fingers ran out of patience and fired another warning shot—this time in a downward direction toward the pier—but missed the pier entirely. And with the force of an assault rifle capable of firing a bullet at the speed of 3,200 feet per second, that shot hit Charlie directly under his knee, right in the shin bone. Blood, skin, muscle, and bone tissue immediately flew everywhere, including onto my own shocked face, because I was still busy holding Charlie, who was now handcuffed, blindfolded, and shot. But in between the impact of the bullet and the sheer weight of Charlie, there was no way I could continue to hold him up. Charlie swayed ominously left, then right, then fell roughly onto the pier. He literally only had one leg to stand on: the injured leg's thigh was now just barely connected to the lower part of his leg, leaving just a couple of pieces of skin where his entire kneecap used to exist. I heard the pilot's voice once again over the radio: "Oh, shit! They just shot him!" Amidst all the craziness, I didn't get to see what, no doubt, would have been an unforgettable reaction from the Bahama Mamas, but I did hear them screaming. And, unlike their discarded bounty of unlucky turtles could have, they must have run like thoroughbreds right the hell off of that pier.

Knowing time was of the essence for Charlie and that he was in immediate need of emergency surgery, I radioed for the aircraft to land so that we could safely transport him to the nearest hospital. Within minutes, the Blackhawk maneuvered as close as possible to the pier, right within that same open space where we'd infilled. I knew the Strikeforce shooter realized the gravity of his mistake when I overheard him desperately ask a passerby if he'd drive Charlie to the landing zone in his truck: "Mon, please, help us take this guy to the helicopter, we have to save his life!" And, thankfully, that's exactly what we did. Charlie was swiftly loaded onto our Blackhawk, as not only a prisoner but also as a medivac patient. But he'd lost a lot of blood, and was going into severe shock. All I could do was treat him for the shock and keep a tight tourniquet on his wounded leg. After about forty-five tense minutes, we landed at Nassau's International Airport, deplaned our prisoner, and got him immediately en route to the emergency room.

As Charlie was being carried in, Pat Shea walked up to me with a wry smile on his face and put his arm around my neck. "Tell me you aren't the shooter?" With my own slight smirk, I replied, "Not this time. So don't worry, you're safe from a mountain of paperwork." Pat squeezed his powerful, college football arm even tighter around my neck and grinned. "Well, finally. Now *that's* some good news."

Later at the hospital, the doctors would have to amputate what was left of Charlie's leg, but he had miraculously survived that horrific day. And given what a character he was even during the whole scene on the pier, I wasn't at all surprised to later hear he now has a nickname, Peg Leg, and is well-known throughout the islands. So, if you're ever sailing through the Caribbean and run into an obese guy with a peg leg and a shirt with a naked woman on it, please give Charlie my best.

As for all the dope that was on Charlie's boat? I paid the truck driver a hundred bucks of my own per diem money to carry it to the Blackhawk, and back it went with us and Charlie to Nassau. As we were loading it onto the truck, the Bahama Mamas crept out from their hiding spot behind a cork tree and came back over for a final encore, yelling: "Hey pretty boy, can you leave some of that for us?"

"Not this time, Mama," I said with a smile, "but the next time I come back, I *will* try some of your turtle." And with that, they waved goodbye, and we took off in the Blackhawk to the infectious sound of their riotous laughter.

CHAPTER 5

OUT FOR A STROLL

T he DEA Training Academy, as one might imagine, is no easy ride. It's a nineteen-week blur of cold, quick showers, little to no sleep, and a whole lot of bellowing "YES, SIR!!!" and "NO, MA'AM!" at the top of one's lungs.

Located within the US Marine Corps base, Quantico is basically an enormous military boot camp, albeit one where, if you fucked up, you could kiss your entire career goodbye as a consequence. To qualify for the DEA, you have to be younger than thirty-seven, so most of the Basic Agent Trainees (BATs) are typically between their mid-twenties to mid-thirties, thus possessing both the energy and stamina needed to successfully handle the Academy's rigorous routine. In my own BAT class (#43, where the class mantra was "So much to remember!"), Special Agent Bill Faiella and I were roommates, and right off the bat, I knew we'd be good together. Despite the fact that Bill was an New York City cop, based in midtown south, and I was a detention officer from Madison County, Alabama, we realized almost immediately that opposites really do attract. And we made quite the pair: Whenever Bill and I spoke to one other, it was always a scene straight out of *My Cousin Vinny*. But even now, a full thirty-five years later, we still speak often. Coming from

Alabama, I had little more than a thimbleful of the experience that Bill had, who'd arrived fresh off his stint with the ever-gritty NYPD. I still remember listening to his stories about the manic, crazy streets of midtown Manhattan, and how they never failed to keep me entertained throughout the entirety of our training.

Fresh out of the Academy, I was about to get a hefty thirty-percent raise in salary and, eager and grateful, I wasted no time reporting for duty. However, Bill would be making less than he had with the NYPD, and I have to think he must have felt somewhat demoted after joining the DEA. He didn't need (nor want) to rush into his new job, so he wound up reporting to the Miami Field Division roughly three months after I did. Bill was impressive in many ways—for one, he always knew where he was going in life, and he always got there. A physically strong, all-around tough, stoic guy of Italian descent (and one who seemed to grow hair from pretty much everywhere hair could grow out of), Bill was also a disciplined and methodical student. Unfailingly professional and tactful in his approach, Bill always played it safe when it came to weighing the pros and cons of any important decision. That is, of course, until he arrived in Miami and met back up with me.

From day one, both of us were champing at the bit to find our own investigation, our own case—something, *anything,* to get our feet wet. Bill had been in Miami barely more than a week when I called him from my desk phone and said: "Dude, feel like grabbing some dinner at my house, then maybe going to check out some possible coke labs after?" Without missing a beat, Bill replied: "I don't know, gimme a minute to check my social calendar. OK, it looks like...I'm single, I just left New York, I'm in Miami, and I have a new badge and gun all ready to go... so uh, yeah, *where do we meet?*" I gave him my address (which was just as new as his badge and gun), and Bill wasted no time in heading over to my place for dinner after work. Looking back, I'm pretty sure dinner was no culinary Herculean effort on my part; the job left me with virtually no time to cook, so I pretty much survived on takeout. After scarfing down whatever boxed-up, lukewarm feast we'd decided to order, we jumped in my government vehicle and took off to southern Dade County, on the outskirts of the Everglades.

In the 1980s, the Redlands were a true no man's land, one that served primarily as a preferred getaway spot for social recluses, citrus and avocado farmers, and, of course, those we were most interested in: fugitives and drug traffickers. Most of the farms were surrounded by large, private fences, or walls specifically built to keep any outsiders from knowing what might be going on inside. Some driveways could stretch as long as half a mile, hardly atypical in this type of privacy-obsessed, rural community. When driving through the Redlands at night, all you could see were the headlights from your car and the stars above. And even with those to guide you, the Redlands was just a very dark place, both literally and figuratively.

At that point, I'd had my eye on a nearby, highly suspicious farm property based on some particularly intriguing intel I'd gotten during a recent Enforcement Group 4 operations meeting. As Bill and I headed in that direction, it struck us both that we were now living a very different reality than the one we'd been grinding our way through at Quantico. As we navigated our way through the darkness, we relished in both the irony and the joy of the moment: mere weeks ago, a typical day would have seen us rising at five in the morning, immediately taking a five-mile run, then capping off the run with a thorough scrub-down of our dorm rooms. The most excitement we ever saw was on the

FBI's firing range (the very same one seen in so many movies, perhaps most memorably in *The Silence of the Lambs*), firing off fifteen thousand rounds with our brand-new Smith & Wesson .357 Magnums. Now we felt more like we'd stumbled onto the set of *Miami Vice*, stealthily cruising the Everglades late into the night, on the hunt for a suspected cocaine lab. This, to us, was Heaven: there we were, in a government-owned car, fueled by government-funded gas, racing along on government-owned tires, just a couple of eager, naive newbies having a damn good time earning our "AUO" (automatic unscheduled overtime pay).

After dreamily cruising throughout the Redlands for hours on end, we at last spotted the farm in question. As we slowly drove by the discreet driveway entrance, Bill and I smelled a very distinct pungent odor, and I immediately recognized it as ether, an extremely volatile chemical diluent. Thanks to our training, we also had a pretty good idea of what it was being used for— in short, ether was the key to being able to dissolve a cocaine base, after which additional, even more toxic chemicals would be added to convert it into the actual cocaine hydrochloride. Bill and I looked at each other in shock. We knew—in no small part because we could still hear our legal instructor telling us—that the smell of ether almost always represented the two words that would change the course of our night: *probable cause*. To our mutual amazement, it turned out we learned something *other* than shooting during our training! Later, Bill told me that when I first asked him if he smelled ether, he thought I'd somehow channeled a hound dog, so quickly did I detect that faint odor.

Confident in our next steps, Bill and I drove about five miles to the only service station in the area, and began our prep. The station, like most of its kind in the 1980s, had only one pay phone, which I hastily made my way to. I immediately called Group 4's

Group Supervisor John Andrejko (a.k.a. "Johnny Arms"), and quickly filled him on what we'd seen and, more importantly, what we'd smelled. John instructed me to continue our surveillance, while he'd go and call the Group 4 "calvary." Roughly fifteen minutes after we'd first detected the ether, Bill and I "picked-up" (surveilled and followed) an SUV, after seeing it exit the farm and disappear into the depths of the desolate, dark streets of the Everglades. Bill and I, thinking ourselves savvy agents but, in reality, just two naive rookies, began to blurt out, rapid-fire, our stream of consciousness thoughts: "Maybe he's delivering some coke he just cooked?" "Maybe he's disposing of chemicals?" and, of course: "Maybe he's dumping a BODY!"

Amped up and jittery, but still adamantly adhering to our professional, disciplined approach, we followed the SUV down the same, solitary road for nearly five miles. It didn't take us more than a mile to realize that whomever was driving would soon figure out he had a "tail," as it was painfully obvious that we were the only two vehicles on the road (and would be for another ten miles). When our suspect reached a four-way intersection, with Bill and I slowly (but not subtly) pulling up behind him, we decided we'd be wise to turn in the opposite direction of the SUV and return to the farm (or, more accurately, return to the clandestine cocaine laboratory *disguised* as a farm). But before we did, I turned to Bill and told him to grab the shotgun, worried that the suspect might turn and fire at us despite our imminent retreat. Without having the luxury of light in order to see, and while also keeping his eyes focused forward, Bill—a truly authentic NYPD cop through and through—reached around to the backseat and, with one hand, grabbed my DEA-issued Remington 870 Pump-Action 12-gauge shotgun and spun it safely back into his lap. Then, in one fell swoop and as naturally as if he were just taking a breath of air, Bill slapped a few rounds of 2 and ¾" inch, 1.8-ounce slug rounds into the 870, racked a round into the chamber ("KA-CHUNK!"), and turned back to me. "I'm ready," he said. In that moment, I knew I'd lucked out when it came to roommates—and colleagues.

Adrenaline flowing, we drove back to the farm and settled back into our surveillance spot. True to his word, Johnny Arms had called out the calvary and, within an hour, had the place completely surrounded. Not long after Bill and I began our vigil for the just-ordered cavalry, the SUV returned and drove through the covert gate that, up until this point, had successfully kept the real use of this property secret. To this day, we have absolutely no idea where the driver went, or what he might have done during that time. During questioning, he refused to satisfy our doubts that at ten thirty at night he was simply "out for a stroll." But that was of little importance to us. When we officially served the federal search warrant (based on Bill and my declarations), there it was: the cocaine hydrochloride in mid-cooking stage, tucked away in a covered shed about fifty feet behind the farmhouse.

It had been an odd night, but all of a sudden Bill and I realized we had our first arrest: Rafael, another Cuban "Marielito" refugee. Rafael was one of the many Miami-based Cuban drug traffickers who'd flocked to the US during this era in a now-infamous mass immigration known as the Mariel Boatlift. The immigration proved problematic for myriad reasons, not least because Fidel Castro had shrewdly exploited President Carter's promise to accept any and all Cuban dissidents, leaving the window open for Castro to expel thousands and thousands of Cuban prisoners and mental patients. Unsurprisingly, the majority of these often mentally ill criminals not only embraced this move to another country, but also the opportunity to continue their lives of crime once they got settled. Rafael was no exception.

And as it turned out, Rafael wasn't alone: he had his eight-year-old son with him. We soon found out that the little boy slept nightly in Rafael's bed, right alongside a loaded .45 caliber semi-automatic firearm. While looking around Rafael's living room, I noticed a huge portrait of a blond, elegantly dressed woman. At first, I thought she might be Rafael's mother. Curious, and slightly bewitched by the photograph's beauty, I asked Rafael who she was. Initially, he made it clear that he refused to answer. But after roughly thirty minutes of incessant questioning, an exhausted, handcuffed Rafael confessed that the portrait was of his late wife, who'd committed suicide the year before. I happened to be holding Rafael's .45 pistol at that point and, as we all silently took in the gravity of what he'd just told us, I heard Rafael begin to speak aloud in his broken English: "Chu 'olding da same gun chi used, mang." He wanted us to believe that this was the same pistol that his belated wife, the mother of his now-terrified little boy, supposedly killed herself with one year ago. But I instinctively sensed that something in his tone rang false, and I hesitated. Without blinking, I looked solemnly at Rafael and asked him, in earnest, if she'd *really* killed herself— whereby I took a long pause, then persisted—or did *he* do it? Shamelessly grinning like a Cheshire cat and with a knowing, overly-exaggerated wink of his eye, he replied: "Nah, chi keeled *erself*, mang." So now I was also arresting a probable murderer, and one who didn't really give a shit who knew about it, to boot.

Men like Rafael were indeed part of the darkest side of the "Marielitos." A great number of these heartless, soulless bastards were also Fidel Castro's handpicked, most-preferred maniacs and psychos, not the more common, well-intentioned refugees so ubiquitous in Miami and South Florida (who'd come from the less troublesome side of that Mariel boatlift). As for Rafael, his own dark, horrific underworld was completely rocked that day, despite his blatant lack of any semblance of remorse or regret. Ultimately, DEA Enforcement Group 4, along with Bill (who was technically from Enforcement Group 3), took down a cocaine lab capable of processing a colossal five hundred kilograms of coke every single week. Rafael was sent to prison—thereby sparing him the chance to ruin the lives of countless potential future victims—where he languished for decades. No doubt it was a day he'd like to forget, but for us, it was a true high point of our then-burgeoning careers.

The following morning, after Bill walked into his office and was busy recounting the details of the bust with his group, his supervisor—a savvy, highly-revered smooth operator named Lew Rice—pulled Bill into the supervisor's office. Without a whiff of condescension or emotion, he said: "Bill, you're new to this, and I absolutely commend your energy, attitude, and ambition. But the next time you decide to venture out in the middle of the night, deep into the heart of the Everglades, on a clandestine search for a potentially deadly cocaine lab run by a total lunatic, can you call me and let me know first?" "Sure, boss," Bill replied, and with that, it was back to business as usual. And that's exactly how the DEA Miami leadership operated back in the 1980s: no whining, no beatdowns, and no bullshit. Just a team of experienced, supportive agents, all of them dedicated to teaching the newbies how to get the job done—and how to stay alive while doing it.

CHAPTER 6

JUMPER

I n Miami, Enforcement Group 4 often used an informant named Miguel, a native Colombian with an amazing nose for drug traffickers and their abilities to sell him anywhere from five to fifty kilograms of cocaine on the streets of South Florida. Miguel sweetened the pot by bringing extremely beautiful Colombian women to accompany him while he met and negotiated with his drug-trafficking friends. I remember sitting with Miguel and his harem of "Colombianas"—each more stunning than the next and each with her own alias that made no sense to me, i.e., *Gordita* (she was skinny), *Flaquita* (who was not skinny at all), *Viejita* (a young lady in her 20s), and *Mamacita* (she didn't have any children)—and listening to their stories of living the high-life with cigarette boats, private islands, lavish parties, and all the money, drugs, and sex in the world. To successfully ingratiate themselves with the who's who of Colombian cocaine traffickers, these gorgeous women had to play the part, and thus were recruited, mentored, and coached by Miguel very effectively. He was one of Group 4's best confidential informants.

In one particular case, Miguel had made contact with a no- torious Colombian money launderer in Miami by the name of Arturo. Arturo had a crash pad near the bustling Dadeland Mall in the suburb of Kendall, where he was supposedly counting a load of money to pay Miguel for the sale of fifty kilos of coke. At the time, Miguel was being handled by one of our agents, Larry Tong (not real name). Tong was better known by his nickname, Radar, due to his uncanny resemblance to Radar O'Reilly, the character played by Gary Burghoff on the hit sitcom *M*A*S*H*. A former top-tier college wrestler from Pennsylvania, Radar appeared to me as an anal-retentive stickler for detail. Determined to nail every detail needed to convict Arturo, he reached out to the group for help with surveillance and arrests. For us, this was just another night on the town, and we were happy to pitch in.

With little intelligence on this particular trafficker, we scuttled out to Kendall around 4pm and set watch on Arturo's apartment. Unbeknownst to any of the agents, Miguel had told Arturo that he would stash and deliver him the cocaine in his BMW. Around 5 o'clock, Miguel showed up and under our surveillance, pulled his BMW into a parking space, got out, and proceeded to walk up to the fourth-floor unit, where Arturo had instructed they meet. Courtesy of Radar, Miguel had been fitted with a microphone, a device we called a "Kel," so that native Spanish-speaking agents Alex Dominguez and Nicanor Ibanez could hear the arrest signal—a pre-arranged verbal cue that money or drugs had been exchanged and the agents could move in to apprehend the traffickers. The hidden microphone would also capture audio recordings to be used as evidence in a federal trial. As with most drug deals in Miami, we waited... one hour turned into two, and two hours turned into four. Eventually, an unidentified man came out of the apartment building and went directly to Miguel's BMW, climbed in, and drove off. Not knowing what was going on, and also certain that Miguel's car did not contain any drugs (we always searched the car before initiating an undercover operation), we let the guy go. Five minutes later, Radar had an epiphany: Miguel must have told Arturo that the cocaine was in the trunk of his BMW, and he was inside the apartment collecting his money for that delivery. Unfortunately, not knowing this tidbit of information, we had just allowed a coke dealer to drive away!

That was a problem with 1980s technology: nearly every time we used a Kel unit, set up a camouflaged video camera, or even while frequently using our car and handheld radios, the technology failed us and we missed information. This was the reality of those times. Another problem with precision targeting involved DEA's "bread and butter," the use of confidential informants: they often make up the rules of an operation while performing their part. This happens even when the controlling DEA agent has delivered a thorough operational brief, with detailed instructions on the informant's participation, including what *not* do, before initiating contact with the target.

In this case, Miguel simply changed directions and acted alone without giving Radar or any Group 4 member a heads up. Most likely, he thought that by wearing a wire, the monitoring agents would pick up on his new plan and follow the driver of Miguel's car for an arrest down the road. But with our failed monitoring equipment, that didn't happen.

Incidentally, Miguel's BMW was found in a canal, under ten feet of water, by Miami Dade PD the following week. For many years after, Miguel complained about losing his BMW and never receiving any compensation, putting all of the blame on the DEA. In this type of situation, the DEA's rule is clear: if you, Mr. or Ms. Informant, fail to follow your controlling agent's instructions or decide to change plans midway through an operation, any material loss that results is *your* fault to bear and not the DEA's responsibility to pay for. Miguel's penance was the total loss of his BMW.

As Radar figured out what had just occurred, he relayed his "aha moment" over the radio in the exact tone that actor Gary Burghoff would use, "Ooooooh, I know what happened! That guy thought there was dope in the car." In a completely haphazard way, we rushed to mount a raid into that apartment, knowing that money had to be inside—money that the traffickers were supposed to have paid Miguel for the cocaine he purported to be selling. Back in the day (1988), we didn't have the "*Rabbit door driver*"—a hydraulic mechanism used to pry any door off of its hinges—so, we relied on a twenty-pound sledge hammer. Because Radar was the case agent, he was the first through the door to make the first arrest, so he carried the sledge hammer to bust open the door. Radar, like the actor who played him on *M*A*S*H*, was of small stature, but he was wiry and strong! He lifted that hammer and slammed it against the door, expecting it to give way enough for us to kick it open, run through, and grab any and all suspects inside, including Miguel. (As a common practice, the informant is arrested along with the suspects to give the impression that no one at the scene is a traitor, reducing the propensity for immediate violence. Additionally, informants have at least 48 hours to prepare a story that denies or deflects their involvement in the operation—or come up with a plan to protect themself and their loved ones against retaliation.)

The door, however, didn't give way easily. Arturo had replaced the standard apartment door with a cork-filled, steel-plated barricade that took some time to defeat. In fact, after swinging that twenty-pound hammer about fifteen times, Radar stopped, looked at me with visible frustration and said, "It's not opening!" I looked straight back and said, "Bullshit, man! Knock the fucker down!" Radar took a deep breath, picked up the hammer, and gave that door another half-dozen or so strikes. Yeah, baby! When the door finally opened, it freaking came off the hinges, with a formidable force! When we entered the apartment, the traffickers, including Arturo, were scurrying around like mice who had just been dropped into a kitty cage.

As the second guy through the door, I spotted four people: a man and a woman on the apartment's outside balcony climbing over the railing and about to jump off (onto the next lower, third-floor balcony, I assumed); a guy sprinting into the kitchen; and another guy (the smartest one of the bunch!) diving onto the floor with his arms spread above him. In a split-second, I had to decide who to go after. The guy on the floor was likely not an immediate threat to me or my buddies. The two people on the balcony were fleeing from the apartment, and I was reasonably sure we had the back of the building secured and covered. So, I went after the guy in the kitchen. The kitchen typically has all kind of weapons that can kill: knives, forks, knives, a fire extinguisher, knives, a gun stashed in a junk drawer, knives. (Okay, I never want to be stabbed to death). And a trafficker about to be arrested, prosecuted, and sent to federal prison for twenty or more years may be driven to kill. In this particular case, however, the trafficker was trying to hide in the refrigerator! As I rounded the corner in a small kitchen, he had opened the refrigerator and was attempting to crawl into the top shelf. I pulled him out, slapped him on the head, and tackled him. As a 28-year-old, weight-lifting crime-fighter, it took me about three seconds to put him face down on the floor and handcuff him. Then, I looked up to see Agent Coleman Ramsey handcuffing the guy on the floor.

Coleman Ramsey emanated the aura of a tough but cool cowboy. One of the senior men on our squad, Coleman had ten years on me, both in age and experience, having worked in the Tennessee State Bureau of Investigation. A tall guy with a handlebar mustache and a deep Southern drawl, he was also a Civil War buff who collected books and battlefield memorabilia. A confident risk taker, he was always in the fight and never cowed down to anyone, let alone a dirtbag trafficker. In fact, Coleman wouldn't shy away from a fuss with other DEA agents, even at the highest level of command. I can remember several times when he pissed off Johnny Arms and other bosses, and it was entertaining. If you were alongside Coleman, you were always entertained. I'd go through any door with him anytime. A good man.

Coleman and I then looked toward the balcony and saw it was empty, meaning the fleeing man and woman had jumped off. We instinctively led our prisoners over to take a closer look. At the same moment, we all observed: the male jumper had fallen to the parking lot below and appeared to be motionless. As my prisoner looked down at him, he exclaimed, "Que pendejo!" (What an idiot!). Coleman and I passed our prisoners to another agent, Alex Dominguez, and rushed to the apartment stairs as to get down to the jumper. A native Cuban with rugged good looks, standing six-foot-three and weighing in at 220 pounds, Alex was also someone I'd go through any door with. Plus, he excelled at interviewing suspects and taught me a very useful Cuban colloquialism: "Morrrrrrrrronga!" What it means, in plain English, is: "You're full of shit, and I ain't buying it!"—just a lot more succinctly put. Morrrrrrrrronga remains a favorite expression of mine to this day.

Before I reveal the ultimate fate of those jumpers, I'd like share a quick story about Alex and Radar. Radar had a simple two-kilo cocaine "buy-bust" that I and Alex helped him on. We called the Miami Police Department because we were operating within the city limits and needed some additional backup in case more than two suspects arrived to deliver the coke. The deal was supposed to go down in a 7-11 parking lot near downtown Miami, so Enforcement Group 4 was set up nearby, with the Miami police a couple of blocks away. The principal suspect kept delaying over and over, telling the informant that he was getting the two kilos and taking us close to midnight before he finally showed up with the dope. Around 10 p.m., Alex and I, who were in the same OGV, got to talking, when Alex blurted out, "That fucker is holding up my good sleep. When he does show I'm gonna barrel roll his sorry ass!"

Sure enough, around midnight our two coke dealers, both around age twenty, showed up in the 7-11 lot. Radar's informant gave the arrest "coke is here" signal and Radar announced, "Let's go!" In a flash, Alex jumped from our OGV and ran a 4.25-second forty-yard dash to the suspects, who were standing in directly in front of the 7-11. When all of Alex's 220 pounds arrived at the point of impact with the suspects, he realized that the store's front wall was made of nothing but glass, and at the last second, tried to stop. Unfortunately, like the Titanic, Alex could not stop on a dime and went straight into those assholes, knocking them into the glass wall and causing Alex to inadvertently discharge his firearm. Although the bullet safely went into the 7-11's ceiling, the sound of the shot caused the suspects to stick to the side of the glass pane like frozen Jell-O. Seriously, like the green tree frogs that stick on to the windows of your house, these two putzes were glued to the glass.

After peeling off and separating the two suspects, we searched their car, recovering not two but five kilos of cocaine. These morons were just dropping off our two kilos and heading to another deal! Such impetuous, stupid boys. By then, the Miami cops, all Cuban born and well-fed power lifters, had arrived and were processing Alex's discharged round in the 7-11 ceiling. Two of the cops were standing about ten feet from me as I was searching the suspect's pants pockets and in one, found a pistol. I asked the already handcuffed lad what kind of pistol it was and he responded ".38 revolver" in a whisper, as if not to tell the two big, uniformed police officers nearby. I immediately stepped away in an urgent stance, yelling "GUN, GUN!"—knowing full well what would occur. The suspect glanced at me in defeat and quietly murmured, "Oh God, no!" Immediately, those behemoth cops looked up, their heads turned towards the kid, and briskly walked up to him. Without hesitation, the uniformed mountains of muscle began placing him in some extremely uncomfortable restraint maneuvers, because he had an illegal gun during a drug crime. Everybody stood around thinking, "Glad I'm not that moron!"

That leads us back to the jumpers...As Coleman and I ran downstairs to the second floor, with our pistols drawn and handcuffs at the ready, we ran into another agent—who had decided to wear neither his bulletproof vest nor his raid jacket that identified him as an agent. Agent Nicanor Ibanez (not his real name) had recently arrived from a duty assignment in Quito, Ecuador, was experienced and smooth, but had lost his touch on domestic enforcement and all of the safety knowledge that comes with street police work. We later heard Nicanor bragging about having two telephone lines in his house: one for DEA calls and the other for anyone else. That way, if the DEA phone rang on weekends or holidays, he wouldn't answer it to evade work. That was just his style. His lack of concern for safety was a considerably more serious matter. When Coleman and I were running down the stairs in pursuit of suspects, we rounded a corner and saw a semi-automatic pistol barrel staring at us. We both intended to shoot first and later investigate who that pistol was connected to. Fortunately, in an instant prior to firing, we recognized that the pistol was connected to Nicanor—which saved his life. The agent almost died right there. Man, that would have been a lot of paperwork!

Thinking that the suspects who jumped from the balcony might be getting away, Coleman and I continued to run downstairs. When we reached the parking lot, we found the male jumper face down in a puddle of dark blood, with more blood bubbling from his nose and mouth. Clearly, the dude was near death. I turned the man over onto his back and came face-to-face with what looked like a piece of lung dripping from his face. Even for a couple of veteran narcs, it was gross. Coleman then looked at me and said in his low southern tone, "Dave, a true civil servant would give him mouth-to-mouth resuscitation." I replied, "After you buddy!" It was clear with that piece of lung hanging out of his nostril that this guy was at the end of his rope. There was not much anyone could do for him at this point.

Out of nowhere, civilians started to walk around us and eventually up to the jumper. That's when Coleman and I realized we needed to control the crowd and spare the deceased from gawkers. As I was attempting to rope off the area with police tape, Coleman was covering the old sot with a blanket. Just when we thought we had it under control, some kid intentionally broke the tape and people started collecting en masse. One of the onlookers started harassing Coleman; for a second, I thought we were going to have another victim because Coleman doesn't take any shit.

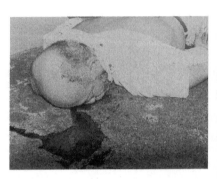 

(Left) The cartel money-laundering "Jumper" in Miami, circa 1988. (Right) DEA Special Agent Coleman Ramsey places a cadaver sheet over the "jumper."

I wasn't sure what had happened to the woman who had jumped behind this guy. There was no one around. I later found out that two agents were assigned to the rear side of the apartment, but during the commotion of the missing BMW and the dynamic Radar entry, they abandoned their posts and were not there to arrest fleeing suspects.

Apparently, when the male jumper attempted to scale from one balcony to another, he slipped, lost his grip, and fell in a spin toward the parking lot where he landed on his face—a bad break, no pun intended. In that parking lot, the jumper took his last bloody breath in front of Coleman and me. The female jumper, who was the girlfriend of the deceased, apparently landed on top of her lover, got up, and limped away. She remains unidentified to this day because none of the other suspects knew her name. Her cellular "burner" or "drop" phone was found the following morning in the bottom of the complex's swimming pool. Back in those days, however, we could not easily retrieve phone data, especially after a phone had been soaked in water all night long. Besides, a "drop" phone is used specifically to evade law enforcement wiretaps. Narcos acquire this phone exclusively for illicit business, and it never tracks back to them. Even if we had managed to recover some data, that phone would have been useless to us in the end.

After the medics certified that the fallen jumper was definitely dead, I searched through his pants pockets and found some keys for a car, and perhaps a house. We used the key remote to locate the suspect's Buick Riviera, which was sitting in the complex's parking lot. In our search of the glove box for registration and insurance information, we were able to ID the male jumper. To honor the dead, I'll call him "Carlos." On his car registration, Jumper Carlos listed a home address in South Kendall, and we all agreed we would be going there. But first, we had to process the apartment where arrests had been made, and we found quite an assortment of twenty-, fifty-, and hundred-dollar bills. There was so much money in the apartment! We had to use seven or eight large paper grocery bags to carry it all down to my vehicle. Yes, I was tasked with delivering the money to the DEA Miami headquarters in North Miami's Koger Center. As a Dade County resident, I got that shitty job.

I remember one thing in this apartment that struck me: a framed mirror etched with the Coca-Cola emblem and on the bottom, a tagline: "Cocaine, The Rich Man's Champagne." What great evidence of the narco mindset! I took it off the wall and carried it with the seized money. Years later, I wondered what had happened to that mirror after the trial. I imagined it was sent to auction with all of the other items seized by the DEA and provided to the U.S. Marshals Service.

Anyways, after arriving at the South Kendall home address of deceased money launderer and high-jumper Carlos, we knocked on the door. A woman in her early fifties, well-dressed and seemingly educated, answered. With her were two teenagers, a young man of about fifteen and his sister, who looked a year or two older. Apparently, they were her children—and perhaps, Carlos's children as well. There was also the family dog—the tiny yapper type, which was generally calm and well-behaved. When we knocked on the door, they were all watching a movie and eating popcorn, the picture of an ordinary, happy family. Was Carlos was related to these seemingly nice people? We were reluctant to break the news of his death.

Because agents were spread out over Dade County looking for suspects, I was the only Spanish-speaking agent on site. I explained to them in my broken Spanish that we were looking to identify a man we had arrested in a drug raid and his vehicle came back to this address. The woman handed me a family portrait and there was Carlos, smiling alongside his proud family. At this moment, I truly did not know what to do, but instinctively told this nice family that there had been an accident and Carlos had been killed while attempting to flee from arrest.

That was a bad decision. Immediately, the woman, who turned out to be Carlos's wife of thirty-plus years, reached her hands up toward the ceiling (or, perhaps, heaven) and screamed in Spanish, "I knew it, I knew it—I should have stopped him!" Then, the two kids got really angry and directed this confused anger towards us—the DEA agents who had dared to come inside their house. From there, the situation only got worse. They both fell to the floor and began to roll around as if they were possessed by the devil. At one point, the boy yelled at Coleman that he had killed his father. Biting his tongue, Coleman told the son to settle down. His father had killed himself by jumping from a thirty-four-foot balcony while participating in a drug deal. Then, all hell broke loose.

During the ensuing hysterics, Coleman, I, and the other agents on the scene took turns following the wife and kids in and out of the house, again and again. The family was shocked, sad, and outraged all at once, and we were just trying our best to keep the situation under control. While entering and exiting the house, that little yapper dog never bothered anyone—with the exception of one agent, AD Wright. Every time, and I mean every time, that AD attempted to set foot in the house, that dog went nutso, violently barking, snapping at AD's feet and pant legs, and seemingly wanting to eat him alive. As we were departing and forming an exit strategy for post- event assignments, the generally quiet AD Wright remarked, "That damn dog was picking on the only Black guy. That's some mutha fukin, bullshit!" In spite of managing danger, death, and the destroyed family behind a drug dealer's greed and stupidity, every one of us cracked up in maniacal laughter. On that day from hell, like many other days, Enforcement Group 4 stayed true to our mantra: *Never Lose Your Sense of Humor.*

After finally leaving the house, we all went our separate ways. I began to head back to the office and by that time—nearly 11 p.m.—I was pretty tired. At one point, while approaching an intersection, someone ran a red light. To avoid a collision, I slammed the brakes—and all of the money rolled out of the bags and flew through the air. Hundred-dollar bills, fifty-dollar bills, twenty-dollar bills... they landed everywhere, from the top of the dashboard to under the seats and even in my lap! I stopped my car and, in a panic, thought, "My God, I've got a lot of money here and the only guy who really knows how much, Carlos Jumper, is dead! What if I lose it? What if someone alleges I stole it?!" Due to the fact other agents were processing the scene or transporting prisoners to jail, I was alone with this money, a lot of it, without a single witness. I was mortified and drove to the office as fast as I could, making sure not to plow into any cars at other intersections.

When I arrived at the office, which was empty, I gathered up all of the money I could find and dropped it in to the non-drug evidence vault. Then, at last, I headed home for the night. The entire drive, I kept thinking about that money, and could not believe I had taken responsibility for that much money by myself. What a stupid move! The following day, an official count at Federal Reserve showed we had seized close to $470,000— enough to retire three times over in the mid-1980s. It all went to the US Treasurer to help pay for another day of DEA operations.

The day and night of the jumpers was eventful, to say the least. Yet, every once in a while, active investigations throughout Enforcement Group 4 would be slow. In a lull, we would have to find things to do. Back in the 80s, a supervisor told us, "You're in Miami, the drug capital of the world! If you're bored, go out and find an informant or a fugitive." And we loved doing both. Often, it involved "sitting on the phones"—conducting surveillance on pay phones at the Kendall Home Depot and waiting for a drug deal to happen. The Group 4 boys and lady (we had a fantastic female Special Agent, Meredith Thompson, who had played college basketball on scholarship for the University of South Carolina and loved running marathons[3]) would surveil the long line of twenty pay phones and soon find a caller who matched the drug deal profile. Call and hang up, call and hang up, call and hang up, and then pace around, all in ten minutes. We would follow the person of interest and watch them pick up a package of dope or money from another drug trafficker. Then we'd swoop down on them. Or, with the help of a Metro Dade Police patrol unit, we'd conduct a traffic stop and discover their product in the car and take them the Miami office.

For small amounts of dope, the US Attorney's Office would declare "nolle pros," short for the Latin term that translates to "Will Not Prosecute." So, we would have to set them free— but not before telling them that they would be going to a State of Florida courtroom unless they cooperated with the DEA. (That's where our skilled use of "Morrrrrrrronga!" often came in handy.) Nine times out of ten, these small-time drug dealers would sing like canaries, and that's how we gained informants. Other times during a lull, we would pick up cases of outstanding fugitive warrants and work toward locating the fugitive, so we could eventually "bag & tag" the perp.

One of these fugitive apprehension cases took us to an island just off the Miami Skyline, Key Biscayne. On this paradise for the rich and famous, Group 4 agents, including Radar, Alonso Petino (not real name), and myself, located a luxury condo being occupied by a high-level Colombian trafficker, along with his Colombian model girlfriend and their two tiny dogs. After confirming the details with the building's security guard and maintenance engineers, we devised a plan to gain access to the targeted fugitive. Using the maintenance engineers' uniform for cover, we would come knocking on Mr. Fugitive's door to inform him that another resident had backed into his Porsche Cayenne while it was parked in the garage. First, we needed agent Alonso Petino to call the unit from the maintenance office and tell Mr. Fugitive (in Spanish) that the condo's maintenance men were coming up to explain an incident resulting in damage to his Porche. This way, he wouldn't be surprised when strangers rang the doorbell. After Alonso made the call, Radar and I, dressed like maintenance engineers, came up to the door, rang the bell, and Mr. Fugitive cracked it open slightly to speak with us. Since Radar didn't speak Spanish and, at that time, neither did I, we blew the door open and tried to grab Mr. Fugitive as he ran to the living room coffee table, where a S&W .44 Magnum was lying in the open. Had he made it to the pistol, Radar and I would have had another terrible day, like the one I had with Sammy in Miami Lakes. But Radar ran forward and caught the guy with a shoestring tackle even Coach Bear Bryant from the Alabama Crimson Tide would have loved. Radar climbed on top of Mr. Fugitive, a man easily twice his size, and used his college wrestling moves to tie him into a pretzel shape so he ended up staring directly at his scrotum. His head was so close to his crotch, he could have licked his balls like a dog. I cuffed the fugitive trafficker, and we took him to jail.

After catching our breath on the trafficker's $10,000 Italian leather sofa, I got up and proceeded to clear the apartment, room by room, closet by closet, accompanied by the gorgeous model girlfriend. In every room, I couldn't help but notice a striking piece of artwork: a life-sized photograph of her in the nude. One with her sitting naked on that sofa, one with her standing naked on the balcony with the ocean in the background, even a nude of her washing dishes in the kitchen. Every time I looked at a nude photo of her and then back at her in the flesh fully clothed, she laughed and said, "Mi favorito" (my favorite). When she asked me which one was my favorite, we decided it was time to leave with her man in tow. This striking Columbiana was already working her charms to try to get out of trouble, but she was never really in trouble. It was Mr. Fugitive's name on the warrant; he was the one we wanted. Another good day on the job!

CHAPTER 7

BLUE MOUNTAINS

Back in the 1980s, my partner, Chris Feistl, was the epitome of a South Florida DEA agent—and hunk. Standing six foot, three inches tall and weighing in at 190 pounds, Chris was athletic (in fact, he owed his undergrad degree to a basketball scholarship). Topped off with blonde hair that fell past his shoulders, he made *Miami Vice's* Don Johnson look like Ernest Borgnine. His physical attributes aside, what made Chris a top-tier agent was his mind.

Chris was gifted with a photographic memory. He remembered, in sharp detail, the precise routes he had taken on every surveillance and undercover mission. He remembered names and dates mentioned in casual conversations between traffickers, even when he pretended not to be listening.

What's more, Chris had a spectacular drive as an investigator; when he set his mind to achieving a goal, it was as good as done. I remember working with Chris on a case in South Miami, involving a Ghana heroin trafficker named Sam-Sam. To monitor Sam-Sam's phone calls and discussions, we needed to place a wiretap in his workplace—a private business. And that meant submitting a Title III wiretap order. Working through the night, Chris prepared a sixty-seven-page affidavit, and sent it off to the US Attorney General's office the following morning. That was unheard of! He completed this massive piece of paperwork from memory alone, pulling all the information required out of his head.

Chris knew how to use being both smart and handsome to his advantage. However, there was one unfortunate occasion when his "rico suave" good looks failed him. There's an inexplicable and rare affliction called Bell's Palsy. It's basically a temporary facial paralysis, often making it difficult to close the eye on the affected side. Well, Chris woke up one day in sunny Miami and started getting ready to go to work. When he looked in the mirror, he was greeted by a half-droopy face. When he tried to blink and refocus, one eye wouldn't shut. Freaking out, Chris called both Alex, his DEA "partner in crime" at the time, and me. (Alex, a Miami Cuban, arrived in the United States very early in his life. A tough yet intelligent man who stood six foot four with a solid physical build and obtained a finance degree from the University of Miami, he could have made a success in almost any career.) Chris was yelling, "I'm paralyzed!" So, we rushed him to the doctor. He was quickly diagnosed and treated—but with Bell's Palsy, there's not much you can do except wait it out. Still, he made the best of it, and humored us. There were days when Alex, AD (yes, the same AD from "Swords Drawn"), and I would offer to buy Chris lunch or dinner with the sole intention of making fun of him. We always got a laugh out of watching the food run out and drop from one side of his mouth. Fortunately, Chris laughed right along with us. (Yes, DEA agents are easily entertained.)

In most cases, Bell's Palsy will pass in time and everything returns to normal. However, because Chris was unable to close his affected eye, the doctor gave him a black eye patch to wear for a few weeks. After two weeks, Chris's facial muscles began to relax, and he started to look like his handsome self again. So, Chris and his eye patch went out bar-hopping. What a reaction that patch stirred up with the ladies! Local businesswomen of every ethnicity imaginable in Miami, ladies in town on vacation, ladies just out on the town—ladies, ladies, and more ladies flocked to my one-eyed brother! A single, tall, muscular guy with flowing blonde hair and an eye patch—Coconut Grove definitely took notice. And the new local hottie had a secret power: the ability to remember every name and detail about each young lady who walked up to him and asked, "Hey good looking, why are you wearing that eye patch?" At that time, as Chris's luck would have it, a popular soap opera featured a blond long-haired dude with an eye patch. That character had all the ladies swooning, and Chris fell right into a bed of roses! AD, Alex, and I just shook our heads, thinking that only Chris could turn Bell's Palsy into a seduction play.

Chris and I were tight (and we still are). Our friendship went beyond the agent partnership. For some inexplicable reason, our careers tracked in parallel: we were partners in Miami; our cases overlapped when he was in Colombia (for the first time) and I in Central America; we worked in the Carolinas at the same time; and from 2004 to 2006, we worked side-by-side in Colombia. As "Brothers in Blue," we pretty much knew each other inside and out.

When we were partnered in Colombia, I remember us training in an open water course for scuba diving. In scuba training, there's an exercise where a pair of divers must go underwater and share a regulator—the oxygen producing mouthpiece that keeps you breathing and alive. The purpose of this particular training is to know how to survive if a regulator fails and one dive buddy has no air to breath while sixty-plus feet deep underwater. The safety principal is to slowly ascend to avoid the risk of injuring your lungs with a rapid pressure change as you return to natural air. With his functional regulator, a buddy takes a nice big breath and calmly passes it to his partner, and then they switch back and forth until slowly and safely resurfacing.

Well, during this exercise in a swimming pool of about ten feet of water, with the Colombian instructor watching us, I passed my functional regulator to Chris, and he began to use it as instructed. This transfer phase went fine, but after twenty seconds or so, I motioned for him to give it back so I could breathe—when he simply gave me the finger. Not an index finger as if to say "give me one more breath," but THE finger. Without saying a word, he was soundly telling me, "Screw you, buddy; I've got my air and you're on your own!" I broke out in maniacal laughter, shooting bubbles out of my nose and mouth while glancing at our instructor, who was doing the same. That was Chris's attempt at humor, clearly at my expense. I almost blacked out from holding my breath and laughing simultaneously on that exercise. At the end of our multi-week training, we both easily passed our final exam—Chris, of course, with a 100% score. As we accepted our dive cards, the Colombian instructor confidently stated that DEA agents were nuts, and he would dive with us anywhere and at anytime.

Chris had a lot of memorable traits, and we worked together on more than a few unforgettable cases. But what most stands out is our Jamaican adventure. It all started when our senior colleague, Senior Special Agent Coleman Ramsey, was trying to negotiate a multi-ton cocaine smuggling load with local traffickers. Coleman needed a couple of undercover agents to meet the traffickers in Kingston, Jamaica. So, Chris and I were left working with Coleman's informant, Hershal, to arrange a meeting with a posse front man, identified as Dred-Dee. (Yes, that's his real name—at least, according to his Jamaican driver's license.) Dred-Dee invited us to join him for dinner.

A thirty-year-old career marijuana trafficker with long thick dreadlocks, Dred-Dee acted the tough guy, but I took him for a wimp. He sported massive gold chains and always wore a tracksuit, usually bright red, solid white, or yellow.

Before getting to that dinner, I'll tell you about Hershal. A native Jamaican with a taste for quality liquor, fast living, and risky business, Hershal would take Chris and me all around his chaotic island. Since his youth, Hershal had frequently dabbled in scams, swindles, and scandals to make a fast buck. He was probably raised that way. One of those schemes involved his appreciation for horse racing. Hershal made lots of money— until Jamaica's national gaming authorities got wise. As they discovered, he injected his preferred horses with amphetamines before the race, and then sat back and watched them outrun the competition by four to six lengths. Hershal wound up in jail and, according to him, worse, was banned from the horse racing industry for life. In fact, he was deemed persona-non-grata from even watching a race at the tracks. Needless to say, Hershal was not one to follow rules or orders, so Chris and I ended up with Hershal at the racetrack. I refused to lend Hershal money, but Chris was more of a gambler. He let Hershal borrow a hundred bucks, and never got a cent back!

Later that evening, Chris and I arrived at the appointed swank restaurant in Kingston to meet our host, Dred-Dee. While waiting, we ordered a couple of Red Stripe beers. Striking up a conversation with another man from the bar who introduced himself as Lloyd, we began debating the benefits of smuggling drugs from Jamaica to South Florida using small aircraft. This kind of discussion was common and wide open amongst friends and strangers alike in Jamaica. As we talked, Lloyd used both of his index fingers to pick his nose. As we sat and watched him shoving his fingers into his nostrils in a five-star restaurant, it became clear that we had picked bad company to kill time with. Shortly after bolting from Lloyd, we called Dred-Dee, who inconveniently cancelled on us, saying he was unfortunately detained with other "clients." Maybe his enforcers had conducted an advance surveillance on the restaurant and saw us engaged in conversation with the village nose-picker. Or perhaps he was a no-show for fear we were DEA. Regardless, Dred-Dee opted out. Instead, he suggested we meet with his second-in-command for a few drinks, and we complied.

Sadly, we had to say goodbye to this beautiful and elegant restaurant; Dred-Dee's associates wanted to get together at a sleazy fish house in the city. After meeting, greeting, and drinking a few mimosas, Dred-Dee's cohorts asked if they could take us on a tour of the town. Again, we complied, and hopped in a jeep with Dred-Dee's second-in-command and his driver. And again, we came to regret it.

They took us on a trek into the Blue Mountains, famed for its rich soil to cultivate coffee beans and weed. While working our way up the mountainous terrain, we hit a roadblock: two posts connected by a chain across the desolate road. It was manned by a guard holding a machete. Our driver stopped the jeep and got out to speak with the guard. As Chris and I were seated in the back enjoying a few Red Stripes, we heard our driver and the guard arguing, increasingly talking louder to each other. When the guard raised his machete, our driver held up his hands, seemingly in defeat, and said, "Leave you be, mon!" Then he walked to the back of the jeep, opened the door, and removed his own machete. Now, things were getting interesting.

You haven't seen a show until sitting in a back seat of a jeep, downing Red Stripes while watching two grown men run around the vehicle while hacking machetes at one another. Chris put his money (another indication of a gambling problem) on the tall skinny guard, and I bet on our short fat driver. After twenty minutes or so, the two warriors became exhausted. The guard agreed that we could move ahead, if we paid him ten dollars, US currency. I had to pay. A typical GS-12 civil servant, I immediately began to think of a way to get my money back. I envisioned my travel voucher explaining the expense in the following way: "Security tariff of $10 US required to avoid being hacked to death by a machete-wielding psychopath."

This story reminds me of another story of creative DEA expense-accounting. While on foreign assignment, an agent purchased a wide-brimmed hat to protect his handsome face from the tropical sun. When he called his supervisor for approval to use the government's money to pay for this $100 head cover, he was succinctly told under no uncertain terms that the government would pay for his new hat. When the agent finished his assignment and returned to his base office, he submitted his typed-written temporary duty assignment voucher with a litany of travel charges. At the bottom of those claimed charges, the agent wrote in longhand, "The hat is in here somewhere; you find it!"

So off Chris and I went to continue our excursion. At last, we arrived at a farm on the top of a mountain, offering us a spectacular yet unique view of Kingston—because there were no other houses in sight. I knew that if Chris and I needed help, there was none; we were all alone. We were "invited," or more like escorted, into a house with bars on all the doors and windows, for "some cold beer, mon!" Our only option was to go with the flow because at that point resisting any "invitations" was futile and would only result in suspicions and likely violence against us. Once inside, we knew we were in trouble. Our hosts locked the doors behind us, sat down in the living room, and promptly began to smoke crack cocaine from a pipe bong. I did a quick, furtive scan of our surroundings and observed only a few pieces of wooden furniture and a couple of AK-47 auto machine guns leaning up in a corner of the main living room. After one of the "posse boyz" burned his rock, he handed me the pipe and said, "Your turn, mon; show me you're not a cop."

It's important to understand what is going through an undercover DEA agent's mind when they're pressed to inhale, ingest, or inject illegal drugs. I'm not talking about a scenario where a gun is pressed up against your head and the trafficker is saying, "Do it, mother-fucker or I'll kill you!" Under those circumstances, every human being will do what they must to survive. I'm talking about an agent working in an undercover capacity and told to try a drug to prove they're not a cop. You just don't do it. The cardinal rules of an agent's behavior are fourfold: no drugs, no misrepresenting expenses on a voucher, no stupid shit involving an official government vehicle, and never break rules, or even bend them, with a confidential informant. Any violation of one or more of these rules will get an agent fired or prosecuted faster than a flea on a dog's ass.

So, how does an agent avoid using drugs when pressured? The evasion tactics are limited only by one's imagination. But first and foremost, the agent must stay calm. Concentrating on breathing techniques keeps the heart from beating excessively. At that moment, one drop of sweat on the brow can give the opposition (a trafficker) all the justification needed to back out of a deal or worse, accelerate pressure that might lead to a violent situation. So, I would program my thoughts into a "don't give a shit" mode, even at the risk of seeming cocky, and calmly explain why I did not want to smoke, snort, swallow, or shoot up. If my undercover position was challenged, I'd stand my ground and let the chips fall where they may. The undercover agent must think like a trafficker, knowing when and how to deflect challenges while making the response seem perfectly reasonable to the dirtbag being addressed.

Second, think three steps ahead. Ultimately, the agent must be willing to forfeit the deal and move on. Personally, if a trafficker threatened my life to use a drug, I'd do it—but you could be damn sure that trafficker would never see natural light again. Even without an awareness of the undercover being a federal agent, the trafficker is responsible for any harm or abuse of that agent. That's why criminals who kill undercover police officers and agents face the harshest penalties possible for their crime, whether or not they knew the victim was a member of the law enforcement "family."

Third, you never admit to the trafficker you're an agent. Some traffickers might think that is the kiss of death for them and uncommonly react with violence, even if they did not possess the propensity to do so. If the undercover agent disagrees while negotiating or brokering a deal, that's okay since most traffickers disagree on how to do business. As such, the undercover is simply blending in even better.

My training immediately kicked in the moment that crackhead passed me his pipe. As I pulled a cigarette from my breast pocket (where my micro cassette recorder was safely tucked away and dutifully capturing every word), I said, "Sure, not a problem, but first go get me a hammer."

I peeked at Chris, who was looking straight at me and must have been thinking, "You've lost your mind! What's a damn hammer got to do with smoking crack? We're gonna die!" Chris, being the cool dude he is, was hiding it well, but I knew him—and he was thinking the worst. I also knew he would never compromise an undercover operation, and I had 100% confidence he would handle whatever I threw at him.

When the crackhead heard my response, he jumped up and shouted, "What you say, mon? You want a hammer? What you need a hammer for, mon?!" I leaned back in my seat, fired up the cig, and calmly replied, "Well, I'm a recovering coke addict, and if I hit that pipe even one time, it'll give me a fucking splitting headache. I just want to slap you in your head with that hammer so we'll both feel the same." I peeked at Chris again, and now his eyes were beginning to calmly widen. Our crackhead host gazed at me with a stony expression and piercing bloodshot eyeballs, trying to detect and discover a smidgen of an indication that I was bluffing. After staring at me in silence for about ten seconds, which felt like an hour, he broke out in maniacal laughter. Then, everybody in the room started laughing, including my relieved partner and me.

Chris and I stayed in that house for hours, watching our hosts fry their brains rock after rock while we drank Red Stripe beer and discussed how rich we would all be someday. We eventually drank those wild-ass jerks out of their Red Stripe. When I went to the bathroom to pee, I found that the toilet was removed, leaving only a hole for dropping any and all bile and excrement. Well, you know what they say, "while in Rome." So, I peed in the hole like everyone else and the stench was overwhelmingly rancid. Suffice it to say, I was happy to get out of there.

While later pondering that hole and the ungodly putrid odor emanating from it, I realized: this secluded "flophouse" has been used as a torture chamber against competing drug traffickers. As an experienced investigator, I was no stranger to the smell of dead human tissue. The pungent disgusting odor was not only of bile, but also of decayed bodies. My gut and nose told me that the expired torture victims were dropped into that filthy dark hole to rot.

Chris and I must have been stuck in that hell house at least for five hours. At one point, Mr. Crack "Hammerhead" walked up to me and abruptly reached out to snatch my pack of cigarettes from my breast pocket, which contained my Panasonic mini-recording device. I immediately slapped my hand against the pocket to block his grab and asked, "What are you doing, mon?" Hammer replied he wanted a cigarette, so I said, "Look, I don't give away my last one, so let me check." I calmly and slowly took the pack out of my pocket and pulled one out to give to my "sky-high" nemesis. I quickly shoved the pack into my pocked and Hammer politely said, "Thank ya, mon."

Finally, after many hours, our crackhead hosts lost their will to stay awake and acquiesced to our request for a ride back to a hotel where we were *not* staying. They too were tired of smelling the stench from inside that prison house. When they dropped us off, we made sure we had "shook them off" and immediately took a cab to our actual hotel.

Later that night, Chris and I agreed that the entire night was a debacle made of our own stupidity, and we swore on our souls to each other that we would never speak of it again. I guess my soul is finished. As I'm sure Chris was, I was so pumped with adrenaline that I could not sleep—of course, had it not been for more Red Stripes. That day, between the trip to Blue Mountains, watching a machete fight, entertaining five psycho drug traffickers high on crack cocaine, and our necessary and routine "Action Backbrief," I must have drunk thirty-five of those smooth cold beverages. Thanks to my excessive imbibing, I had a sleepless night flooded with constant belching, frequent flatulence, and urinating every twenty minutes. Did I admit to the stupidity of this less than honorable event?

Sometime in the morning, I awoke and looked outside my hotel door to check for surveillance, when I noticed a garbage pail sitting outside Chris' hotel door. Each room opened out directly to a porch outside, much like the old motels here in America. Slowly wandering over the pail for a glimpse, I was aghast to find a freshly soiled pair of underwear inside. I figured Chris had the shit scared out of him the night before. But no, as he later explained, the beer and spoiled jerked chicken was to blame. It had coursed through his system like a goose on a Jell-O diet, which I understood perfectly, as my "movements" were equally loose that morning. Gross? C'mon, we're all human. Even hunky DEA agents.

When agents from domestic offices are working overseas, protocol requires us to check in with the DEA country office on a daily basis, if possible. That way, the local office—in this case, Kingston—would collect intelligence as to who is trafficking drugs, as well as provide us personal security while on risky operations. In other words, if Chris and I were to come up missing or dead, the local DEA and their Jamaican police partners could find our bodies. To check in, we had to go to the American Embassy, where the Kingston DEA office is located.

Embassy security is tight with three layers: the US Diplomatic Security Office, whose Special Agents manage personnel and conduct investigations of security lapses and violations; the

US Marine Corps Security Detachment or Group (SMG); and a cadre of poorly uniformed Jamaican security guards who execute the day-to-day traffic of visitors and basic outer perimeter patrols. When Chris and I arrived at the embassy's front gate, we registered our names, showed our DEA credentials, and walked through the magnetometer, commonly known as a metal detector, to enter the grounds. As usual, both of us were armed with our DEA-approved handguns. So, when we walked through the magnetometer, all hell broke loose. Whoop, whoop, whoop! Bells were going off and red lights blasting over the embassy grounds as Chris and I obliviously strolled into the chancery building, in obvious, violation of US State Department rules.

By the time we were well inside the building, a couple of Marines who were barely into their twenties caught up with us and asked, "Excuse me, sirs, are you carrying weapons?" Chris responded in the affirmative while simultaneously flashing his badge and credentials at close proximity to one of the Marine's bulging eyes. At that very moment, I couldn't help recall a scene from a Cheech & Chong movie, where one says, "We don't need no stinking badges!" Well, apparently we needed more than badges and creds to walk through the chancery with our sidearms. Politely yet firmly, the young Marines made sure our weapons were checked in their front gate station before we took another step.

When Chris and I finally arrived at the DEA office, the local DEA Agent informed us that the "boss" wanted to speak to us. We were quickly ushered into the DEA country attaché's office, where he made it very clear that we were never again to bring weapons onto the embassy grounds. "Okay, boss, no worries," I replied. I later heard that the ambassador, a Ronald Reagan political appointee, chewed the country attaché a new ass over this incident. Well, I thought, it's better to be judged by twelve than carried by six! Anyways, it wasn't my ass.

Later that day, we returned to the hotel, where the complimentary pale of soiled drawers remained on the porch, and I called Dred-Dee to break his balls about blowing us off. His girlfriend, Palombo, answered. I had met Palombo once when she was with Dred-Dee, and she was the most beautiful woman I had ever seen. She was about five foot, nine inches tall, with flawless mocha skin, piercing green eyes, and long, straight, glowing jet-black hair. Plus, she had an hourglass figure with the attitude to show it all off. When I first saw her, I thought I had died and gone to heaven. (At least, I hope heaven has a few Palombos hanging around.) During our brief phone conversation, Palombo informed me Dred-Dee was not around that day (he was definitely avoiding us, a clear indication the deal would not go this time). She was home all alone, and asked if I wanted to come over and "spend time" with her. I said, "Wait a minute, let me get this straight. Dred-Dee is away, and you're home alone, wanting me to come over to 'spend time'?" Palombo replied, "Yes, you won't tell Dred-Dee, will you?"

Chris was in the room as I was talking to Palombo. Getting the gist of our conversation, he propped himself up in the chair, gazed directly at me, and started vigorously shaking his head from side-to-side, clearly conveying, "No, no, no, stupid!" I was very tempted by Palombo's invitation; in fact, I told her yes, I would be there. Not long after, however, I listened to my inner conscious (named Chris) and called her back to cancel, telling her I had too many appointments to work her into my busy jet-set lifestyle.

As soon as I said no to Palombo, it hit me: divorce was imminent in my life back at home. I had actually entertained the idea of being with another woman, envisioning the excitement of straying with a gorgeous international mistress. I did not do it, but I definitely thought about it, and that's not healthy in a marriage. Although this experience was not the single factor in our eventual breakup, it followed me until our divorce in 1992. Red Stripes, crackheads, and a life-changing awakening from a fantasy affair—my time in Jamaica was certainly eventful.

CHAPTER 8

THE CANUCK

With only three years on the job under my belt, I was incredibly busy, thriving, and more than happy to be working closely with my then-senior partner, Special Agent Ken Peterson. Kenny had previously worked for well over a decade back in Buffalo, New York, building complicated cases centered around high-profile members of the New York Mafia, as well as Canadian and US-based international drug traffickers. Both the Canadian and the US traffickers were incredibly successful at the time, consistently supplying both cocaine and heroin to the countless biker gangs then dominating the local drug trade, and meeting most of the drug-related demands of countless Canadian neighborhoods. (Some of these biker clubs, including the Hells Angels and the Pagans, are still around today.) One day, Kenny got a call from an old pal of his from the RCMP (Royal Canadian Mounted Police), a Mountie he'd worked with in New York a few years prior. That cop, Nick Ronaldson (alias: "Nick the Narc"), and not his true name, turned out to be one of the funniest jacks I'd ever met. After twenty years of undercover work spent posing successfully as a hardcore biker, Nick could spin, dominate, and master any conversation, and flawlessly so. He had an acerbic, sharp wit, a unique charm, and an equally unique look, replete with a long ponytail and Fu Manchu mustache. Nick was the rare agent who was blessed with the ability to sell ice cubes to an Eskimo, and he was widely considered to be the best narc in the RCMP.

Nick (each time I write his name, I want to write Nick the Narc instead—in fact, we almost never used his birth name) had recently identified and opened up an RCMP case against a prominent heroin trafficker, but still didn't know how the heroin was being smuggled into Toronto. From an informant he'd recently recruited and culled critical information from, Nick soon found out that the heroin was actually being imported through the trafficker's father, a sharp-dressed man in his sixties named Leonard Bosnell (not his real name), a man so impeccable and elegant in both appearance and language, in fact, that he could easily have been mistaken for a Classics professor at Harvard with a Sunday school-teaching gig on the side. Leonard wasn't tall or physically imposing, but he had a lean, athletic build, one sculpted after many years spent mastering judo. He was also unfailingly eloquent and soft-spoken, with a slight British accent that only added to his charm. In addition, Leonard (who insisted my partner and I call him "Lenny") was impressively well-traveled, having made countless trips to Southeast Asia and the Middle East in order to support his (legitimate) Toronto-based import/export business.

At one point, Lenny's son, Archibold (also not his real name)— the heroin trafficker Nick had been busy tracking—convinced him to pick up some high-quality, ready-to-sell Turkish heroin on his behalf during one of Lenny's business trips (on this occasion, while passing through Bahrain). After making his pre-planned stop, Lenny pulled off what would actually turn out to be his first real heroin-smuggling venture, ultimately bringing back over twenty ounces of heroin sewn directly into the soles of his own (also impeccably elegant) shoes. It was that first trip, actually, that further cemented my belief that the adage "success breeds innovation" is true because from that point on, Lenny just got more and more creative. Employing a variety of smuggling methods and making at least two trips a month, Lenny segued seamlessly into the practice of consistently smuggling pure-grade heroin into Canada. Each time he did, Archibold would then take the heroin, cut it up, multiply the volume enormously, and casually proceed setting about his usual business of selling it. Unlike most other burgeoning businesses, however, this joint venture brought them both millions and millions of US dollars in an incredibly short amount of time. And while their particular kind of success may have been uncommon, their mutual greed was not: Archibold immediately bought himself multiple brand-new Porsches and other high-performance cars (along with expensive watches, which no doubt proved useful when checking the time when waiting for one of his new Porsches to arrive), while Lenny wasted no time either, buying a mansion outside of Toronto for him and his young wife to luxuriate in alongside their two little boys. As an old Southern boy might put it, they were "living in high cotton," and loving every minute of it.

As our Mountie friend Nick explained to Kenny, the plan was to choose a viable and reliable informant, coach him through the process of infiltrating the group, then have the informant offer Lenny an opportunity to trade their heroin for our Miami-supplied cocaine. (It's worth noting that at the time cocaine had reached peak-performance pricing, averaging somewhere between sixty and seventy thousand US dollars per kilo in Canada, then equal to about $77,500 to $90,000 Canadian dollars.) Lenny, being a savvy and superb businessman, realized that he could easily double his already vast fortune simply by adding the cocaine into his trafficking endeavors, right alongside the ever-profitable heroin. So, almost immediately after the informant made the offer, the deal was on. Not wanting to waste a moment, and eager to get the ball rolling, Lenny requested a meeting in Toronto with the Miami-based cocaine suppliers (a.k.a. Kenny and me) to discuss future business plans and how to set them in motion. Again, Lenny truly was a formidable businessman. With him now completely in charge of business, things moved quickly.

Recognizing the very real chance that the RCMP could actually take down the entire Bosnell organization with some assistance, Nick asked Kenny if he'd officially join forces. It didn't take Kenny all that long to make a decision: now, years later and without reading his mind, I imagine his thought process went something along the lines of: "A chance to lock up a scumbag heroin smuggler, *and* spend a ton of long-overdue face time with an old friend, *and* enjoy limitless bottles of Labatt's Blue all the while? Sign me up." In his defense, what better motivations could one have?

Kenny next convinced our supervisor, John Andrejko, a.k.a. "Johnny Arms," (he was another recipient in our grand tradition of assigning nicknames) to let him take me along as his "UC trainee" (a.k.a. his de facto bag carrier). "Look, John," he said, "If I get hit by lightning tomorrow, we're still gonna need another guy to keep this case alive!" (Kenny was nothing if not a Jedi Master of mixing bullshit with genuinely valid requests. Actually, I think that's in large part what made Kenny such a great agent. He was confident, convincing, knew what he was doing, and almost always succeeded in whatever that was, no matter the challenge.) Having smooth-talked his way into adding me to the trip, Kenny and I left for Toronto the following week. During our check-in at the Miami International Airport, a clearly volatile and unstable woman approached Kenny, demanding to know where he was traveling to, for no apparent reason. We quickly bailed, and the irony was not lost on us: Here we were, two stealth and stoic agents who, by all accounts, lived lives rife with danger and risk, forced to essentially race around the airport just to hide out from a seemingly batshit-crazy fellow traveler. Once we were finally safe and seated (and crazy lady-free) on our flight, Kenny took a smooth, shiny brass flask out of his bag (totally full, of course) and brazenly knocked back a hefty swig of bourbon, then handed it on over to me. As you can see, those were the old days in commercial aviation. We were openly drinking, and for all I know, the people behind us were drinking *and* smoking.

When Kenny and I at last arrived at Toronto's International Airport, we dutifully followed alongside the throng of fellow passengers on our way to Her Majesty's Customs and Immigration Services. While riding a packed escalator headed up toward the immigration booths, Kenny and I observed the usual swarm of people on the opposite side of a large glass wall, all of them anxiously awaiting the arrivals of family and friends. Grandparents, wives, children—all of them equally excited and waiting impatiently to see their loved ones return from wherever it was they'd been. Amidst this enormous, bustling crowd of joyous, expectant faces, one face instantly stood out among the rest. Melodramatically smashed up against the wall, mouth gaping open, and a slobbery tongue quite literally pressed to the glass, was—who else?—subtle as ever, our boy. It was, of course, Nick the Narc.

After picking us up, Nick (a.k.a. our favorite defacer of glass walls) took us straight to the hotel, where we unloaded our luggage and got settled. We also quickly tucked away the one kilo of "sham" cocaine Nick had so graciously given us as our little homecoming gift. This sham packet was actually for us to use to "flash" Lenny with, a little added flourish we deemed necessary in order to successfully convince him that we were authentic, competent cocaine traffickers. When Nick handed me the little brown paper bag with his "gift" and I took the packet out, I looked right back up at him in horror: the powder itself had been tightly packed in clear, *cotton candy-pink* plastic wrapping—not exactly the norm. "NICK!", I said, "Cocaine is NOT pink!" Nick, ever the practical agent (and ever the practical joker), just shrugged and said, in his disarming Canadian accent, "Don't worry, Bosnell's never seen coke—so just tell him it's Peruvian Pink!" Kenny and I both laughed, but we also balked at taking any chances, wisely deciding to conceal the color completely with duct tape. For his part, Lenny seemed genuinely impressed, thinking we'd brought him a complimentary kilo on our very first trip. "No, Leonard," said Kenny, "you can't open this package, because this is actually for another client not too far from here. *Yours* will come as soon as we see your smack." Again, Kenny was always without equal when it came to these exchanges.

Seemingly born to become an effortlessly natural undercover agent, Kenny was not someone you'd describe as physically fit or youthful in his appearance. At the time, he was sporting a long beard and had atypically long hair for a guy his age (about forty-six). I, however, was far less convincing on this front. I was twenty-five, very much in shape, and physically a far cry from your typical Miami drug trafficker. In fact, Lenny once stared me down during one of our meetings and asked: "So, tell me, just *how do* you keep in shape, Dave?" I gave Lenny what I thought was the quick and credible answer, explaining that because I traveled so much, I always relied on plenty of jogging outside, along with basic exercises in my hotel room done while waiting for visitors like him to arrive. Lenny just squinted his eyes, looked me up and down, and said, "Really? That's what cops do." Lenny had been a fierce judo competitor and was known to randomly fly off the handle, so I braced myself for the very real possibility that he'd grab me and check for a wire. Immediately, I decided to get ahead of that potential disaster: "Lenny, you think I'm a cop? If I was a cop, I'd have already busted you just for admitting you smuggle horse. You'd be wearing striped pajamas and pissing in a can right now, man." To my enormous relief Lenny relaxed, gave me a big smile, laughed, and agreed. And I was able to breathe again.

After numerous meetings with Lenny held at hotels, restaurants, and even his own, monster-sized mansion (all to discuss the weight exchange pricing model and exactly how we'd smuggle the coke into Canada without getting caught), we all agreed that on our next trip Kenny and I would finally bring our cocaine and trade it for his heroin. Just two weeks later, Kenny and I arranged our return trip to Toronto to meet Mr. Leonard Bosnell one last time. We didn't really *both* have to go, but at that point Kenny and I were having so much fun with the Mounties that we couldn't pass it up.

And really, they *were* fun. On one of the more memorable of those infamous trips, Nick took us to a bar called Miss Hayward's Home for Wayward Girls (we loved it immediately, for the name alone). Along with copious amounts of booze, they also sold hats and shirts with that unforgettable name emblazoned on them. For me, a sale was a no-brainer. I bought two hats and still wish I'd gotten more. Growing up, my two daughters Talia and Laura frequently wore those hats occasionally requiring some explanation to their friend's parents before they could do sleepovers.

Dark, seedy, and tucked away far out in the countryside, Miss Hayward's Home for Wayward Girls (really, I never tire of seeing that name in print) boasted a staff who all prided themselves on both the bartender, Smiley (who, in fact, was always frowning) as well as their free, unlimited, and unshelled peanuts (the shells of which covered the entire floor), which gave severe gas to everyone in the place but that everyone ate by the fistful anyway. As we were busy discussing our next plan of action to help further improve the case (while also loudly farting and shoveling in beer, whiskey and peanuts), a beefy, short, rough-looking guy with a porn moustache and BO more pungent than all our farts combined sauntered up and promptly challenged me to an arm-wrestling bout. No one in our group had any idea who this guy was, but he'd apparently overheard us talking, and wanted to be part of the team. I had zero interest in arm wrestling with a drunk, unpredictable, brawny stranger, but Kenny and Nick seized the opportunity to mess with me, and relentlessly egged him on. Resigning myself to my obvious fate, I finished my beer, took off my sweater, and, with my sleeveless tee exposing my considerably less girthy arms, sat down and said, "Okay, Hercules. Bring it on." What followed was totally unsurprising: we arm wrestled, I quickly won, and he sulked. (This personal victory did not come easy, incidentally. Sensing his imminent defeat, the Ron Jeremy of Miss Hayward's hooked both of his feet around the table legs just as I was finishing him off, and as I slammed his arm down the entire table lifted up, making it look less like a wrestling match and more like a séance where we'd just raised the dead.) Still, he didn't want to leave us alone, and after a good half hour more of his pestering, we decided we'd have to soon bail or be stuck with him all night long.

We all foolishly assumed that plotting our collective Irish goodbye shouldn't be too difficult: Nick would distract him, keep him occupied with more of the "cop talk" he was so fascinated by, then each of us would separately and covertly sneak out and make a dash to Nick's car. Unsurprisingly, things didn't exactly work out as we'd hoped. After we'd each successfully made it out to the car, Nick—with the swiftness of a gazelle, and only after waiting for the perfect moment—called his own Code Blue and fled the scene, only to look back and find our wannabe groupie right there behind him. All of a sudden, we found ourselves in a *Rebel Without a Cause*-type situation we neither asked for nor wanted. The still-sulking James Dean of Miss Hayward's jumped into his 1972 Gremlin (not exactly the ideal car for a drag race, mind you) *just* as we were spinning out of the gritty, grassy parking lot, and proceeded to furiously chase us until, at long last (and honestly, what was probably no more than two miles felt like forever), his lights faded into the pitch black behind us and then disappeared altogether. Nick, meanwhile, had seemed suddenly possessed by Evel Knievel, calmly averaging about a hundred miles an hour while we'd all held our breath (and held on for our dear lives). At one point, we shot up and over a hill-based bridge, and the car (literally) flew about four feet into the air, then made it a good forty or fifty feet forward before slamming back down into solid ground (this was on a tiny, quiet, two-lane country road, by the way). Just to make things more surreal, while soaring mid-air and watching our lives flash before our eyes, we somehow spotted a stray cat illuminated in the outer edge of our headlights just as we were descending directly above it. Nick, blithely shifting from his Evel Knievel persona to, apparently, his "Burt Reynolds in the original *Cannonball Run"* persona, shrugged his shoulders and said: "As my wife would happily confirm, boys, I've never passed on pussy that fast in my entire life!"

On another day, Nick took us all to the RCMP Mess, a bar located inside the actual RCMP Headquarters in downtown Toronto. (Yet another reason to love the Mounties: they have a full *bar* in their very own headquarters, and, even better, are encouraged to use it.) But that perk comes with one big, fat caveat: before you can leave the Mess, you must first kiss the Buffalo.

Sadly for me, it turned out that "kiss the buffalo" was *not* a euphemism (though it would make a great one), and it also clearly requires further explanation: the Buffalo in question is, in fact, RCMP's mascot, and is also pictured—front and center—on both of their official emblems. As a mascot, the buffalo is genuinely beloved by all, so it wasn't a surprise to learn that, positioned more than thirty feet up on the main wall of the Mess, is the biggest, grandest, craziest-looking buffalo head you've ever seen (and trust me, they grow them big in Canada). So, if you one day find yourself mindlessly imbibing there, be forewarned: no matter how many beers you manage to knock back, you are *not* leaving that room until you climb up a rickety thirty-foot ladder (of highly-questionable stability), and kiss that damn buffalo. Some of us, of course, had to learn this the hard way.

By the time I got up to leave and learned of this cruel challenge, we'd already spent a solid three hours in the Mess, all of us steadily downing Molsons the whole time. So, it was hardly a tough decision I faced: either I stayed and drank more (and really risk death once I worked up the nerve to climb that ladder) or faced my inevitable fate and got right to it. I stared long and hard at that wobbly ladder, then all the way up to the buffalo, and down again. Then, while loudly cursing that last Molson, I took a deep breath and braced myself for potential disaster.

Majorly buzzed and entirely unsure if the ladder was shaking from my knees knocking together from the nerves, the ladder's own decrepit state, or both, I tried to keep my eyes on the prize—or, rather, the buffalo—but focusing was no easy feat when all I could hear were the howls of my Mountie brothers including Nick the Narc as they drunkenly "held" the ladder and promised to break my fall with their heads (a scenario that would not have turned out well for any of us. Except, of course, the Buffalo). At last, by both the grace of God and the skin of my teeth, I made it to the top. Knowing better than to stay aloft and savor my (almost) victory, I kissed that beast smack on the nose and found my way back down in one piece. Everyone cheered, my life and countless Mountie heads were spared, and, to no one's surprise, I then wound up staying and drinking Molsons until they closed. At that point, I figured I had damn well earned it.

Not all of our trips were filled with such levity, of course. Later, on what would be our final trip to Toronto, Lenny finally made good on his promise to tell us all about his heroin business, and also made the move we'd been waiting for: the actual offer of a sample. This was enough evidence to not only arrest and prosecute Lenny (and his entire organization), but to also seize and forfeit his ill-gotten gains, i.e., his mansion, his vehicles, the entire contents of his wine cellar, etc. This also marked the very first time the RCMP had enforced new seizure and forfeiture laws. In this case, I can say without question, crime truly did not pay.

During Lenny's arraignment, I had to take the stand and testify to Lenny's involvement in heroin smuggling, distribution, and money-laundering. After answering Her Majesty's Prosecutor's final question, I stepped down from the box, relieved and more than ready to leave and mark this entire endeavor down as a success. However, my walk toward the exit, as it turned out, took me directly past Lenny and his defense attorney. Before I reached the door, something in me forced me to take one last look at Lenny, who, with his usual steady composure and calm, looked back at me and softly said in his British accent: "Dave, you are no longer welcome in my home."

To add insult to injury, when Kenny and I returned to our hotel and walked into the lobby, we noticed Lenny's *wife* standing in front of the café entrance. To our great surprise, we realized that she wasn't a hotel guest: she was the café's hostess. She was of course *also* the same woman who'd accompanied Lenny on at least a half dozen of our meetings to discuss our cocaine for heroin trade. And in that moment, I realized that maybe crime *doesn't* always pay: the very same, overly-spoiled woman who'd once lived a lavish lifestyle (thanks to the millions her husband made from smuggling heroin) was now the hostess at her local hotel café. In this case, karma really was a bitch.

Darting past the café, we made a beeline for our room, called Nick, and informed him that his recon skills were dissipating as rapidly as his hair. And that was, of course, our last day there. As soon as we hung up, we packed, covertly left, and dutifully avoided any boozy, bar-based challenges, Buffalo mascots, or Lenny-related distractions. Needless to say, we stayed at a different hotel that night, before reluctantly leaving that much-beloved city (and our even more much-beloved RCMP friends) first thing the next morning.

CHAPTER 9

DOS HUEVOS

As a journeyman criminal investigator, aka street agent, with the DEA in Miami, I followed up on as many informant prospects as possible. As my first supervisor, Johnny Arms, once told me: a successful agent never stops recruiting informants. If one "snitch" out of a dozen was useful, consider yourself lucky. And over my years on the job, I had to remove tons and tons of earth to find a gem in the dirt. One of those gems was "Dos Huevos." A tall man with a gift for articulate if loquacious conversation, Dos Huevos kick-started my career at a new level, and I never looked back. You see, a newbie street agent typically begins by working ounce or pound drug cases and gradually ascends to complex conspiracy investigations that yield seizures of drugs weighing in the metric tons and cash adding up to millions. Dos Huevos (a nickname that will be explained a little later) offered me an opportunity to get into the big leagues.

A college-educated professional in the publishing industry, Dos Huevos earned more than a hundred million in the 1970s as a marijuana smuggler. After losing almost everything he had worked for, he began dabbling in the world of cocaine use. In 1988, he tried crack cocaine for the very first time and, as he later told me, it was love at first puff; he knew he'd never go back to powder. Sadly, he instantly became a crack addict and that addiction nearly ruined him, literally. In December 1987 alone, Dos Huevos smoked an entire kilogram of crack cocaine.

I'll start with the story of how we got acquainted. One night while manning the anonymous tip line—a required night and weekend duty assignment for junior agents—I received a call from a Miami attorney named Mike, who told me he had a client who wanted to cooperate with the DEA. I asked Mike if, to his knowledge, his client was facing arrest or prosecution for anything. He answered no, but his client did have a history with drug trafficking and drug abuse. That caught my attention because most good informants have worked in the business. It is extremely difficult for an agent to find productive informants when they're recruited from churches or the Boys/Girls Club of America. So, I agreed to meet Mike and have him introduce me to the man I'd eventually come to call Dos Huevos.

We met at a small deli around the corner from the DEA Miami office. Because the call from Mike was unsolicited and I didn't know him or his client, I asked another agent—my partner, A.D. Wright, a common-sense kind of guy—to join me for the meeting. A.D. and I intentionally arrived ten minutes earlier than our agreed upon time in order to watch the attorney and my future informant roll in and see if others were tagging along with them, or if they were being followed by someone. To our surprise, Mike and Dos Huevos, or D.H., were already in the deli, seated in a corner booth and quietly waiting for me. We walked right up to the two men and introduced ourselves.

A.D. was an imposing figure; a former defensive football player with Florida State University, he stood at six-foot-two and easily weighed in at 250 pounds. I was carrying a slightly smaller frame, at six-foot even and a svelte 235 pounds. (In fact, by power-lifting in the DEA Miami gym at 0600 every morning, I had quickly added so much weight to my frame that Chris nicknamed me "Lumpy," a term of endearment that has stuck with me for almost four decades.) A.D., an African American, and I, a whitey Scotsman, must have made an impression on the attorney when we walked in because he nodded to me. "Let the games begin," A.D. murmured as we approached the odd-looking couple.

Attorney Mike was an average-looking man with a decent athletic build, wearing a polo shirt and wire-rimmed glasses. D.H., however, appeared to have been teleported from H.G. Well's 1895 novel, *The Time Machine.* He was wearing penny loafers, business slacks with a button-down shirt that had seen better days, and a smoking jacket with patches on the elbows, topped off with a food-stained white ascot. This was in Miami, for chrissakes! Mike stood and shook our hands, but D.H. waited to stand until Mike turned to properly introduce him. When he stood up, I blurted out, "Good God, man! Where's your bean stalk?!" At six-foot-eight, D.H. towered over us like the Jolly Green Giant. After a brief, awkward laugh, the four of us sat back down and started to figure out why we were together.

Mike opened by explaining that D.H. was a graduate of the prestigious University of North Carolina at Chapel Hill (a school I could not get into; I had to settle for NC State) and had been quite successful in the publishing business before he fell into the world of drug trafficking. It started in the late 1970s when he was introduced to the spoils of marijuana trafficking by a college buddy, who was netting roughly five million dollars a year picking up loads of Colombian weed in the Atlantic Ocean and bringing them into the Gulf of Mexico on shrimp and fishing vessels. Impressed, D.H. decided to set up his own smuggling business, complete with transporters, receivers, distributors, and logistics. He upgraded from smaller fishing vessels to full-sized freighters that shipped more than twenty tons of weed on each trip into the Gulf. All of that good business was earning D.H. a steady net income of seven to ten million a year until 1982—when one of his freighters was boarded by the US Coast Guard and seized upon the discovery of *eighty metric tons* of pot onboard!

After paying for lawyers to represent the thirteen crew members and losing the valuable asset of a hundred-and-twenty-foot boat, on top of the lost revenue from that eighty-ton pot purchase, D.H. was, understandably, finding it hard to make ends meet. After all was said and done, he spent close to fifty-five million dollars (equal to a hundred and fifty million today) to resolve that one seizure off the coast of Louisiana, and it busted his business. As far as I could tell, D.H. had pled to a lesser charge of conspiracy to import marijuana and only served several years on probation. I assumed he had cooperated with another agency to get such a deal, but was never able to confirm my suspicions. After the demise of his weed smuggling business, D.H. fell into cocaine addiction. Naturally, while using cocaine at increasingly alarming levels, he became less and less dependable, which led to his long-term unemployed status. No one was willing to lift his poor tired soul back in the publishing business. He was simply lost.

One fateful day in December 1988, D.H. was introduced to crack cocaine when another addict gave him a rock to smoke. He fired it up and was instantly hooked. Within the next thirty days, D.H. had single-handedly smoked through a whole kilogram of crack cocaine. (For those of you who are not crack users, that would be like smoking a ton of weed in one month!) He was eventually admitted to the emergency room and a recovery hospital, and that is when he reached out to his old friend Mike for help. In their relationship, Mike sometimes played the role of a family member, maybe a loving uncle, and sometimes acted like D.H.'s social worker. As his attorney, however, Mike suggested that D.H. work for the DEA and get on the right side of the law. This way, if D.H. were ever arrested for prior indiscretions, or became the target of a former competitor's or partner's reprisals, he would have the United States' premier and most qualified drug enforcement team at his back. Or Mike could have simply wanted to shove D.H. onto another putz so he would be relieved of the responsibility. As you will soon understand, it was a combination of these theories.

Away from his client's earshot, Mike told me that he knew D.H. was destined for death if he didn't turn a new leaf and clean up his life. Mike's hope was that, with DEA supervision, D.H. could attain a normal life once again. That idea turned out to be more difficult than I originally thought.

At the time, I was a twenty-six-year-old agent with little to lose and a lot to learn and accomplish. I cared less for my personal safety than the right and privilege to take calculable risks for big successes and a heavy caseload. As DEA agents frequently say, "little cases, little problems...big cases big problems!"—and I wanted big problems. Working with D.H. offered me my first taste of big problems, and how bitter it was.

D.H. was still in contact with several significant drug suppliers from his Colombian-marijuana supply business, and by the mid-1980s those suppliers were in the cocaine business. One of these traffickers was Roberto Davila, known for being connected to Santa Marta traffickers and politicians. Near the birthplace of famous music artist Shakira, Santa Marta is a small yet growing city on the Atlantic Coast of Colombia, approximately sixty miles north of Barranquilla.

D.H. introduced me to Davila as his brother-in-law and potential partner in a deal for the supply of five hundred kilograms of cocaine. Afterwards, the three of us had regular phone conversations, with Davila making calls from his jungle hut in the Guajira Peninsula to a landline number that reached D.H. and me at my office in the Koger Executive Center. (Remember: this was before cellphones were everywhere.) Case developments were going well—with agreements on the type of aircraft I would use to pick up the coke load in the Guajira, who Davila would bribe and conscribe for support to allow the plane to be flown into Colombia and then fly the load out, and even the matter of expenses and service fees. All we were waiting for was the right time when given the green light to send my pilots and plane to the specified clandestine airstrip's grid points, in the center of the wild Guajira jungle. Due to issues of weather and Colombian military patrols, our communications went on for weeks as I responded to every call and need of Davila and his traffickers. I would drop whatever I was doing to continue the communications. (I remember one time I was cutting my lawn when my wife ran from the house and passed me the DEA-loaned "brick" antennae mobile phone I was using for undercover calls.) Timing would be perfect when few Colombian Army patrols were present at the zone of our designated airstrip, the weather was right, and a supply of cocaine was packaged and ready to go.

D.H. and I were speaking with Davila via UH radio and telephone on a daily basis—sometimes, two or three times a day. D.H. was staying at an old roach motel in North Miami Beach, and I wanted him closer to the DEA office for faster response to Davila's calls. I moved him to the Miami Airport Sofitel and arranged for a government rate of forty-five dollars a night. I figured that within two days, we'd have our instructions for the smuggling venture and I would have my hands on five hundred kilos of coke before the weekend—finally, the big leagues! To make business you have to invest in business, right? So, after leaving my DEA travel Mastercard on file with the Sofitel for D.H.'s room and expecting to claim the ninety bucks, plus tax, for two days lodging on an expense voucher for investigative charges, I left D.H. at his new fancy hotel with instructions to stay there until I met him the next morning.

Early the next morning, I awoke to a call from Davila on my "brick" phone: he wanted to pass along the exact contacts for who we would meet at the airstrip during the "drop." Davila knew that D.H. was familiar with the characters, so I agreed to call Davila back in one hour. I had to leave my house and dart over to the Sofitel to pick up D.H., get to the undercover phone in our office, call Davila, and figured one hour was just enough time to do it all. In five minutes, I was hauling ass to the Sofitel, calling ahead to reach and inform D.H. of my plans. Room #422 did not pick up. "Okay," I told myself, "he's in the shower or the phone's off the hook. Stay positive, Dave." When I arrived at the hotel, I went straight to the front desk to pay for the single night. The polite receptionist handed me a bill for four hundred and eighty-five bucks! "What the hell?!" In one night, D.H. had ordered four plates of room service and four bottles of champagne! Suffice it to say, it didn't take me long to get to room #422.

I knocked on the door like a pissed off cop would do, and there was no answer. Then, I banged on the door, and there was still no answer. Finally, I spoke in a calm and sweet voice, almost singing the words, "Heeeeello, I know you're in theeeere. Answer the door, and we can discuss your bill." At last, I heard the security chain being unlocked and the dead bolt release as the door slowly opened. D.H. bent his six-foot-eight frame down, stuck his head out of the door, and said, "Good morning, Dave!" I pushed the door open and immediately noticed that D.H. was naked. But I took that in stride until what I saw next: his male lover in the room, also naked; food—high-end food, not sandwiches—splattered all over the walls and ceiling; and assorted furniture turned over and broken. And I was responsible for every bit of it! In a flash, I understood exactly why attorney Mike had wanted to turn over the task of handling and controlling D.H. to the DEA. Even a newbie agent could figure that one out!

Calmly but sternly, I instructed D.H. and friend to immediately get dressed. As soon as they were decent, I kicked the playmate out of the room. D.H. began to explain that he met his old buddy and they found a crack supplier who "forced" him into breaking his promise-to-self, and they got high all night long.

For a second, I wanted to choke the life out of D.H., or, at the very least, give him a good beat down. All I had worked for was about to come crashing down. But, after taking a breath, I knew our operations could be salvaged within a matter of days. So, I said, "Okay, let's just get the hell out of here and deal with it later." D.H. and I returned to the office as quickly as possible, got on the phone with Davila, and agreed on a rendezvous in two days at the airstrip in Guajira, Colombia. D.H.'s part was done, and as far as I cared, our agent-informant relationship was over. I hated to be around this guy.

Still, D.H. was expecting me to fund his room service meals and bar tab for the next few or several days. But I had a better idea. After settling that whopping bill, I had closed the room charges, so he no longer had a place to stay. For the next ten days, I avoided D.H.'s calls and attempts to visit. At day ten, he finally caught A.D. in the office parking lot and told him, "A.D., in the past week I've only eaten two eggs! I'm starving, brother!" From that point on, my informant was known as Dos Huevos or Two Eggs.

In my mind, D.H. was the epitome of an American failure story. He had an education, a prestigious career, and the intellect to succeed in life, yet he lacked purpose and drive, and he squandered it all. Could I blame cocaine on this particular failure? Perhaps he was a troubled individual who might fail no matter what, but the crack cocaine addiction certainly didn't help. Regardless, I was going to finish my case with or without Dos Huevos.

We eventually brought back that load of cocaine, along with a thousand kilos of weed they forced on the pilot at the last minute. Unfortunately, we had a few more problems along the way. For this operation, DEA Miami chose to use a pilot I'll call "Cecil," a defendant turned informant who'd been caught running plane loads of cocaine for several Colombian and Venezuelan drug cartels. A native Canadian red head with pasty white skin, short in stature and wide in girth, Cecil was an experienced pilot who specialized in water-landing aircraft, so he could bring his cocaine loads well inside North America and land on lakes, rivers, or reservoirs without being detected by law enforcement. A Canuck Barry Seal, if you will.

One time in the early 1970s, Cecil was flying a DC-3 loaded with Colombian marijuana for a Canadian client, when he experienced mechanical problems and was forced to do an emergency landing in the Caribbean Island nation of Dominica. Unfortunately for Cecil, his forced choice of an airstrip was in the middle of a sugar plantation employed by local natives. At the time, native plantation workers were livid over the Dominica government's decision to cut subsidiary benefits to the sugar manufacturing industry, making their already meager existence downright miserable. On this tiny island, the only aviation visitors to the plantation were government-sponsored flights. Even worse, those Dominica government flights involved the same aircraft that Cecil was piloting that fateful day. The natives assumed that Cecil was with the same government that had cut their benefits and damaged their livelihood. As such, the natives grabbed Cecil out of the broken DC-3 and dragged him off of the airstrip to a sandy patch where they staked his hands and feet in a "spread eagle" position, face up. Over threats of cutting off his arms and legs one by one, Cecil tried to explain in his best pigeon English that he was not a Dominica government agent, just a marijuana trafficker! Eventually, he was able to convince them. After Cecil agreed to share part of his high-grade Colombian load with the natives, they let him go with all of his appendages intact. He later told me with a Regina twang, "That day, I really almost lost me head and few other body parts on that operation!"

In his usual coke smuggling operations, as long as Cecil had a land crew willing to meet him and off-load his cocaine, he would never have a problem. However, a crew member he entrusted with his "drops" was also a defendant informant and set up Cecil for DEA. From that point, he was no longer working for himself but for us, and as an agency, we worked Cecil really hard. Skillful pilots are hard to come by in the narco world, and finding one with the balls to fly directly into high-risk, remote environments and land a Merlin 350 IIB jet prop aircraft on dirt airstrips is even more rare. Cecil fit the bill and was the perfect performer on aviation operations almost anywhere. Not only did he have the balls, but Cecil's experience and knowledge were profound.

Cecil's downfall: he loved cold beer. I was told that he had a habit of carrying a large ice cooler full of beer with him to pick up loads, and that's how he passed the time on his way to South America. It's hard to believe that a pilot was drinking booze while flying, but apparently, it happened. Cecil defended it by saying, "I'm the only one in the airplane, so if it crashes it's on me." That habit finally caught up with him on a trip to the Guajira. Flying a Merlin 350 IIB jet prop aircraft, Cecil was on his final approach when a flock of buzzards flew up and entered his jet engines, knocking out one of them. With only one functional motor and perhaps ten beers under his belt, even Cecil met his match and could not avoid the crash. He landed catawampus and shot directly into the jungle that hugged the clandestine airstrip he had intended to land on. Although bruised up, Cecil survived that crash and was eventually provided a fake passport and identity by Davila and made his way back to me.

I remember waiting for Cecil the morning he was slated to return from Colombia with that load of coke. I waited and waited at the Tamiami Airport, in Southwest Dade County, hoping he would call my mobile "brick" phone and inform me why he was late and when he'd been arriving. Finally, at around noon, a DEA supervisor named Bill, who oversaw Cecil's parole and informant services, called me. Although Bill was waiting to hear from me, he first received a call from Cecil's wife, who told him that Cecil had called her on the UH radio he kept at home. "Mrs. Cecil" was understandably upset that her dear husband had crashed his airplane in the Colombian jungle, was injured, had no way to get home, and was having trouble contacting his DEA friends! When Bill got this call, he was a little perturbed, to say the least, and expressed that frustration directly in my ear.

"You swinging Johnson! How fucked up of an operation are you running down there?!" I replied, "Sorry, Bill, I didn't know he'd crashed. I was giving Cecil a little more time to contact me before I pulled the emergency alarm. I'm at Tamiami now, waiting for him." Then, it got ugly. Bill, a seasoned, old-school agent from South Boston, shot back, "Well, you're going to wait a long fucking time, you fucking Johnson! I can't believe you're standing there with your prick in your palm! Find out now what happened and get it fixed. You got that?" "Yes, sir, Bill, I got it" was my only reply.

Within two hours of my memorable one-sided conversation with Bill, I got a call from Cecil. He told me to wait for a call from him the next day, and every day thereafter, at noon Miami time, until he was able to obtain a false passport, courtesy of Davila's contacts in the Colombian government, and catch a commercial flight back to the United States. This would wind up taking another two weeks. During our phone call, Cecil told me that upon impact his airplane slid off the runway into the jungle and rested amongst papaya trees. As his landing gear collapsed, he slid through the mud for two hundred feet, which severely damaged the plane's undercarriage. Within twenty-five minutes, a local farmer working for Davila showed up with a backhoe and dug a thirty-foot-wide hole to bury the plane, which he did after Cecil and his ground crew pulled out all of the avionics that could be removed and salvaged. Cecil teared up as the plane fell into that massive hole. Within a half hour of burying Cecil's sole means of income, the Colombian Army was scouring the zone overhead in US-donated Huey helicopters and fixed-wing surveillance planes.

Well, as they say, the show must go on! I now had to find another pilot to pick up my coke. I sent out some "feelers" to other DEA offices to check on the availability of an informant pilot; after a few days, I was lucky enough to find an operator in Florida. Stam was a well-trained South African pilot with the balls of a Spanish matador. Unlike Cecil, however, Stam was extremely particular about details, to the point of bordering on anally compulsive neurosis. For instance, if he were scheduled to meet someone, Stam would not wait ten seconds longer than the prescribed time. Stam would not debate a single point if it involved an issue with his aircraft. Stam was Stam, a damn good pilot but difficult to sit and drink a cup of coffee with. It took one agonizing week to work out the new details with Stam as my new pilot, but the operation moved ahead. We eventually went back to the Tamiami Airport to wait for Stam's arrival with my elusive load of coke.

As coordinated, Stam was to land at Tamiami around midnight, after departing the Guajira at dusk in Colombia, heading northwest towards Miami. Our team of agents was "locked and loaded," with a cargo truck ready to go. We arrived at the airstrip around 11 p.m., anticipating Stam's arrival at midnight, sharp. But midnight came and went with no Stam. Then 1 a.m., 2 a.m.....and still, no Stam. I thought, "Good Lord, after Cecil's misfortune, please don't let Stam fail! Please don't let me fail!" I had at least seven DEA agents and two Customs agents waiting all night long at this rinky-dink airport, and I didn't want to go back without my dope! At last, we heard a distant hum, a hum from an aircraft in flight. Could it be Stam? Then, out of nowhere, an airplane dropped from the sky and landed at Tamiami at 2:30 in the morning! That must be Stam, I thought. The airport does not open until 5 a.m., and this plane came in so quick! But why didn't he call me?

All of the agents climbed on to the cargo truck and ran down the airstrip in the direction Stam had landed, but there was no plane at the end of the runway! Where did it go? What happened to the plane? Was it our imaginations, a mirage? Several agents besides me saw it, so the plane had to be here! When we realized the plane had taxied directly and rapidly turned into a darkened hangar, we began our search. Clearly, this plane was not Stam's: it was yet another narco pilot who landed his drug smuggling plane right under DEA's noses! We spent the next hour running around like keystone cops, approaching aircraft lined up on the tarmac and touching the engines to see if one of them was warm. Later that morning, while discussing this matter with our supervisor, he sharply observed, "It's a good thing none of you found the plane that had just landed, or your hands would have melted the second you touched that scorching hot engine!"

We never found that ghost plane at the Tamiami Airport; I'm certain, from the way it landed and disappeared from sight, that it was another drug flight. That's how Miami was in the 1980s, drugs and smugglers were everywhere! In fact, once while on a mobile surveillance in North Miami Beach, I grabbed my "brick" cell phone to call my supervisor with an operational update when I heard another drug deal between two guys over the air waves on my phone. Although I carefully listened to determine a meeting place, the conversation was in native Spanish, and at that time, I only understood bits and pieces. Since then, I've learned to speak, read, and write Spanish fluently. It was a requirement to do this job right.

At 4 a.m., I finally heard from Stam on the radio, as he was heading in with a full load. We greeted Stam as he arrived and loaded the cargo truck with several hundred kilos of cocaine. We never expected marijuana as well, but Davila's associates wanted to supply their weed distributors in Florida. They sent an additional thousand kilos of weed, so Stam took it—and so did we. Dope is dope. We were happy to take some weed off the street and the money for it out of the cartel's hands. Less revenue for them to murder with. When infiltrating international drug traffickers, the unexpected comes with the territory.

CHAPTER 10

THE CONGRESSMAN

A fter Stam had safely landed at the Tamiami Airport, and we'd secured the load of cocaine along with the "bonus" marijuana, Davila let me know that his South Florida-based cocaine distributors were ready to receive, and that my job (in an undercover capacity, of course) would be to deliver both the coke and the weed directly to them. The first recipient on my proverbial hit list was Jaime Ceballos, an older man who'd once served as a Colombian congressman for the State of Guajira. I first met Jaime at Café Americano, a quiet little spot in Miami. I can still picture just how flagrantly suspicious he was of me, and will never forget the intensity of his gaze, almost as if he was angered by my mere presence. But I'd been on the receiving end of this type of dynamic many times before, and thus knew perfectly well that he was just trying to see through me to identify who I *really* was, what I was thinking, and perhaps even what my intentions might be. The motivation behind such a high level of scrutiny was entirely understandable. On one hand you have an infamous, successful, Colombian cocaine smuggler and distributor, one who's built his reputation in Miami through many years of lucrative dealing while pretending to be an upstanding, law-abiding, distinguished diplomat who simply visited Miami

145

often for (legal) work purposes. On the other hand, you have a total stranger, a young, white, blue-eyed gringo who *says* he's not a cop, and then not much else. In fact, it had already taken me a good three or four "auditions" with Chi-Chi, one of Jaime's underlings, before being granted that first sit-down with Jaime at the Café. And even after that, it then took an additional six or seven meetings with Jaime before he felt comfortable enough (a.k.a. trusted me enough) to finally introduce me to his son/ drug trafficking partner, Martin Ceballos. Together, Jaime and Martin were two of the most dominant cocaine traffickers in all of northwest Colombia.

During a lengthy series of successive business meetings, Jaime and I fleshed out the details of our plan, a complicated one involving me first passing my cocaine over to Jaime and Martin, to be immediately followed by them passing it over to their distributors in Miami, Atlanta, and New York. And, in the usual nightmarish path that always followed these kinds of transactions, from those major cities the cocaine would then be disseminated to hundreds of smaller towns and rural communities throughout the eastern United States.

For an undercover agent, the "Grand Slam" of success when it comes to narc deals is to seize both the drugs *and* the money from the trafficking organization, and to then use those seizures as the additional nail-in-the-coffin evidence needed to successfully prosecute at the absolute highest level possible. In this case, we (the DEA) had choreographed and executed, through my undercover role, a drug smuggling plan for/with the Davila organization. Typically, with this kind of arrangement, the smuggler would be paid in cash, or some kind of combination of cash and illegal drugs. Knowing that the Ceballos team had a history of drug distribution in the United

States (primarily in Los Angeles, Houston, and Miami), and that they were sitting on funds I could potentially get my hands on to use as prosecutorial evidence, I demanded a small payment of $175,000 (cash—and, within that world, $175,000 really *was* a drop in the proverbial drug bucket) before I'd deliver the drugs to Davila's US network (a.k.a. the Ceballos team). I figured that requiring a payment of under $200K wouldn't raise any red flags, but this sudden demand for cash set off internal alarms, and I shouldn't have been too surprised. More often than not in the 1980s, the usual drug-trafficking deal involved more of a consignment-type arrangement, where the drugs would be delivered and the payment received only after "moving" the illicit merchandise to (in this case, the US-based) distributors. Money moved "upstream," so when the congressman was paid, I would get paid. By telling the organization that I wanted a preliminary taste of my payment before actually giving them the dope, I stood out to them as not just atypical, but perhaps also as a greedy, untrustworthy operator. Even after I explained that this payment done in good faith was requested simply to assuage my anxiety over any potential theft or seizure, my attempt at a quid-pro-quo maneuver created both alarm and a small but significant delay in the overall negotiations with the congressman.

As a result, Martin demanded that I "flash" (a.k.a. show) him the cocaine that had been supplied to me by Davila. The impetus behind his demand was obvious enough—most likely, Martin had begun to suspect that my delaying the Davila coke delivery was because I'd already sold it and was now busy trying to find new, potentially lesser quality product to pass off to Martin. In reality, the actual motivation for the delay was that I needed to squeeze money out of the Davila organization (in this case, money we'd charged them for having us fly down to Colombia to pick up the load of cocaine). And I unfortunately had no other choice, because my cumulative case expenses at the time had grown exorbitant. Not only did I owe an obscene amount of money to my Canadian informant for the missing aircraft, I also had the South African pilot still (impatiently) waiting for his own service fees to be paid.

So, I knew that if I was going to keep this deal going *and* save face with my supervisor at the same time, I'd have to agree to flash the sample. Three of my fellow agents—AD Wright, Alex Dominguez, and Chris Feistl—joined me to brainstorm and come up with the perfect place. We all ultimately agreed that we'd prefer to stay relatively close to the office, where there were several nearby, discreet truck yards to choose from and suggest. One of them, in particular, was atypically desolate and private, replete with an enormous, open-fenced area. We all deemed it perfect.

A day or two later, with my three partners in anti-crime camped out in their (undetectable) respective surveillance positions, Dos Huevos and I were en route to pick up Martin in DH's '78 Cadillac Coupé de Ville. The decrepit de Ville was then (literally) falling apart, and on our way to get Martin we were pulled over by a well-meaning Metro Dade patrol unit for—of all things—not having properly functioning brake lights. With only my undercover (as in, entirely fake) driver's license on me, I had to plead with the officer to let me call our Miami base (a.k.a. the communications center), so that they could vouch for my status as a DEA agent and we could be on our way to Martin, brake lights or no brake lights. Amazingly the cop complied, and we mercifully avoided blowing an entire case over something so insignificant as a busted backend. Needless to say, there's no way that could ever have gone down like that today.

As part of our prep work for the meeting, we'd already stashed a full kilo of cocaine in the trunk of our undercover car we'd parked in the yard, and I'd assured Martin that my car (with the coke) was in a secure, safe place. As is the norm in the drug-dealing world, each kilogram was marked with a unique, highly-specific emblem, and as Martin was already well familiar with Davila's product, we were careful to stash a kilo with the correct markings. Already consumed with worry about how precarious the situation had by then become, we were leaving no stone unturned and taking absolutely no chances. The kilo was marked, well-hidden, and would unquestionably ring true to Martin as being one of Davila's.

When I turned and pulled into that creepy, almost cinematically foreboding lot, I watched as Martin's complexion quickly turned white—nearly as white as mine (no easy feat). He visibly recoiled and began flailing his arms, and I at once realized that all the precautions we'd taken to set up such a private, "safe" meeting spot turned out, in reality, to look a lot less like a secure, abandoned lot and a lot more like a scene straight out of *Miami Vice* (worse, the kind of scene that would alert the audience that a major bust and/or showdown was about to happen). Needless to say, it scared both the shit *and* the color straight out of Martin. Still flailing his arms, he began yelling, "No, no, no, no!" Visibly confused and desperately unsure what to do, he then covered his eyes with both hands, as if they would protect him from the worst he feared. With no other viable choice, I made a swift U-turn and hauled my Don Johnson-seeming ass out of there (to be clear, I was *not* wearing a white linen blazer and sockless loafers at the time). Later, on the way back to Martin's car, he told us—while still slightly trembling and sweating profusely—that his preferred place for doing any kind of flash or swap was never anything other than a busy, public parking lot in places like a supermarket chain, a Home Depot, even a Walmart. Anywhere, basically, where it was would be a guarantee that there would be both a ton of cars and a ton of people. So, when I'd first driven into that lot, with its total absence of life or semblance of activity, he almost went into cardiac arrest. Which, of course, would not have been good for our case, and most certainly would not have been good for Martin.

A couple of days later, I was able to finally show Martin one of "Davila's" kilos. Along with his father, Martin immediately agreed to give me $175,000 (in cash, and up-front) to cover the transport fees, which thankfully enabled me to pay Cecil, Stam, and, of course, Dos Huevos. As per the norm, a cash ledger was prepared and certified by my supervisor for every single payment made to the informants, along with the completed, signed, required DEA Form 103, with the also-required minimum of two DEA agents having witnessed the payment. And while those details may seem mundane, they actually represented a great deal more than just a paper trail. Ultimately, the money held great significance: as soon as Jaime and Martin delivered the cash, our arrest spree began. In rapid succession, we arrested Jaime, Martin, and a host of other offenders. And I, after a whole lot of near-misses and incredibly close calls, had finally entered the Big Leagues.

CHAPTER 11

MANGOS!

nformants have always played a critical role in the work and
ultimate successes of the DEA. I recruited one of the most
memorable ones of my career in the same easy, seamless way
I had with Martin Ceballos: by simply checking him out of and
escorting him from the Federal Metropolitan Correction Center
in southwest Dade County. This particular informant was a
Cuban trafficker, and was also associated with the Ceballos
organization. We called him Chi-Chi.

To my great surprise, it turned out that Chi-Chi and I got
along incredibly well, which was especially unusual given the
circumstances of our first "introduction." Once we were away
from the prison and settled into the newfound safety of my
car, we quickly fell into an unexpectedly lively and engaging
conversation. He listened to my undercover stories about
my drug-dealing "friends" in Canada, while I listened as he
reminisced about his travels and adventures throughout Florida.

This, of course, was very much the antithesis of the *actual*
first time we'd been in a car together.

During my initial series of undercover meetings involving the
Ceballos case, and despite the fact that I had an exceptionally
credible cover story, Jaime and Martin Ceballos had zero interest

in meeting with me—a Miami-based, Bama-speaking, bench-pressing white boy—to talk about cocaine (or anything else, for that matter). At that point they'd been in the drug business for a great many years, and were savvy (and wary) enough to know better than to potentially expose themselves too early. But their interest had been piqued, so they decided to send an emissary on their behalf. That's how I came to meet an eager, charming, and energetic young man named Isidrio Vasquez. Slight but sinewy, with greasy, slicked-back hair, Isidrio had a comical little habit of twisting his thin, jet-black moustache between his thumb and forefinger whenever pondering his (often fabricated) answers to my very direct questions. He gave himself the alias name "Chi-Chi," which stuck with us, and also suited him perfectly.

Chi-Chi and I had our very first meeting in the parking lot of a Miami car dealership and, almost immediately, I could tell he was nervous. As it turned out, his cousin owned the dealership, so I'd just assumed that mine was not the first of many meetings Chi-Chi must have already held in that lot. Still, I could sense the tension. I also knew that what he'd been told didn't exactly amount to an abundance of background, but it should have been enough. My story was that I was a Canadian coke dealer and the brother-in-law of Jaime and Martin's favorite, most-preferred smuggler pilot. Also, for additional credibility, we added that I'd been in business with the brother-in-law for many years, and that Jaime and Martin knew me quite well. This was untrue on more than one level: The part about me being a relative of the pilot was my base cover story, of course, but the part about them knowing me personally was pure BS. If the team and I ever decided to take down Chi-Chi on a conspiracy charge (with the goal of getting him to snitch), I knew Jaime and Martin wouldn't care. It was painfully obvious that they'd happily sacrifice Chi-

Chi if that meant knowing for sure whether or not I was who I said I was (there truly is no honor among thieves). Regardless, I decided not to touch Chi-Chi until we had the Ceballos boys in handcuffs too: I wanted the whole enchilada, baby!

In the series of meetings that followed, I relayed various stories and bits of relevant, credible information I'd gotten months earlier from another informant. That informant, Cecil, had been of enormous help, having given me a wealth of good material to use, all culled from his own smuggling experiences as a known, Caribbean-based drug pilot. It was those vivid little details, along with the calm and confidence with which I delivered them, that ultimately gained Chi-Chi's confidence. And sure enough, not long after he went back to the Ceballos group and assured them that I was the real deal, Jaime and Martin immediately came forward to talk money.

Eventually, my collective undercover operations involving the Ceballos organization led to the seizure of literally hundreds of kilos of cocaine, not to mention the arrests of countless drug traffickers and their properties. And, of course, they also led to the infamous Chi-Chi.

When we actually indicted Chi-Chi (along with Jaime and Martin Ceballos), he ran like the wind, sparking an exhausting search that lasted nearly three months. I knew right off that bat that I didn't want anything to do with checking the "fugitive" status box on the DEA Form 202 (the official paperwork an agent must submit when someone is arrested or deemed a non-arrestable suspect, a.k.a. a fugitive or deceased). To submit the form would have exposed his identity to the US Marshals Service, and my thinking was: I'll be *damned* if he's gonna wear anyone else's cuffs but mine. So, along with my partners AD Wright, Alex Dominguez, and Chris Feistl, I searched what must have been nearly every single street corner in Miami. The four of us eventually befriended a few people in the neighborhood where he'd last lived, making sure to tell them that we'd absolutely make it worth their while if they'd just let us know when Chi-Chi reappeared. And, as always, greed proved to be a powerful motivator: Three months later, one of his neighbors called me one night to tell me that he'd just seen a moving truck pull up alongside Chi-Chi's old house. The source went a step further, relaying the new rumor that Chi-Chi was supposedly staying with his sister, and even going so far as to give us the exact address.

This all happened on a Friday, when everyone was doing what they'd usually be doing on a weekend eve: Chris was already at his favorite bar in the bustling, hip area known as Coconut Grove; Alex was settled at home with his wife and baby girl; and AD was up in Broward County in his tv room playing video games. But once the tip came in, all four of us immediately stopped what we were doing and hauled our asses over to Chi-Chi's old house. I did make sure to give Chris an extra kick in the ass in terms of hustle, because—considering he was busy flirting with pretty women, as opposed to changing diapers or wearing down an Atari joystick—I knew he'd most likely take a little longer to motivate than the rest of us.

I was the first to arrive and sat silently in my car, eyes locked on the moving truck still parked in the driveway. Alex joined me next, followed by AD, and, lastly, Chris, who arrived in great spirits after managing to get a beautiful girl's number on his way out of the Grove. Chris was actually using his personally owned car for this surveillance (his 280Z, of which we were all jealous), because, technically, agents are prohibited from using an OGV for personal transportation (especially to a bar). All of us now accounted for, we—our own Fab 4—were more than ready to pounce when we saw someone walking casually out of the house. However, that someone was clearly not Chi-Chi. This was a stranger to us, and we all watched as he began moving out the furniture along with another man, one we'd also never seen. When the two of them finished, they hopped into the truck and took off, while we pulled out and covertly followed. AD, Alex, and I followed the mystery movers, while Chris was perched outside the reported hideout keeping his eyes peeled for "the Chich" (as Chris liked to call him), who was nowhere in sight. After a short drive, the guys in the truck pulled into a shopping center lot in Hialeah (one of the dozens of small municipalities in Dade County), parked, got out, and left the truck sitting there in its parking space. They then got into a nearby car, and were clearly gearing up to leave.

But, after three long, frustrating months of fruitless searching and digging, we'd had enough, and snagged them both before they even made it halfway out of the lot. Technically, this was an investigative detention, not an arrest. Unsurprisingly, when we asked the men why they were moving Chi-Chi's furniture, they quickly denied even *knowing* anyone named Chi-Chi. Eventually, Alex (the only one of us who spoke Spanish, and perfectly), got into a heated one-on-one with the more vocal of the two, and that's when I heard Alex shout out my longtime favorite, much-beloved word: "Morrrrrrrrrronga!" Alex didn't stop there, following up his preferred slang with the fact that if these two didn't stop feeding us their bullshit, they'd be screwed.

Neither put up much of a fight after that, soon telling Alex all about Chi-Chi's apparent plan to relocate to Port St. Lucie, Florida, in order to hide out for as long as he needed. They even told Alex the exact location Chi-Chi was currently hiding out in (back in Hialeah), and offered to take us there. From two faithful, tight-lipped friends to gracious, wannabe chauffeurs, all in under an hour. We passed on their offer and took off, leaving them securely in the hands of our new enforcement supervisor.

When we arrived at Chi-Chi's hideout we checked back in with Chris, who was growing impatient, having abandoned any and all opportunities for romance only to wind up sitting alone in his car, with nothing at all to report from the entire time we'd been gone. In fact, the Chich, Chris remarked, had chosen his hideout spot incredibly well: This was a particularly quiet, even tranquil, neighborhood. Forcing ourselves to be patient, we all sat and waited for activity of any kind. At this point it was approaching two a.m., and still no Chi-Chi.

Suddenly, we saw the unmistakable glow of headlights in the distance, and we all held our breath and watched as a car slowly drove up and approached the house. After the car stopped short, the driver turned off the engine, but—to our surprise and also to our great frustration—they then just sat there, no movement, no nothing, for a full fifteen minutes. It was still pitch-black outside, so we couldn't see who the driver was, let alone if they might have any passengers with them. Finally, the driver door opened, and we saw a guy jump out and walk swiftly to the front door. Chris was the first to make the ID—"It's the Chich!"—but we all knew it was critical that we go in slow. Still, despite our silent, steady approach, Chi-Chi must have heard something (or perhaps realized that there were far more cars on the street than usual), and he suddenly spun around and made a run for it. But with a pack of eager, enormously impatient Enforcement Group 4 agents on his ass, he didn't get far. To no one's surprise, Chris snagged him first, and the rest of the group quickly had his back, forming a circle and surrounding Chi-Chi completely. It was immediately clear to us that Chi-Chi was in shock and perhaps even a bit scared—in those days, even if the guys who just ran up to you were wearing DEA vests, it could actually turn out to be a drug hit. For a minute, Chi-Chi probably thought he was a dead man. After we surrounded him, Chris asked the Chich if he knew me, as I'd been the undercover agent who'd met him not that long ago. Chi-Chi hesitated and then gave him a resounding no, at which point I grabbed him in a bear hug and took him down to the ground. In my own broken Spanish, I just stared at him and said: "Me conoces ya?" ("Do you know me now?")

Chi-Chi went straight to jail that night. When we arrived at the correction center, I gently removed the handcuffs from his wrists. Somehow, Chi-Chi didn't hold any semblance of a grudge against me for either the tackle or the arrest and, in fact, we ended up being genuinely friendly to—and even fond of—one another.

And so, it was months later when my partner Alex and I picked him up from prison that first time. It hardly hurt my endgame that we'd already established our easygoing rapport (one that, I think, was surprising to us both), and it didn't take long for me to successfully recruit him as my informant. One day soon after, I checked Chi-Chi out again from his miserable stint at Club Fed, with the plan of having him point out the virtual dozens of storefronts where cocaine loads were dropped (and stashed for later distribution), as well as some of the money-counting and laundering hubs throughout Dade and Monroe counties. While passing through a serene, atypically bucolic neighborhood in Hialeah, I heard Chi-Chi gasp. Naturally I feared the worst, but, to my relief, the cause of his shock and excitement was far less sinister than I had expected: All I saw was one stunningly perfect, enormous, fully-loaded mango tree, literally overflowing with all manner of ripe, juicy mangos. To be clear, mangos were most definitely *not* on any federal penitentiary menu (in fact, I don't

157

think they offered the prisoners any fresh fruit at all, unless you counted the occasional stale, Dole fruit cup) and for someone like Chi-Chi, who no doubt grew up eating (and loving) them, this was akin to seeing a mirage in the desert then discovering it was real.

With a frenzy usually reserved only for small children on Christmas morning, Chi-Chi spun around, nearly snapping his wrists right out of the handcuffs attached to the door handle in the process. And, like any good father on Christmas morning, I was helpless to resist. I hadn't even finished asking him if he wanted to stop and get *one* before he hollered "Si! Si!!! Quiero maaaaaaangooooooos!" We pulled over, and as I contemplated the potential consequences of my next move, Chi-Chi sat beside me, breathless and impatient. I paused, then made a judgement call I still don't regret. Reaching over to uncuff him, I tried to adopt a convincingly foreboding, overly stern tone: "Okay, *go for it,* but don't you dare run off, or I'll shoot you in the back, I swear to God." Chi-Chi stared back at me, then down at my S&W 9mm semi-automatic, then back on up again. He nodded, solemnly. "I'll be right back."

For the next three minutes I sat there in my OGV, watching Chi-Chi gazing up intently at the mango tree, carefully examining every single piece of fruit in order to determine the very best one. Finally, he chose his favorite: Chi-Chi being Chi-Chi, though, he had to make it difficult. This mango was more than fifteen feet off the ground and seemingly unattainable, so now I really *was* riveted, wondering how the hell he was gonna get it down. And he did not disappoint. Careful to select only a rotten mango as his tool (he wouldn't dare waste a fresh one), Chi-Chi threw that old mango into the air at least five times, as focused as a closing pitcher in the bottom of the ninth in game seven of the world series and, on attempt number five, he nailed it. After gently catching the mango mid-air, he turned toward the OGV and smiled at me. Still beaming, he began his triumphant walk back. But just as he nearly reached the OGV, he stopped—just for one split-second—and looked up and down the street. I held my breath ("Don't you run, you bastard, don't you do it"), then took one enormous sigh of relief as Chi-Chi lowered himself back into the passenger seat, prize in hand. In retrospect, I don't think he was truly considering a make a break for it. I think Chi-Chi just wanted to take in his one brief, quiet moment of freedom before having to return to living the nightmare that was prison and mourning the life he'd lost by getting involved in the drug business in the first place.

After I buckled him in and locked the doors, I sat and patiently waited while Chi-Chi savored every single bite of that mango. When he was done, he turned to thank me, and what he said next (in Spanish) has always stayed with me: "Gracias, Dave. You just never really know the pleasure of the little things, until you can't have them."

Later that day we pulled up alongside a bustling hot dog stand at a busy intersection. Like the majority of the ubiquitous hot dog stands throughout Miami, this one was topped by an enormous beach umbrella, and helmed by several young, beautiful, bikini-clad young women. Chi-Chi's eyes fixated immediately on one particularly busty one, and he turned to me with a smile, slyly saying that he suddenly wanted more mangos (the kind that were *also* not on the prison menu). This time, though, I didn't stop the car.

It's difficult now to remember exactly how many successful cases Chi-Chi's cooperation helped Enforcement Group 4 with, but there's absolutely no doubt that he proved to be one of our greatest assets. Both because of his help and his unfailingly good behavior, he had time taken off his prison sentence and was eventually released.

To this day I'm actually grateful to Chi-Chi, and that's not something I find myself saying often about a former criminal. At least, I hope he's still a former criminal. My one wish for Chi-Chi—besides permanent access to countless mangos of all types and sizes—is that he never returned to his old profession and instead went on to live a happy, safe, crime-free life.

CHAPTER 12

OPERATION SNOWCAP

n 1990, after five long, increasingly stressful years spent fighting a seemingly endless drug war in Miami, I was in desperate need of a break. Most of the cases I'd been tasked with had no discernible schedule, ranging in hours from all day to all night, to a blur of both. Beyond burned out, I was beginning to feel a sense of visceral discomfort with my surroundings in Miami: Even the largest of cities can start to seem claustrophobic when you're working in the world of drug cartels every waking (and sometimes sleeping) moment. To add to my anxiety, not only were Colombian drug traffickers beginning to know my actual identity but one of them, Carlos Montoya (who'd recently been identified as a money launderer for the Ochoa Cartel by Enforcement Group 4), was *literally* my new neighbor. When I discovered that he was living in my very own southwest Dade County neighborhood, that was it. I no longer felt safe, let alone anonymous, in my own home.

One night after watching a World Cup finals game, I looked outside and noticed at least a dozen cars parked in front of Montoya's house. Knowing full well that most Colombians live and die for their fútbol, I assumed that they were all friends of Carlos (and no doubt, fellow drug traffickers), gathered there en masse to drink and party after the game. Of all random things, a mundane televised sporting event had just provided me with a potentially critical work opportunity.

I immediately called my partners Alex Dominguez, AD Wright, and Chris Feistl, all of whom were, as always, selfless enough to drop whatever they were doing and pick up. My proposal to them: Get their asses to my place ASAP, so we could seize this rare chance to conduct a surveillance and potentially ID the majority of the Who's Who of Miami's Medellin Cartel. They all rushed over, we began our watch, and at about ten that night we made our first move. After seeing a Hispanic couple drive off from the party, we asked a Metro Dade patrol unit to stop them, request identifications, and search for any possible contraband they might have in the car.

Not long after we made the request, two patrol units pulled them over less than five miles from Montoya's house, and we discovered that the driver was, in fact, a high-level cocaine trafficker (not to mention a member of Medellin's infamous Pablo Escobar cartel) named Zaragoza. And it got even better: His female passenger turned out to be Jorge Ochoa's sister and had with her more than fifty thousand US dollars, made up entirely of hundred-dollar bills bound tightly together with a rubber band. Together, Pablo Escobar and Jorge Ochoa were widely known as Medellin's most powerful—and equally violent and vicious—drug traffickers and, amazingly, their own closest relatives and capos were at that very moment busy partying and watching fútbol *on my street*. As insane as it sounds, that was simply Miami in the '80s, but that night I finally hit my breaking point of worry over my own personal safety and well-being. There goes the neighborhood, indeed.

Recognizing that the drug war was continuing to spiral out of control, the DEA took further action. In early 1990, an entirely new group of agents were recruited from all over the US for a newly developed jungle interdiction program to be held in Peru, Bolivia, and Colombia. This groundbreaking venture was known as Operation Snowcap.

A great many domestic Division DEA supervisors—including the Special Agents in Charge (SACs)—detested Operation Snowcap from the very start, not least of all because it took from the department's overall available (and much-needed) resources. In their minds, it also (and perhaps even symbolically) took the focus away from the countless number of US-based cases their Special Agents had been spending most of their time on, thus detracting from the overall US-based drug enforcement effectiveness and engagement. If an agent was busy destroying cocaine clandestine labs in, say, Peru, then he or she quite obviously wouldn't be free to make any arrests in Detroit, Dallas, Miami, etc. Every single DEA supervisor lived and died by their respective group's statistics, and the Snowcappers only weakened those numbers. Some supervisors went so far as to theorize that these "Snowcrappers" weren't even working on cases against major drug traffickers, which was patently untrue. Unfortunately, those executives simply weren't fully informed about what was going on outside of their divisions.

For instance, some of the largest Colombian cartels were using coca brokers whose clan labs were scattered throughout the Chapare jungle in Bolivia and the Upper Huallaga Valley in Peru. By targeting these specific brokers, the DEA was helping break the direct supply link to both the Medellin and Cali cartels. That wasn't where the Snowcappers efforts ended, either: FAST (which stood for Foreign Advisory Support Teams) was a quickly established descendant interdiction program under Snowcap, and a critical one at that. The agents within FAST worked in both Afghanistan and Central America, ultimately taking down many of the most important targets in those regions, and often achieving what countless other DEA agents did not.

In October of 2009, during my tenure as Chief of Global Enforcement Operations at DEA Headquarters, I was fast asleep when I was suddenly startled by the sound of my phone ringing at two a.m. On the other end was our Afghanistan Regional Director Mike Marsac, who told me that a Chinook helicopter had just crashed in Badghis Province, Afghanistan. The chopper had been carrying thirty-six passengers—only twenty-six of whom survived—and had gone down while en route to execute a pivotal raid and arrest involving one of the biggest heroin traffickers in the country at the time.

What had happened was both shocking and tragic: All of the team members had been in great spirits and ready to go, having just executed a near-flawless infiltration ("infil") and raid. However, during their exfiltration ("exfil"), one of the two Chinooks inexplicably and suddenly went down, crashing forcefully in what we call a "white-out." A white-out is truly uncommon, and only happens when the rotator on a Chinooks stirs up so much desert dust, sand, and smoke from incinerated drugs that it reaches a point where no pilot—regardless of how gifted or skilled they might be—could possibly be able to adequately judge the distance from a nearby obstacle (in this case, a close mountain range). Once the second Chinook lifted, a natural forward hover carried it even closer to the mountain, before forcefully thrusting it forward. So, to their surprise and horror, when the pilots finally saw the mountain, it was far too late to be able to break right, swerve to avoid it, and keep the

Chinook safely flying. Again, I need to emphasize this: These amazing US Army 160th pilots were as talented, experienced, and quick-thinking as any you could ever imagine, or could ever hope to meet. But in cases like this, fate takes over. Experience means nothing.

A sudden stall mid-air prompted the initial MH-47G fall, but the pilots were able to position the Chinook belly-first (a critical, brilliant tactic on the pilots' part, and one that reduced loss of life by a significant amount). Still, any rapidly-moving aircraft crash-landing into the dry desert reaps nothing but total calamity, and on that terrible day, ten hero passengers and three DEA agents from the FAST program all lost their lives. A fourth Supervisory Agent was seriously injured but miraculously survived and—despite the "hot" rounds that were firing off in every direction from the flames inside the aircraft—also managed to help every single survivor from that Chinook before it eventually exploded. Special Agents Michael Weston, Forrest Leamon, and Chad Michael were the three fellow agents who hadn't been as lucky as their Supervisor, who survived the explosion. But all three of them left incredible legacies behind, not least that day's success: the arrest of the most significant heroin trafficker in Afghanistan. The names of Agents Weston, Leamon, and Michael are all displayed on the DEA Wall of Honor, yet another assurance that they will never be forgotten. Agent Weston, who'd also served as a US Marine, was buried at the renowned Arlington National Cemetery, with honors.

I made sure to be there at the Dover Air Force Base when Agents Weston, Leamon, and Michael were brought back to us, along with the other fallen US military personnel. I was specifically designated as the escort to Agent Leamon's family, responsible for bringing them to meet the Air Force

C-141 Starlifter that had brought back their patriarch. DEA Administrator Michelle Leonhart and Attorney General Eric Holder were also in attendance, with Supervisory Special Agent Curt Clements tasked with the unenviable job of overseeing the entire event. In the end, Special Agent Clements did an incredible job, choreographing every detail, from the liaison with the US Air Force funeral services division to assuring that all family members were comfortable, seamlessly-transported, and fully-accommodated. And, per DEA tradition (a tradition every agent prays their own family never has to suffer through, no matter how poignant), he made sure to carefully line up all of the FAST Division agents for one final DEA salute just as the families and fallen agents passed by the chapel and the tarmac. It was an incredibly moving and memorable scene to witness, to say the least.

An event like this is an unusual thing. Though the mood is overwhelmingly somber and melancholy, there is also a universal sense of pride for the fallen agents, as well as the jobs to which they had dedicated—and ultimately given—their lives. After a difficult five-hour wait, the aircraft at last landed, with Curt's FAST team honored to be the ones at the front of the pack and eager to greet. Sometime around two a.m., President Barack Obama arrived and met with each and every family member, from DEA and military families alike. Gracious, kind, and sincere, he was there for one reason and one reason only: to offer his personal, deepest sympathies. While President Obama didn't have a military background himself, he knew full well the importance of these men and the investigations they had spent their entire careers working on. These were men—and jobs and accomplishments—worthy enough of their own President of the United States to openly praise and acknowledge, in person. To the families, and certainly also to us, it was a gesture that meant everything.

So, unsurprisingly, I held a different point of view than some of those domestic SACs when it came to the Snowcappers. That outlook, combined with what had turned into an undeniable mid-career malaise combined with a very valid, rapidly-growing fear for my own personal safety (and in my own neighborhood, no less), sparked a pivot from admiration to appreciation to actual interest. I had nothing more to prove in Miami just by staying in the US to do my job (nor to gain, for that matter). I craved a new, exciting, challenge, and working overseas (while also learning how to cultivate foreign contacts *and* master the Spanish language at the same time) was an intriguing option, one I couldn't stop thinking about. I also knew from my case experiences that a seamless continuum existed between the foreign narco supplier and the US-based narco distributor. So, I didn't take long to make up my mind, and by the time I applied for the Snowcap program I was, after much hard work, already a full journeyman, grade GS-13 Criminal Investigator. Now, I can look back with genuine gratitude for my Spanish-speaking capabilities (still bueno), along with all of the foreign experience under my belt, and recognize that it was the best choice that I could have made for myself.

Not that it was an easy road. To be officially accepted into the Snowcap program, an agent had to pass a rigorous physical examination, have an exceptionally excellent work record, and, by far the most daunting challenge, be able to pass two legendarily brutal trainings. First, a nine-week US Army Ranger Training Course in Fort Benning, Georgia (the first week of which is widely known as "Hell on Earth"), immediately followed by eight intense, grueling weeks made up primarily of a hardcore combination of warfare and survival training. Inspired (and, no doubt, motivated) after years of hearing my father's stories of his own experiences in the Army, to me it all seemed a perfect fit. I was still only twenty-eight, strong, fearless, and constantly running toward every possible challenge, never away from one. On a more thoughtful level, I also realized that taking a break from Miami would most certainly help to clear my mind, break out of what had become a rut, and focus just long enough to finally select my true career path.

DEA Ranger Stamina Training,
Ft. Benning, Georgia, circa 1990

As it turned out, my gut instincts had led me in the right direction once again. While the US Army Ranger School training wound up being among the toughest weeks of my life, there's no question that they were also some of the best. Certainly, they remain some of the most important.

After successfully completing (rather, after successfully *surviving*) all aspects of the training, including six months of intense daily Spanish language instruction at the Defense Language Institute (DLI) in Monterey, I was deployed on a jungle interdiction assignment over to the Chapare jungle region of Bolivia. My team leader was Bob Hartman[4], an Army vet and all-around outstanding guy who came to the DEA after many years of demanding police work. After everyone had arrived, about a dozen DEA guys were partnered with men from the US Border Patrol BORTAC[5] team. Our mission was to work together with the National Rural Police (referred to as UMOPAR) in order to collect intelligence we could then use against drug cartels— more specifically, the most successful and brazen of the cartels, those thriving off of their use of the Chapare jungle as a collective home base for a staggeringly high number of cocaine conversion laboratories. During that time, in fact, the vast majority of notorious Colombian cartels chose to headquarter their cocaine conversion labs right there in Bolivia and Peru.

Our joint efforts to take down the cartels included defendant debriefings, both land and air reconnaissance missions, "raid and arrest" planning, and reliance upon intel and assistance from myriad, well-cultivated informants. The process was typically as follows: Snowcap agents would first collect the information needed in order to build a solid case, then hand it over to the UMOPAR, working elbow to elbow with them to both execute the arrests and, ideally, incarcerate the traffickers involved. Of course, that makes it sound far more seamless in practice than it actually was, not least for the Snowcappers. First, we (the agents) flew a US Air Force C-141 to La Paz, Bolivia, planting ourselves deep within the Chapare jungle, along with our six Toyota Landcruiser SUVs and enough rations and supplies to easily last us four solid months. We next drove a day to the base camp, Chimore, where we then made our new home away from home. Chimore was certainly a no-frills base; still, it had everything we needed, replete with a small airstrip and several buildings containing barracks, a kitchen, and even a weight room. Since this was pre-Wi-Fi (back in the dark ages that was 1990), there most certainly was no television, no cable, no internet, and no phones of any kind. For communication purposes, we relied solely upon a UHF radio, one "owned" and operated by our comms man Don Taylor, who'd done an almost unheard of five full tours in Vietnam and recently retired from the US Army Special Forces. He is now greatly missed: I attended Don's funeral in 2019, and by all accounts, he was an unfailingly kind and good man to all of his friends and family, not to mention a true patriot (a moniker so often overused but totally applicable in this case) and a loyal warrior on behalf of his country.

Myself (*right*) and DEA Agent Jerry Salameh (*left*) with Umopar police on a raid of a cartel communications center in the Chapare jungle of Bolivia.

During our four-month-long deployment, we conducted riverine operations, air interdictions, and quickly stacked up the kind of seize and arrests statistics that Operation Snowcap had never seen. I wish I could say that those successes were a credit just to us; rather, they were in fact a credit to the teams who came before us and who'd worked so diligently to build the groundwork that made such success even possible. While we worked hand-in-hand primarily with UMOPAR authorities, our partner in transportation was the Bolivian Air Forces' Diablos Rojos (also referred to as the Red Devils). Hands down, these guys were some of the absolute ballsiest pilots I'd ever met—still are—and would have landed us down perfectly on a gnat's *ass* if we'd asked them to (assuming gnats have asses). To fight our enemy on their ground, we frequently had to infil on isolated riverbanks, cliffs, remote jungle areas—even sometimes on top of the water—and without fail, the Diablos Rojos delivered every single time.

One night, we worked our way to an FOB (a Forward Operations Base) buried deep within the Beni plateau. This particular FOB was in the most remote and desolate of regions, where many of the most powerful cartels built their fincas: farms in which they stored thousands of kilos of cocaine, along with the millions of gallons of precursor chemicals needed to convert the coca base into the pure, precious, snow-white cocaine hydrochloride off of which they made their living. Not long after we'd settled, I went on a reconnaissance mission with a Diablos Rojos pilot, the two of us taking flight in a single-engine Cessna 182. My one goal that day was to confirm (or dispel) an informant's report of an enormous, clandestine lab, one located a mere sixty kilometers from our own Camp Chimore. The Cessna we were using was unusual, however, having been recently seized from drug traffickers and put to immediate use, which told me two things: 1) It almost certainly had not been properly maintained; 2) Today was not the most ideal day for me to be serving as co-pilot. Thankfully, we did manage to complete the mission with our lives intact, albeit also disappointed because we hadn't found the clan lab. Our pilot commander Jorge, however, wasn't going to let our failed attempt dampen our spirits. While still mid-air and en route back to Chimore, Jorge let go of the Cessna's wheel, turned to me with a slightly unnerving, clearly mischievous look, and, in a matter-of-fact tone, said: "Dave, you go ahead and fly now." I waited for the punchline, and when I saw that his expression remained unchanged, just stared back at him in shock and finally said, in Spanish, "But I'm not a pilot!" Calmly shrugging his shoulders, he then made that universal kind of expression/shrug that instantly signals: "Well, there's not much *I* can do about that." Realizing he was not going to back down—joke or not—I grabbed that damn steering wheel and held on to it for dear life.

Damn him: It was no joke. Jorge made me fly that bird—my first time doing anything even remotely like that—to Chimore, and then even land the airplane at the airstrip. He talked me through it, with not one hint of humor, but once we were at wheels-down, he broke into riotous laughter before we'd even made the second bounce. When we at last came to a stop at the end of the strip, I tried in vain to take my hands off the wheel: Unsurprisingly, my hands were frozen in such a death grip that I couldn't unclench them for at least two or three interminably long minutes. "Jorge, tu eres un pendejo!" I said. (I'll let you use your imagination as to what that means, but I will say that "pendejo" is *not* a pilot's preferred nickname.)

During a later, equally memorable (but far less terrifying) FOB, we overnighted on an abandoned narco farm in the Beni and, as we hung blissfully in hammocks strung around an enormous Eucalyptus tree and savored the rare moment of actual silence, a rooster began to crow. This was no somewhat-annoying, early-morning Midwestern farm-based, modest decibel-level kind of crow gently nudging us awake at two in the morning—this was the kind of crow who could raise the dead, only to have the dead wish for immediate death again. Collectively we held our breath, each of us testing our own patience limits and wondering just how long we could stand the noise. In retrospect, the fact that we made it almost an hour is a testament to our endurance (and perhaps our present-day hearing loss). But eventually, enough was enough—and at that one-hour mark, Jorge begrudgingly lowered himself out of his hammock, squinted his eyes, examined our tree more carefully than if he had been giving it an annual physical, then grinned without regret as he located our torturer and promptly knocked that rooster square in the head with a long, broken limb taken off the tree itself. I still have no regrets when I tell you that the following day, we all enjoyed a delicious, supremely satisfying, perfectly *quiet* grilled chicken feast.

Wildlife nemeses properly disposed of (and digested), we went back to the business at hand. Our biggest raid on a narco-controlled village happened in Santa Ana, where the team had to first fly via a Huey II (a helicopter dating as far back as the Vietnam era), land aside a riverbank, then boat for over two hours into the village, all under the cover of total darkness. Not only did we have to remain blanketed in that black gloom (with reliance only upon the dim glow of our flashlights), but we also had to maintain complete silence at all times. At one point, I rolled over and inadvertently aimed my flashlight toward the water, whereupon I immediately saw at least a thousand illuminated, muddy-yellow eyeballs staring right back. And, on the ghost of that rooster (RIP), I never used my flashlight on that trip again. Just a few hours later—and as surreptitiously as possible—we advanced into Santa Ana, the light slowly breaking, as by then it was just before dawn. The tranquility of the setting didn't dampen our instincts or expectations for one minute (thanks no doubt to our hardcore training), and almost immediately we found ourselves fighting with not only myriad traffickers, but the actual community the traffickers had been protecting. After we managed to secure the tiny town airport, over six hundred

UMOPAR were flown in. Riots then began—and continued—for over two days straight.

On the third day, universally starved, the team began to desperately crave something, anything, to eat: just *anything,* even the tiniest bit more flavorful than the usual military MREs (Meals Ready to Eat).[4] Clearly inspired by our recent hunt, I remembered that en route to Santa Ana—where we'd stopped to search a large, now-abandoned farm that was once the headquarters of a still-active narco—I'd spotted several large hogs left behind, aimlessly wandering around the nearby fields, clearly growing wilder by the day. Leading mainly with my appetite, I checked with Bob and asked if I could take a few Bolivian UMOPAR police on a "recon" flight and bring back some pork to barbeque. Bob being Bob (the man led with his appetite even more than I did, if that's even possible), he immediately deemed it an outstanding suggestion, and off we went to the abandoned farm, with its unsuspecting main course/residents. After shooting a couple of six-hundred-pound hogs with my DEA-issued M-16 .223 automatic rifle and waiting an hour for them to bleed out, we swiftly tied them in a cargo net and sling-loaded them under the Huey II. Back in Santa Ana that evening, while we knew we'd now officially gone on to make yet more enemies of the wildlife of the region, our only regret was that we hadn't found any others. And that night, every single trooper and pilot ate what each of us would still swear was the freshest, most delicious, most hard-earned barbeque sandwich of our lives.

CHAPTER 13

LAND OF ETERNAL SPRING

B y early 1991, it had already become very clear to me that I wanted to extend the focus on my overseas work. I loved what I was doing, so once again I requested a temporary assignment. This one was based in Guatemala, where (as with Operation Snowcap) I'd be joining a militarized group of DEA agents in order to conduct investigations and intercept aircraft used to smuggle cocaine from Colombia directly to Guatemala. The operation was deemed "Operation Cadence." Ranger school had trained all of us on nearly every possible aspect of warfare, and the DEA had trained us on nearly every possible aspect of how to best conduct criminal investigations. By fusing these skills, the resulting hybrid DEA agents—myself included—were in high demand.

I'd never been to Guatemala before and was immediately taken with the near-perfect weather and overall enchanting mood that made up Guatemala City. From its aesthetic to its native residents, it's obvious right from the minute you arrive just why it's known as "The Land of Eternal Spring." Our base was about ten minutes from the Aurora International Airport, and we had easy access to a slew of aviation-related resources we'd use in missions involving the pursuit and interdiction of criminally-operated airplanes and speed boats.

One of the first of those missions saw us operating several US Department of State UH-60 Blackhawk helicopters (helmed by talented Guatemalan pilots) in order to find a last-known directional isthmus of a speed boat we knew was smuggling approximately two metric tons of cocaine. After launching into the Pacific Ocean off of Puerto San Jose, we established our isthmus, then began patrolling. It didn't take long for us to locate the fifty-foot speed boat, which held four passengers and, of course, their cocaine.

Our Blackhawk was equipped with an M-60 machine gun, which was very ably manned by an expert Guatemalan gunner. So, when the occupants refused to stop their vessel at our command, the gunner opened fire in front of the boat in order to slow them down. The tactic was successful, albeit only briefly. At one point Michael Braun, our Cadence team leader at the time, was wielding an enormous megaphone, yelling and attempting to direct them to go to the beach—but in English. Not getting the response he wanted, at one point Mike stopped mid-sentence, laughing, and asked me: "Dave, how do you say beach in Spanish?" ("Playa, Mike.") Too late: Successful translation or no, those maniacs instead chose to speed up and drive deeper into the open ocean, prompting our eagle-eyed gunner to open fire in front of them a second, and then a third, time. With so many crazy things all going on at once—and all of them as we were flying about a hundred feet above the ocean's surface, dangerously weaving back and forth to keep up—I honestly can't say for sure if any of those M-60 rounds even penetrated the vessel or any of its five 300 HP motors. But whatever the cause, the vessel eventually capsized roughly a hundred meters from shore, and we all breathed a collective sigh of relief.

Mike then gave orders for the Blackhawk to be lowered to about ten feet off the ground, and I—along with two other men— jumped out of the copter and onto the beach. Fortunately, the dense, chalky, white sand broke my fall. Far less fortunately, however, as I not so deftly sprung from the helo door, my range pants got caught on one of the door parts, causing my britches to rip loudly all the way from my belt loop down to my boot. I was left with one full leg exposed, and I can say with the utmost confidence that Angelina Jolie posing on the Oscars red carpet, I was not. I was mortified, but I was also incredibly sick with the flu at the time, and that tempered my embarrassment in a major way. I hardly cared—I wasn't thrilled about ruining the pants, but there were far more important matters at hand.

At that point we still didn't know if all or any of the smugglers had made it to land, because the waters had gotten increasingly rough, with ten-to-fifteen-foot waves consistently breaking one after the other as they crashed onto the shore. As I was meticulously collecting kilos of packaged cocaine bricks, I glanced up and saw one of the men from the smuggling boat on his hands and knees struggling to crawl out of the water, followed by a second, and eventually a third. There had been four men aboard when we first started pursuing them, and it soon became pretty clear that one of them had met a far less ideal fate.

After the three surviving smugglers wearily bobbed and weaved their way onto dry land, they were soon followed by a wave (no pun intended) of cocaine bales floating atop the surf. It took us hours to collect all of it, and we were left exhausted (and, of course, it didn't exactly help that I was both flu-ridden and nearly pant-less). More aircraft and support vehicles were requested by Braun, and we ultimately succeeded in getting both the (surviving) defendants and their copious amounts of cocaine to the appropriate places: jail and the Guatemalan Military drug warehouse and laboratory, respectively. The remainder of my pants, however, went right into the trash.

Another memorable investigation from this time in my career involved myself and Edward Marlowe, an agent from Texas. This mission sent us to the northern towns of Puerto Barrios and Lake Atitlan with the goal of locating ill-gotten assets—in this case, assets belonging to a US citizen who'd made millions off of smuggling marijuana and cocaine back to the States. Agent Ed was a true, tough Texas cowboy in every way. Ed and I had been great friends ever since the very first moment we met, all the way back in Ranger School at Fort Benning.

The owner of the vessels we were pursuing was a Georgia-born, down home country boy kind of fella who'd been hiding out somewhere in Guatemala City. His eighty-foot sailboat and forty-foot speedboat, however, were housed in the north country, so off Ed and I went (along with a team of Guatemalan military officials) to seize them. This was a great example of a perfect day's work: teamwork, collaboration, and success. We found the vessels and seized them both for forfeiture to the Guatemalan government.

A third case from my days in The Land of Eternal Spring involved the interception and interdiction of a Gulfstream II airplane from Colombia that had been forced to land on a rocky dirt strip in the middle of a Guatemalan sugarcane field. Multiple significant arrests were made and approximately one-thousand kilos of cocaine seized, but the *real* prize to us was the Gulfstream itself. The G-II had no discernible flight logs aboard, and the dash looked like it had been repeatedly trashed, but one of the Guatemalan pilots and I boarded that baby and flew it straight out of that sugarcane field and right on back to the

Aurora Airport. As far as I could tell, the only actual tangible, truly functional thing on that flight was a picture of La Virgin Madre Maria, the mother of Jesus Christ, because in all reality that plane could and should have fallen from the sky and crashed at any time. I couldn't help but think remarkable that this criminal pilot felt he needed a photograph of the Virgin Mary as opposed to flight logs and adequate avionics (weather radar, geo-point systems, communications, etc.) in a jet aircraft that was traveling internationally and over open oceans. Less than a year after that miracle flight, I heard that the Guatemalan president was, incredibly, using that G-II as his own presidential aircraft.

During those four memorable months in Guatemala, I was also fortunate enough to spend a good amount of time training the national police on interdiction and raid tactics, along with more time working other cases against the countless Colombian smugglers who chose to use this beautiful country as their waypoint for cocaine smuggling to the USA. But, for all the strife and illicit activity and adventure, it's still the natural beauty of that incredible place that has stayed with me most.

CHAPTER 14

CROCS OF CAUCA

I t was 1994 and I had been assigned to the DEA Costa Rica Country Office for two years. After my work in Miami and Operation Cadence, where I chased narcos from Guatemala to Panama, I set out to find a permanent position in Central America. It wasn't just a smart career move; I was getting divorced and needed a new place to land. I knew I could use what I had learned in Miami in Central America—all of Latin America, actually—and do even more damage to the cartels south of our borders. Besides, to participate in OP Snowcap and Cadence, I had learned to speak Spanish fluently, after six months of training at the US Defense Department Defense Language Institute (DLI).

In late September 1991, DEA headquarters gave me the choice of two language schools: The Foreign Language Institute (FLI) near Washington, DC, or DLI in Monterey, California. I instantly said, "You want me to choose between Washington, DC, and California for six months through the winter? Cali here I come!" The instructor-student ratio at DLI was one-to-one. While taking essentially private Spanish lessons for six hours a day, five days per week, followed by at least three hours of daily homework involving workbook and audio training, I began to pick it up. To supplement my formal instruction, I read books written by native

Hispanic authors and watched Hispanic television every night (I loved the telenovelas.) I learned and came to love this foreign language that once seemed alien to me. After qualifying at the three/three level, I thought: Why not make the most of DEA's investment in me, and use the skill I spent so much time and effort on developing? So, upon graduating from the DLI program two weeks early, I was immediately deployed to the jungles of Bolivia to raid cocaine production laboratories and arrest those behind these laboratories and the coke trafficking that resulted. After one year in the program, I asked for a permanent change of station (PCS) transfer to Costa Rica and Nicaragua.

By 1992, the Colombian and Mexican cartels had already entered into agreements to smuggle cocaine from South America to Mexico, bypassing the Caribbean and South Florida corridor to get to where the Mexican cartels had an international distribution network to the USA. The Mexican routes and distribution cells were already set up from their 1960s and 70s marijuana supply business. Corrupt men like Miguel Angel Felix, brothers Miguel and Gilberto Rodriguez Orejuela, and Pablo Escobar Gaviria used their criminal enterprises to smuggle thousands of metric tons of cocaine across the border to satisfy the insatiable demand from dealers in the United States. And I wanted to be in the middle of it.

I reported to Costa Rica in April 1992 and quickly found myself a third wheel in the office. Two more senior agents had been there for a couple of years and were partnered in their cases. Both agents, Jose and Glenn, were cordial to me and did everything they could to make me feel welcome—but for the first time in my career, I felt a void. I had gotten used to having a regular investigative partner; together, we'd do case work, debrief and manage informants, and hang out after the busts.

After running my cases and operations like a lone wolf for about six months, the office supervisor informed us that an agent from the Bogota, Colombia, office was being reassigned to Costa Rica. His name was Jim Rose.

Jim was working in Bogota when his lovely bride became pregnant—at a time when all agents were required to be stationed without their significant other, also known as an unaccompanied tour. The reasoning behind this policy was that the narcos would target DEA agents' family members, making the job even more risky than it already was for the agents working to bring justice to the most violent drug traffickers in the world. So, when Jim found out he was to be a daddy, he asked for a transfer, and, with coaxing from higher ups, DEA headquarters decided to transfer both him and his wife to Costa Rica, where the threats against agents were almost non-existent. When Jim arrived at the office, the logical choice to partner him with was the third wheel. Jim and I rapidly formed a liaison and recruited informants, co-wrote intelligence reports, and conducted investigations together. We became partners, and what a great partner Jim came to be.

A wiry, athletic type and highly competitive, Jim was skilled in almost every sport you could imagine and loved to exercise on a daily basis. Jim was originally from Cincinnati, Ohio, but had worked as a police officer in Colorado. Prior to working for the DEA, Jim was a narcotics detective with the Colorado Springs Police Department and, in fact, was the inspiration for the character of "Flip Zimmerman," the white undercover detective in Spike Lee's *BlacKkKlansman*.

In real life, Jim's undercover role in that investigation not only dismantled the local chapter but also knocked the Klan's Grand Wizard David Duke off his tracks from successfully entering into national politics. Jim is a cool cat.

After Jim and I had a couple of years of working in Central America with outstanding foreign police partners like Gonzalo Bado from Costa Rica's OIJ (a hybrid version of FBI/DEA) and Captain Leonel Espinoza of the Nicaraguan National Police, I felt confident I could control, manage, and work any informant that was thrown at me. One of these cooperating informants was Andres Cardona, whom we called "AC." AC was an actual "walk-in," meaning he simply arrived at the American Embassy asking to speak with a DEA agent, and I happened to be that agent. Both Jim and I met AC and debriefed him as to what he knew of drug trafficking, how he had possessed such knowledge, and what he was willing to do to help the DEA dismantle the trafficking organizations.

AC was a Costa Rican businessman who owned a food distribution company in San Jose. A large man, standing six foot two and weighing two hundred and forty pounds, with an assertive, no-nonsense attitude, he had made it in business and was doing well in life. On a large scale, AC would ship and receive tons of rice, beans, flour, and assorted canned goods between the USA and Latin America. One of his clients was Leonides Rhadames Trujillo, known as Rhadames, the son of the Dominican Republic's dictator, President Rafael Leonides Trujillo. Rhadames had excellent business contacts throughout Latin America due to his father's tight grip on the DR for forty years, and AC liked using the famed Trujillo name to create more business.

One day, Rhadames approached AC in Panama and told him about his contacts with Gilberto Rodriguez Orejuela and brother Miguel, leaders of the infamous Cali Cartel. Rhadames personally knew these men; in fact, he was in business with them, smuggling tons of cocaine in containerized cargo shipped to various ports in the United States, including Long Beach, Galveston, Miami, and New York. Rhadames was seeking to expand his shipping network and asked AC if he would be willing to embed cocaine into some of his food shipments to Mexico and the United States.

AC realized that there was money to be made here, but he also possessed the integrity and personal ethics to realize he would be far better off to inform the DEA of this illicit enterprise. Besides, AC knew that the US government paid for such valuable information and that the Cali Cartel was already in the crosshairs of the DEA. Additionally, AC knew that if any of his containers were stopped and seized for improper permits or mild infractions of US commerce regulations, friends at the DEA could help smooth out any problems. As I said, AC was a shrewd and good businessman.

AC approached the DEA (that is, Jim and me) in San Jose and reported on what he and Rhadames had discussed. AC wanted to work undercover against Rhadames and the Cali Cartel, but he wanted assurances that he would not be investigated for doing so and that his containers and legit food products would not be seized. If his information led to a seizure of cocaine and criminal indictments, he would receive an appropriate payment from the US government as a reward. This motivation for cooperation—patriotic and monetary—is the best combination, which I fully understand and empathize with. Jim and I documented Andres Cardona as an informant, and AC immediately began documenting and recording his discussions with Rhadames.

Jim and I also had to "reel in" our principal Costa Rican police counterpart, Gonzalo Bado. Six feet tall and just over two hundred pounds, Bado, which is what everyone called him, was the spitting image of the Marlboro Man. His customary dress was blue jeans, cowboy boots, and a loose-fitting, long-sleeved, button-down with a breast pocket for his signature red pack of cigarettes—yes, he smoked the bad ole regular Marlboros. He knew that Costa Rica was the "trampoline" for Colombian drug traffickers to smuggle their cocaine and, as an inherent fighter for justice, he viewed that as a national invasion! Bado and his sidekick, Victor Mullens, would ensure that DEA intelligence was given top priority and acted on in a moment's notice.

I'll share an example of Bado's dedication to DEA. Once, the Costa Rica DEA office identified Colombian money launderers in San Jose for a big party to celebrate a shipment of money they had received from the United States. It was hundreds of millions of dollars. The four Colombian "businessmen" were staying at the San Jose Palacio Hotel, located off the Alajuela Airport highway in San Jose, in the presidential suite. We informed Bado of this small detail—and within two hours, he had his anti-drug squad at the hotel and executing a "Knock & Talk" at the penthouse suite's door. When one of the well-dressed money launderers answered, Bado slammed the door open and had that scumbag turned around, up against the wall, and frisked before he knew what was going on. There were US criminal indictments and arrest warrants for all of the Colombians in that room, and they all went to jail. Due to the party atmosphere, the now vacant suite was full of Dom Perignon champagne, shrimp cocktails, and freshly prepared platters of exquisite cheeses and meats, that I for one could certainly not let go to waste. We were in the presidential suite searching for evidence for some time, and it was nice to be treated to fine dining while doing so!

I also knew that Bado loved his job; he was a police officer with every fiber of his being. His loyalty to Costa Rica's sovereignty was beyond reproach. When we grabbed a meal, went out for drinks, or did just about anything else together, we talked about dope and drug enforcement. When Bado, Jim, and I met, our joint casework was primal and that's just about all we talked about, except for one other activity: soccer. If Bado, Jim, and I went to a soccer game or the subject of a soccer team came up in conversation, Bado was one hundred percent focused on soccer. It was an obsession!

Anyways, I wanted to brief Bado on the Rhadames case and the fact that Jim and I had Andres Cardona as an informant in Costa Rica. Bado was a cop first and a diplomat second, so he concurred with our use of AC. But he made one point very clear to Jim and me: "If I catch that guy running drugs outside of pre-approved activity with you or my government, I'll bury him under the jail!" From that point on, Jim and I shared all of AC's movements and meetings, both inside Costa Rican territory and beyond, with Bado.

Roughly one month after signing on as an informant, Andres called me from Barranquilla, Colombia, with a matter of urgency. "Dave, you have to come up here immediately!" he said. "I am at the Prado Hotel and met a narco who wants me to ship his money in my containers from Panama to Colombia. He says he has four hundred million dollars stacked and waiting near the canal to be transported!" I asked AC for the guy's name, and he answered, "Jorge." Really? You want me to book a flight to Colombia on a "Jorge?" AC calmed down and said, "Don't worry. I will get you a full name and call you back in one hour." Sure enough, within an hour he called with the details. "He calls himself Jorge Eugenio," AC emphatically declared, as if he had just discovered the cure for cancer. He also informed me: the guy was associated with the Montoya Sanchez family, a notorious drug cartel.

I quickly checked the DEA intelligence network database and BING, BING, BING! Jorge Eugenio Montoya Sanchez shot off the screen like a roman candle: "Money launderer for the Autodefenses Unidas Colombiana." This was the AUC, a drug cartel pretending to be a civil vigilante defense group. The AUC, a right-wing paramilitary criminal organization, began their notoriety by claiming to strictly fight against Colombia's leftist guerillas, the Colombian Revolutionary Armed Forces, also known by the Spanish acronym, FARC. The FARC attempted to overturn the populist government by bombing government buildings and targeting politicians in car bombs and ambushes. To develop a revenue stream, they kidnapped wealthy and middle-class Colombian citizens for ransom. Thousands of Colombians simply "closed shop" and fled to the USA, Europe, or other Latin American countries to avoid the FARC's threats and violence.

The AUC was established to defend Colombia from this Communist scourge; however, when the FARC began protecting narcos and eventually became a formidable drug cartel themselves, the AUC turned to drug trafficking in order to build a revenue stream sufficient to compete with the FARC in terms of warfare. "Once a narco, always a narco," said Colombian President Alvaro Uribe, and he eventually designated the AUC, along with the FARC, as a drug cartel. Jorge Eugenio Montoya Sanchez was the AUC's chief financial officer. He was staying at the El Prado Hotel in Barranquilla, and Jim and I planned to meet him in a few hours.

I was sitting at my desk in Costa Rica, urgently arranging for a flight to Barranquilla, or "BQ" as the agents called it, when my partner walked up and dropped himself into the cheap government chair in front of me. Jim had been out for a day or so dealing with personal business and knew nothing of this exciting development. So, with one hand covering the telephone earpiece,

I started telling him about the case. His hand rose up, palm open towards me, and he said, "I'm getting divorced." Since I was still on the phone with the embassy travel agent, I immediately responded, "You want a window seat or aisle?" Jim stoically looked at me for five seconds and said, "aisle." That proved to be a very wise choice. At the time of this brief conversation, I didn't know that Jim's claim of a future divorce was simply a feeble attempt to vent out marital frustrations and did not mean those words. I suppose that's marriage.

While at the San Jose airport café, Jim ordered a coffee with cream, and that cream was bad shit! Really something evil, made personally at the hands of Lucifer. Midway through the flight to BQ, Jim began sweating profusely and turned three shades of green. I also happened to be sitting in an aisle seat, directly across from him, and followed his physical metamorphosis. Within forty-five minutes, Jim went from looking like a statue of virility to a green titty-baby.

When certain vomiting became inevitable, he desperately searched for a barf bag, but the pouch in front of his seat was void of one. At that moment of self-awareness, Jim's eyes widened as if he were destined to soil at least four travelers on this flight, including me. I quickly handed him my bag, and as quietly as I have ever heard anyone barf, Jim filled that bag up to the top edge. I swear, if he burped another drop, it would have overflowed! Not wanting to miss a moment, I kept intently examining Jim to see what his next step would be. With a green face and vomit dripping off his bottom lip while holding a full bag of puke and ready to get divorced, Jim was about as vulnerable as you can get. So, naturally, I laughed.

Jim, realizing he had finished, slowly raised his head and looked at me with a steadily developing smile that never stopped until I saw every vomit-laced tooth in his mouth. About that time, a gorgeous COPA flight attendant named Valeria walked by, stopped, and immediately relieved Jim of that loaded bag. As she walked away up the aisle to the nearest lavatory, Jim looked at me again with his best "James Dean" expression, smiling and winking one eye. He didn't say a word, but I knew he had things under control.

While at the Prado Hotel, I truly can't say what happened to Jim. Apparently, the lactose bug came back, and he was in his room, probably the bathroom, during our entire stay. But I was alive and well. I did a debriefing with AC and then photographed Montoya Sanchez and his colleagues poolside for my intelligence report. In the end, AC never closed a deal with this major drug trafficker. Years later, in January 2007, Montoya Sanchez was finally arrested by the Colombian National Police and extradited to the USA for an all-expenses-paid "vacation" in the federal penitentiary system.

When we returned to Costa Rica, I made an unprecedented operational case decision. I reached out to a "sister" US agency (who shall remain nameless) for communications intercept capability by providing one of their people a cellular telephone that I was giving to AC for his ongoing interactions and engagements with Rhadames and, hopefully, the Rodriguez brothers. My former Miami partner, Chris Feistl, who had successfully recovered from our time in Jamaica (remember the Red Stripe beer and jerked chicken incident?), was already working on the Cali Cartel in Colombia. Chris succeeded in his work and was the principal character reflected in Season Three of the Netflix series, *Narcos*. If I was able to capture locations of the Rodriguez brothers, I would pass that information to Chris so the Colombian National Police could finally arrest them.[5]

When I approached the sister agency, I briefed them on AC's background and what we were planning to do to capture the Cali Cartel Kingpin traffickers, Gilberto and Miguel Rodriguez Orejuela. "Sis" was very accommodating. After a few hours, they brought back my cell phone and said, "We'll let you know everything that goes on." I was ecstatic with the satisfaction of how easy it was to work with these folks and how much assistance I was going to receive from our sister. I had heard horror stories about this group not cooperating with DEA in the past, but damn, not only were they supplying technology that I didn't have, but also doing the legwork of audio intercepts and transcripts to support our DEA case. Wow, let the good times roll! Well, not so fast...

For the first month, sister continually provided me with transcripts of conversations between AC and everyone he knew, it seemed—his wife Georgina, his kids, his business colleagues, his mother, his siblings, his friends, and oh yes, Rhadames Trujillo. The volume was so large that I asked if they'd minimize the work to only conversations with Rhadames and other narcos who were speaking on the phone. Sis replied negative; they do not minimize. But if I wanted, they would hire my wife, a native Spanish speaker, to do the translations and transcripts and therefore get me what I needed without having to wait. WOW! Now they're giving my wife a job! Is this too good to be true?

It was. On week five, I found out (although I can't share how I found out) that our dear sister had been withholding some of the intelligence from AC's activity. In particular, sis was expanding their intercept capability by bringing in "big brother" to monitor communications of all the numbers linked to calls made and received from AC's phone.

This was an extraordinary amount of drug trafficking intel that was not being returned back to the DEA, not even to the agent who provided our sister the lead in the first place! With intercepts of another trafficker from the Cali Cartel, sis was able to notify their law enforcement counterparts in Panama and seize a Cali Cartel load of five thousand kilograms of cocaine at the Panama Canal. Up to that point, this was Panama's largest seizure, and I'm sure "dear sister and big brother" were high-fiving as they wrote their activity reports to their respective headquarters. Or perhaps, it was the headquarters' people who were complicit in such interagency betrayal, and they were high-fiving while writing their notices to the field offices. I will never know. I, however, had to worry about the Cali Cartel coming back to my informants, and perhaps even me, to kill all of their weak links and threats to more of their revenue generating business.

Jim and I told Andres Cardona about the seizure, but refrained from divulging other details about our investigative methods and techniques. After all, an informant doesn't need to know how DEA does its business. Although he was told by Rhadames about the massive seizure and that Miguel Rodriguez was very upset, AC believed he had no connection to that five thousand kilos operation. So, why should he worry? Why would the Rodriguez Orejuela brothers suspect him, now or in the future? Besides, AC suggested that with Panama being a "hot zone," the Cali Cartel would likely come to him for cocaine smuggling in Costa Rica. Andres saw dollar signs in his eyes and was ready to step up and finally grab his pot of gold, with DEA's concurrence.

While AC was champing at the bit and ready to take over the Cali Cartel's Central American smuggling operations, I had a different point of view. This was AC's most vulnerable position, I strongly felt, and he had to remain in a low profile to assure his safety and safety of his kids, who were also in the transshipment business. About a week later, AC called me from his "covered" cell phone with a surprising, to put it mildly, announcement. He and his wife, Georgina, were at the Juan Santamaria International Airport, ready to board a flight to Cali, Colombia, to visit Miguel Rodriguez. Miguel was celebrating his birthday at one of his ranches in Cauca, and both Rhadames and AC were invited. AC was bringing his young sweet wife because it was going to be such a festive occasion.

On this call, which I later heard again from our sister agency, I voiced my intense objection to AC traveling to Cali at this time. In a tense and serious tone, I said, "Andres, this is a terrible idea. You can't go. They're probably setting you up to find out who's responsible for those five thousand kilograms seized in Panama. If you go, you may never come back! Andres, I'm begging you to not go, but if you refuse me and go, please do not take your wife. You two would both be in danger!" Seeming to brush off my warning and reflecting his immense individual confidence, AC responded, "Okay, Dave, okay, I'll think about it. I have to go now. Bye!"

AC and Georgina boarded that flight to Cali for a birthday party in Cauca that never happened. I never saw either of them again.

A year or two later—I had already transferred from Central America and was now fighting new cartels in Hermosillo in northwestern Mexico—I received a call from Chris, my former partner. "Dave, sorry to tell this, bro,'" he said, "but we know what happened a while back to your Costa Rican informant and his wife in Cauca, and it's not good."

Special Agents Chris Feistl and David Mitchell, his very astute, fearless associate, whose character on *Narcos* aptly reflects his courage, were deployed together in Colombia and set their investigative sights on dismantling the Cali Cartel and capturing its Kingpins, Gilberto and Miguel Rodriguez-Orejuela. In close coordination with the Colombian National Police units, Chris and David were able to infiltrate the Cali Cartel and arrest several key players, including Sean, who led the cartel's security team. In an interview with Sean, the details of Miguel's festive birthday party were described.

Sean starts talking. "They (the Rodriguez brothers) knew that the Rhadames network was somehow responsible for the 5,000 kilos seizure in Panama. This really pissed off Miguel and he ordered that Rhadames and his people be interrogated to find out how it happened. So, they orchestrated a celebration in Cauca and told Rhadames and Andres to come and spend time with Miguel and Gilberto and that both were interested in expanding the business away from Panama and throughout Central America. They took the bait and showed up for the party. There were five: Rhadames, his personal assistant, a big Panamanian soldier who was his personal bodyguard, and Andres and his wife from Costa Rica.

"My security team picked them up at the Cali Airport in Mercedes SUVs and offered them drinks en route to the ranch. It was a nice trip to the ranch with our guests laughing and enjoying the views of Colombia's countryside. When we arrived at the ranch, everyone went inside the villa, where we had an enforcement team ready to interrogate. Of course, they were shocked when told to be seated for a quick discussion about the cartel, especially the woman, but they still thought this was part of how Miguel operates, just to be extra cautious.

"As we began to tie their hands and feet together, the Panama bodyguard tried to fight. He was first to die. Besides, we knew he was least informed and knowledgeable about how we lost the merchandise in Panama. My enforcers beat him down, tied his hands and feet, and placed him back in the seat. The five were seated in a row and in the same room.

"First, to let Rhadames and the others know how serious the situation was, they covered the bodyguard's head with a clear plastic bag and asphyxiated him to death. This guy was a tiger! He fought to the point his body gave out and he went limp in exhaustion and then it did not take long. The others were stoic, except the woman, who was crying. One by one, they interrogated each–first Rhadames, his secretary, Andres, and finally the girl– ending each of their lives with a clear plastic bag over their heads.

"After the last one breathed her last breath, we wrapped them in curtains from one of the ranch houses and transported the bodies to the Cauca River, where crocodiles thrive and flourish. The bodies were dumped off the bridge, one by one, and we watched them float into the crocodile's feeding grounds. This part of the river is where the best fed crocodiles in the world live— after all, they've been feeding them this way for many years. The crocs are twenty feet long and weigh more than a ton each. When they reach for prey and close down on the bodies, the sounds of crocs snapping bones resemble the deep pop of a splitting oak barrel that echoes throughout the valley.

"We didn't find out who was responsible, because they all denied knowing how it happened, but our other objective was accomplished: Don't fuck with the Cali Cartel!"

Chris later told me he had a Colombian forensic unit go to the exact location where the bodies were thrown over the bridge and comb the river banks and river one mile downstream in an attempt to locate some evidence of the murders. They found nothing, not even a scrap of clothing.

There is no adequate way for me to express how disappointed I was over the outcome of this friendly partnership with our "sister" and the results of her betrayal to me, the DEA, and the informant who lost his life. I later found out that my case was not unusual and occurring throughout the world. DEA headquarters was addressing it at the highest levels.

In DEA, there are programs to aid families of informants who are killed in the line of their duties. This was a case that qualified for aid, and the families of AC and Georgina were financially compensated over this horrific incident. Jim took care of making sure this happened, as I had already been transferred to Mexico and was focusing on a whole new group of "fish to catch." I knew that Jim was on top of it because we still spoke frequently, as if we were still partners. Like I said before, Jim is a cool cat.

Both Gilberto and Miguel Rodriguez Orejuela were eventually caught by the Colombian National Police and extradited to face criminal drug trafficking charges in the USA. My former partner Chris was crucial in helping the CNP capture Miguel as he hid in a secret compartment behind a false wall within one of his Cali-based homes, breathing on bottled oxygen. Both brothers were convicted and are serving time in US prisons. The crocs of Cauca remain and are being well fed.

CHAPTER 15

MY NICARAGUAN PILLOW

During my permanent assignment in Costa Rica, I had the formidable job of serving as sole collateral DEA agent, responsible for any and all investigations in Nicaragua. At that time, the DEA was without an office in Managua, so cases were managed remotely from the Costa Rica Office. My first trip to Nicaragua, in April of 1992, was most certainly a memorable one. The agent I was replacing, Frederico, was a seasoned investigator who'd recently been promoted to serve as the Country Attaché based in Quito, Ecuador. Fred accompanied me on my first visit to Managua to familiarize me with the Embassy and introduce me to everyone, including the new NNP (Nicaraguan National Police) contacts. The NNP was then in its nascent stages, having just been created as a result of the end of Nicaragua's civil war. Subsequently, the traditional Leftist Sandinista Government, including the Sandinista Police, were transitioning into a new era, led by President Violeta Chamorro. I soon realized, however, that the ranks of both the Nicaraguan military and National Police now differed only in name, not spirit.

On my first six or seven trips to Managua I stayed at the Camino Real Aeropuerto Hotel, situated directly across from the Managua International Airport. After the war, times were still tough in Nicaragua, and the country was forced to ration electricity. Nicaragua, incidentally, is an incredibly hot and humid place, one with a tropical climate and temperatures often well above 90 degrees year-round. Even on one quick walk to my car, I'd inevitably break into a sweat. The hotel itself only used electricity from six in the evening until seven the next morning, with the sole off-hours' exception being (not to my displeasure) the hotel bar. So, whenever I was there during that stretch, needless to say, I spent many an hour working and cooling off there.

After consistently spending at least one week per month in Nicaragua, I began to develop a real rapport with the cops. Nonetheless, I soon discovered that every time I returned to my room from my travels around the city, I'd spot a lit cigarette perched in the ashtray next to the bed. I didn't smoke, so I knew full well that one of two things was happening: either the Camino Real had incredibly incompetent and impolite housekeepers, or the "new" Sandinista cops and/or intelligence officers wanted me to know that they were everywhere, and that I shouldn't be doing any business without their knowledge and approval. Briefings with US folks "in the know" soon told me the latter assumption was indeed correct.

Often, while driving in my rental car, I'd pass by an enormous statue of a grandiose, shirtless man who apparently represented the strength of Nicaragua itself. In one hand he held out a shovel to his side, and in the other, above his head, an AK-47. I never did stop to closely inspect the statue, but heard that it is also, in fact, a monument to the Nicaraguan worker and Patriot. With the newly discovered daily surveillance and constant invasions of my privacy top of mind, I frequently imagined that I might actually be kidnapped or attacked in some way. So, each time I passed by the monument, I couldn't help but visualize being roped up and hung from the arm of this intimidating stone Patriot, all while trying to hide my true identity and screaming in both German and Spanish: "Sprichst de Deutsch? Soy Aleman!" ("You speak German? I'm German!") You might say that back then my imagination, like my exotic surroundings, had a tendency to run wild.

However, after a full year of sharing solid, productive drug trafficking intelligence with my Nicaraguan counterparts, they began to warm up to me, and began to include me in their social engagements along with the narcotics work we all needed (and wanted) to do. Eventually, I even stopped worrying about the Patriot. My primary NNP contacts were Captain Leonel Espinoza, whom I joking referred to as "Capitan Espina" (loosely translated as Captain Thorn-in-My-Shoe), as well as Officer Luis Canas. By the time I left this assignment, I considered these Russian-speaking comrades to be two of the best cops I'd ever worked with.

One of the many cases we took on was coined "Operation Oceano." My colleague from the Costa Rica office, Special Agent Grayson Stevenson (not real name), had obtained recent, highly specific intel from an informant, which he'd planned on sharing with Espinoza and his team. I offered to accompany him, knowing that Espinoza would only be receptive if we came equipped with unquestionably reliable details (in this case, ones involving a scheduled airdrop of Colombian cocaine in San Juan del Sur along the coast of Nicaragua). However, while Grayson's informant knew both the time and place of the drop, he knew very little about who might pick up the drugs in Nicaragua and distribute.

Grayson and I made haste to Managua, but not too much haste. The route we'd taken, the Pan-American highway (which connects Costa Rica and Nicaragua), is an overly crowded, two-lane road that, like so many others we'd frequently encountered, offered up the kind of perils one doesn't typically associate with DEA work: *wildlife* (and not the kind involving parties and liquor). Successfully navigating a tight, two-lane road crawling (literally) with cattle, horses, monkeys, pisotes (a kind of raccoon), and myriad other animals—not to mention other vehicles, and the ubiquitous banana trucks—always necessitated yet another highly-specific skill-set, albeit one perhaps not as seemingly glamorous as all the others. Still, accidents were bound to happen, and I'd soon learn this the hard way only a year later when, swerving to avoid one jaywalking cow, I wound up hitting another (RIP, Bessie), while also managing to trash the car in the process. So even a simple drive could be rife with potential dangers, and as a consequence we stayed extremely focused.

When Grayson and I arrived—safely, this time—in Managua, we briefed Espinoza and his team and, to our great relief and joy, they were excited to take on the case. But this time, the case at hand turned out to be different than most others: in an atypical move, Espinoza asked both Grayson and I to accompany them to the airdrop in San Juan del Sur, tucked far out in the boondocks. This was a true vote of confidence in the two of us on Espinoza's part, as it marked the first time any DEA agent had been included in an arrest and seizure operation in Nicaragua. It was, also, a decision that would ultimately change Espinoza's life.

Of course, we didn't hesitate. We both immediately and excitedly said, "Sign me up!" With very few roadways—none of which were paved—and only a handful of tiny fishing villages making up the majority of the San Juan del Sur region, Grayson and I knew we'd soon be (literally) waist-deep in a true jungle operation. For me, too many years had passed since I'd been in the jungle (not since my Snowcap days), and I couldn't wait to get back in the bush. On the day before the scheduled airdrop, Grayson and I met with the NNP at their headquarters, and prepared for the remote coastal infiltration. After spending a couple of hours reviewing the operations brief, we all dispersed to the parking lot and began loading up our collective gear. Grayson and I each had our usual essentials with us: a backpack with an extra pair of dry socks, extra underwear, our respective DEA-issued sidearms and, most importantly, several navigational devices used to determine where we might be found in case the US government needed to retrieve our cold, lifeless bodies (a scenario we tried our hardest not to dwell on). The NNP guys, on the other hand, were fully geared-up with grenades, rocket-propelled launchers, more AK-47s than the Chinese Army could ever need or use and-an unexpected courtesy in our honor-their own sidearms, no doubt packed to spare us the embarrassment of wanting to carry ours. With everything accounted for and organized, we were off.

By 3:30 a.m., we spotted a site in the bush suitable enough for a quick rest. To get there, we drove three hours—as far as our all-wheel drive vehicles could get us, that is-then walked another three hours deep into the jungle, stopping a half kilometer or so from the coast where the airdrop was set to take place. By the time we stopped I was so damn exhausted, it was all I could do to just sit down and feel around on the ground for a spot level enough to lay down on. In a surprising stroke of good fortune, I was lucky enough to find a wonderfully smooth rock, one rising just slightly from the ground. Hallelujah! My very own Nicaraguan pillow, courtesy of Mother Nature herself. So right there in that very spot, cloaked in the black night of the jungle, I closed my eyes and slept like a baby for two hours. Around 5:30 a.m. the woods were waking up-along with all the birds and carnivorous animals-but even with all of the screeches and whistles and deafening cacophony around me, I awoke feeling more rested than I could ever remember.

I quickly pulled my military Battle Dress Uniform (BDU) shirt up to my neck, then nestled one side of my face back into that smooth stone I'd been so lucky to find just when I'd lost hope of getting any rest at all. After a minute or two, I officially rose, looked up at the brightening Nicaraguan sky, and began to prepare myself for the 0700 airdrop, with the singular hope of catching the local criminals set to pick up the cargo and putting them directly in jail. As I got my bearings, I looked around at Grayson and the other just-waking NNP officers and got their attention. I then said, in Spanish, "Well, boys, I sure got a great night's sleep with my natural pillow." Capitan Espina looked over and started to laugh-and I mean absolutely roar-and swiftly replied: "Bien, Dave. Mira a tu almohadita!" ("Great, Dave. But look at your little pillow!"). I glanced down and to my utter shock, realized I wasn't looking at my beloved stone savior but, instead, an enormous dried-up cow pile (or, to put it more bluntly, a week-old pile of cow shit.) Of course, as I sat there attempting to furiously scrub my hair clean of actual crap, the entire group burst into maniacal laughter, including Grayson. Thankfully all these many years later this story has, understandably, become a favorite amongst my family and friends (and even total strangers at a party). It never, ever fails to get a laugh. Turns out, my Nicaraguan Pillow lives on to this day!

At 0710 hours, with all of the team in place, several snipers all well-hidden in trees, and the Operations Commander perched atop high ground with a view of both the landscape and pristine beach ahead of us, a twin-engine Cessna 310 approached. After descending down to two hundred feet the hatch door opened, and bale after bale of cocaine was thrown into the ocean, subsequently floating as if they were all merely harmless pieces of driftwood. Almost immediately we saw roughly thirty "pangas" (fishing boats) speed directly over to the bales, whereupon the men inside began calmly retrieving each with timely precision. Obviously, they'd done this before.

The Cessna couldn't offload all of its cargo in one fell swoop, so it swiftly circled round and returned a second time, flying even closer to the beach-so close it seemed to be nearly on top of it. Immediately ten or so additional bales were dropped, some even hitting land. At that point I was directly next to the captain and heard from his radio: "Capitan, Capitan! I have the plane in my sights, may I fire?!" Espinoza looked at me and said, "Disparamos, Dave?" ("Should we shoot him down, Dave?") Without missing a beat, I asked, "Well, what weapon is he shooting with?"

When Espinoza explained that it was an RPG (a bazooka-type, rocket-propelled grenade that could blow up the plane in dramatic fashion) I immediately replied, "No, Capitan, no dispare." ("No, Captain, don't shoot.") My reasoning: there was a village nearby, and if the Cessna were to be hit by an RPG it could potentially spiral into the village, killing innocent civilians. I also knew that if that were to happen, not only would our efforts toward successfully opening a DEA office in Nicaragua be all for naught, but also that Grayson and I would no longer be working DEA agents, and would instead be heading directly to prison (and one thing I knew for certain was that I *definitely* didn't want to spend the rest of my days in a Nicaraguan prison).

From his observation point Captain Espinoza spotted where the boats had returned to off-load along with the Jeeps and SUVs there to facilitate the pickup, after which they would transport the cocaine to the designated stash houses nearby. We all knew from previous cases that, eventually, the cocaine would ultimately be relocated and repackaged into containerized cargo set for transport through Mexico, and finally into the pre-determined markets within the United States. So, if we didn't grab the coke at the stash houses immediately, we'd risk losing the cargo-and that was simply not going to happen on my watch.

After trudging through dense, snake-infested mangroves, snagging our AK-47s on every branch all the while, and running for miles just to reach the road where our targets would transport to their stash houses, we set up our roadblocks. Ultimately our team seized roughly 1,800 kilograms of cocaine and arrested over twenty smugglers that day. That evening, I gifted one of the NNP cops-a young man who'd been a champion boxer in his native Nicaragua-my DEA cap, which he immediately put atop his head and wore with immense pride. At that point, I knew that the NNP and their Sandinista cops now trusted me with their own lives. The Cessna, however, got away. But that didn't dampen my spirits or even my sense of accomplishment, because no one had been killed, we achieved our main goals, and, today, the DEA has a bustling and productive office in sunny Managua, Nicaragua. It was an incredible and memorable day, and I still consider Leonel "Espina" Espinoza and Officer Luis Canas to be two of my dearest comrades.

Ultimately, Operation Oceano represents a terrific example of how law enforcement success is so often a result of true teamwork, combined with positive, symbiotic working relationships-in this case, one between the DEA and the NNP. In fact, that case, along with the many others that followed, led to both a permanent DEA presence in Nicaragua as well as a lasting partnership, one mutually relied upon in order to continue to fight drug traffickers throughout Central America. Unfortunately, not long after Operation Oceano Captain Espinoza was transferred from narcotics, because Sandinista traditionalists in Congress had soundly criticized his partnership with the DEA. According to one Sandinista nationalist congressman, Espinoza had violated his oath as a sovereign nation's "comrade" simply by allowing the DEA to operate in Nicaragua, which in retrospect was just typical of the common, anti-American rhetoric of the time. And although Espinoza and his Police Director Fernando Caldera both vigorously lobbied for improved and increase cooperation with the DEA, some of Nicaragua's most powerful communist leaders could never get over the United States' support of Nicaragua's Contras during their eleven-year civil war. Ultimately, it seemed, they just didn't want any more gringos in town.

El comandante Leonel Espinoza, jefe de la *Operación Oceano*, el subcomandante Amín Gurdián y un oficial de la DEA analizan la situación de la zona, dos horas antes de la llegada del avión narco. Abajo, uno de los oficiales norteamericanos atraviesa un estero durante la operación.

While on Operation Oceano working with the Nicaraguan National Police, I'm working with Captain Espinoza on an OPS plan and later navigating through an estuary with my AK47.

CHAPTER 16

DOUBLE AGENT ACADEMY

A quick note to the reader: This chapter is not about the primary FBI or DEA Academies in Quantico, Virginia. Rather, the focus here is on one particular program run within the DEA Academy: The Sensitive Investigations Unit Academy, more commonly known as SIU.

Since the mid '90s, the DEA has hosted, mentored, and trained thousands of foreign law enforcement officials, with the goal of sending each official back to their respective home nations (everywhere from Afghanistan and Pakistan to Mexico and Colombia), ready to conduct criminal investigations and implement drug enforcement at the highest possible level. Countless drug-traffickers, money-launderers, narco-terrorists, and all-around career criminals have been taken down as a direct result of the concerted efforts of these impeccably-trained DEA partners against crime.

US-based training of foreign agents is hardly a new concept. Between the 1950s and the 1980s, the CIA actively trained foreign contacts to combat the leftist guerilla subversive groups that had been challenging democratic institutions around the world. The US Department of Defense operated the School of the Americas, training foreign officers in how best to enhance their national security apparatus. And in 1996, the DEA developed a similar concept with SIU, taking the development of modern investigative technique and foreign drug law enforcement training one step further.

Recently, I came across an article by journalist Delia Estevez about the DEA's use of an SIU program to help infiltrate international drug trafficking organizations, and was momentarily encouraged by the fact that it seemed as if SIU's were finally receiving the credit they so immensely deserved for their longtime commitment to the training of foreign counterparts to help us battle a global, ever-growing scourge. Then I took a closer look at the article's title: *The Double Agent Academy.* My heart sank. In lieu of praise, Estevez was reporting that some graduates of the SIU course had become corrupt, and aligned with the very drug cartels they 'd sworn to fight against. At first, I just rolled my eyes at the hypocrisy. But the more I thought about it, the more it disappointed me. The title was clearly nothing but a "gotcha," one used to inappropriately characterize a DEA program that had, in fact, been successful for many years. It's no secret that some people (including both US *and* foreign agents, and even entire governments) sometimes succumb to the temptations of immense amounts of drug money. But the idea that the DEA Academy would actually be recruiting and training double agents, or just to even imply as much in a misleading headline? It was absurd, and especially for someone who'd spent so many years on the other side of that headline, it was offensive.

The SIU program itself was developed after the DEA realized that the most efficient form of intelligence-sharing by far was with our most-trusted foreign counterparts, the ones with solid track records of actionable results against DEA investigative targets. Prior to the SIU, DEA agents working abroad were forced to individually recruit and partner with foreign counterparts in any way possible, usually with great effort. While this approach worked for the most part, with the rapid international growth of DEA offices and agents it soon became time to formalize a new, better concept, one in which the DEA could confidently share US intelligence with its partners in order to more successfully combat cartels and narco-terrorists around the world. Indicators for suitable locations of DEA SIU's were, of course, drug seizures, money seizures and arrests, but most importantly, it was clear that our foreign counterparts—also exhausted and motivated by the ceaseless threat of cartels and traffickers—were more than ready to graduate to the next level. Enter the SIU.

The SIU program is, at its essence, a formal operational platform used to establish high standards of performance with the foreign police and security forces with whom we work, in order to help enforce US drug policies in their native countries. Candidates are all hand-picked by DEA Country Attachés, and required to pass a battery of tests including DEA-administered polygraph examinations, drug toxicology tests, psychological assessments, and the passing of a five-week instructional course in Quantico focused on intelligence-collection and investigative techniques (commonly referred to as the SIU Academy). By the time an SIU agent graduates from the Academy they're considered "vetted," ready to work alongside the field-experienced DEA agents in his or her native country battling some of the most powerful, dangerous, and brutal criminals in the world.

SIU graduates have also proven themselves to be far more than just part-timers who eventually drift off into other interests. While they all begin their post-SIU careers as young, ambitious foreign officers, many become influential leaders in their own countries after years of dedicated work in the field. Hardworking, excellent SIU graduates have worked their way up to formidable success and truly impressive roles: Director General of the National Police, Administrator of Intelligence Services, Attorney General, and successful career politicians.

There's no question that this program and its graduates have paid off in big dividends for the DEA and US government, much more so than any other single US foreign service program.

However, as with any other training program or group of graduates, there comes the bad with the good when it comes to personal choices, and also when it comes to fate. Three examples—the three that haunt me the most—are described in further detail elsewhere in this book, and none of them were a result of corruption. These were bad things that happened to good, honest, men and women, foreign colleagues who'd been singled out and targeted by cartels just by virtue of their DEA association. Once they'd made the noble decision to join the US fight against drug-related crime in their native countries, they became targets. Adding to their bravery is that fact that they knew that they were putting themselves in danger the minute they signed up, but they did it anyway. For the greater good.

Just one year from graduating from the SIU course, an entire Mexican SIU class was shot and killed while conducting a surveillance in Michoacan, Mexico, against the "Familia Michoacana" cartel. The lone female graduate of the group suffered the most, as she was also subjected to rape and torture before her death. These were, every one, exemplary students with promising futures. I'd handed them each of them their own diplomas, personally.

Another heroic Mexican was a man named Omar Ramirez

Aguilar, a well-respected and incredibly driven SIU Commander. He, too, became a casualty of cartel violence, simply because he chose not to be corrupted. Having turned down a million-dollar bribe from the infamous leader of the Los Zetas cartel, Miguel Trevino Morales (in exchange for his loyalty and his promise to stop investigating anything to do with the Zetas), Aguilar was ambushed and murdered as he drove to the office of his supervisor. He left behind a large, tight-knit family, including a wife and three young children. It pained me to witness, but virtually none of his colleagues attended his funeral, either because they (falsely) believed him to be already corrupt, or because they feared they'd suffer the same fate he did, should the cartels find out they'd dared to pay their respects. I'd had a long lunch with Aguilar only a few hours before his murder. Having just turned down the temptation to profit off a potential betrayal to the SIU (and betrayal of his own morals) he had to have already been actively afraid for his life. But he didn't show it—not for one minute.

In Colombia, another entire SIU team was wiped out by a group of corrupt Colombian Army soldiers, all of whom were on the payroll of the North Valley Cartel. After setting up the SIU team with their own informant "plant," and luring them into what the team thought was a mission to intercept a cache of cocaine in the mountains of Jamundi, Cauca, these amoral animals ambushed the team, then executed every single one of them with Army-grade weaponry, rocket-propelled grenades, automatic weapons, and even hand grenades. They didn't stop there: after the massacre they proceeded to kill their own informant as well, in an effort to make sure they'd completely covered their tracks.

One evening many years later back home, a Netflix series called *SOMOS* caught my eye. Given my own vast amount of experience and history in its subject matter, I was disappointed when I realized that it had taken more than its share of creative liberties, implying that the SIU Program *itself* was responsible for the death of innocent civilians in Northern Mexico, via the hands of the Los Zetas Cartel.

The episode's plot revolved around a DEA intelligence tip to SIU that was subsequently leaked to the Zetas, resulting in a spree of revenge murders throughout the small northern town of Allende, Tamaulipas, Mexico. In reality it hadn't been the DEA's fault: the blame lay squarely with the Mexican government and their total lack of control and inability to hold their own personnel accountable for their corrupt maneuverings. As always, the DEA did what they could to limit that corruption, but the process, unsurprisingly, failed. And yet again, we were forced to ask ourselves: why?

The fact is, SIUs differ dramatically from country to country, especially in regards to the quality of field work, overall management, and personnel. I've long borne witness to this wide range, with the best of that berth including both Colombia and Central American police, who so often excelled in the SIU program as a direct result of their personal commitment to the Nobel Experiment (and cause). Watching these men and women over the years was, overall, no different than observing the diverse level of dedication and effort in any group of trainees, in any program, in any country: some classes had a great deal of excellent, hard-working students, ones who eagerly threw themselves into their training. But just as those exemplary students existed, so too did the lazy ones, recruits whose interests revolved mainly around taking advantage of "The Big PX" (Post Exchange). In other words: endless shopping.

It's always been up to the DEA to determine which students pass and which don't, and often those decisions become incredibly complicated both because of foreign policy considerations as well as the desperate need to get "bodies on the ground" (a.k.a. new agents in the field). Adding to the complexity and tenuousness of the situation is just how rapidly an SIU candidate (even those deemed "clean" upon graduation) is targeted by cartels upon returning to their own country. Hence the critical need for consistent use of post-graduation, consistent polygraph testing.

To be clear: I'm certainly not implying that corruption never exists within the SIU, just that it figures no more prominently than it does with our own police and police administration. It's no secret that some of our own American officers begin their careers with every intention of forever honoring their oath, only to fall into a trap of deceit, greed, and betrayal. Sometimes this avarice goes unchecked and they get away with it. And sometimes this avarice ruins their careers, lives, and families.

Again, just as there are noble men and women everywhere in all walks of life and in all manner of professions, there is also a flip side. But to imply that the (all too) common acts of disloyalty, corruption, malice, and betrayal are decisions only government and government-trained employees (foreign or otherwise) make is patently absurd. Some people will always make poor choices, and give into weakness and the seduction of money and power, in every sector, every office, every household.

This is not a new concept; this is human nature. And the SIU is just one small facet of that, and of the myriad modern drug enforcement challenges we still face. However, that doesn't mean we have to just sit back and watch as our trusted colleagues and allies continue to fall victim to greed and temptation. We can instead ask ourselves: exactly how might we mitigate and reduce some of this corruption?

The best and most feasible of my recommendations include:

- Develop a strict pass/fail curriculum for *all* students in the SIU Program (both officers and non-officers) to ensure that *only* the fully-qualified, highest-performing individuals graduate and begin a career with DEA support. The overall assessment should not include input from DEA Country Offices, rather, it should come directly from DEA training and headquarters representatives.

- Pursuant to graduation, all SIU graduates must take (and pass) polygraph examinations on a monthly basis, administered only by DEA and/or FBI polygraphers (or retired FBI and DEA Agent polygraphers, if certified by the National Polygraph Institute).

- All SIU-related foreign officials who fall under the chain of command—regardless of their rank or political position— must also be required to take monthly polygraphs. Any officials removed from the chain of command must be fully debriefed by a DEA field SIU agent (or agents) as well as a field office supervisor prior to officially leaving the program.

- With the singular goal of ensuring bilateral program integrity in mind, all DEA agents directly assigned to *any* of the SIU field offices should also be subject to DEA or FBI polygraphs (though on a random, as-needed basis, should an action come into question or an allegation arise). Because these agents take on quite a few new, additional responsibilities that go hand in hand with their new roles and locations, they should be entitled to a stipend of at least ten percent of their respective salaries. No one holding any functional Headquarters-based position, however, would be eligible for the stipend: it would be given only to SIU field agents and intel analysts, as certified by the Regional Director and approved by Headquarters.

• SIU equipment inventory checks must be conducted on a quarterly basis, and only by the DEA agents assigned to the SIU. Any irregularities or anomalies must be reported immediately to the DEA Regional Director.

Without a doubt, the SIU Program has been a formidable, invaluable investigative tool, one relied upon to help maximize the DEA's impact in international investigations. While the program is far from perfect, it's imperative that it continue on as a critical part of the US's drug control policy. At the time of this writing, a Department of Justice (DOJ) assessment of the SIU program is underway, with hundreds of our foreign counterparts (and their leaders) closely watching, waiting to see how we choose to keep up (and improve) our commitment to our international allies. And without a doubt, no one involved with the program— including myself, God knows—wants to see them disappointed. The fact is we need this to work, because another thing no one wants is for our citizens to suffer the consequences of having even more deadly drugs on America's streets. The fact is, if our international partners in DEA's "Defense in Depth" strategy fail, we all fail.

CHAPTER 17

MEXICO'S HEROES, ZEROES

Mexico is a fascinating country, one rich in diversity and history. But Mexico is also a country that doesn't just undervalue its police officers, but also blatantly disrespects and mistreats them. It's been that way for decades, and remains that way to this day.

When I first took on the role of DEA Regional Director in Mexico City, I was leafing through a local publication one day when I came across a statistic in a national survey that surprised me. When given a long list of possible career choices from which to choose, the vast majority of children between five and eighteen all selected the exact same profession as their *least* desirable: police officer. This was a far cry from my youth, when the police were viewed as local heroes. But back in Mexico in the 1990s, it had long been the norm to view the federal, state, and municipal police officers as universally corrupt, lacking in ethics, morals, and integrity. There were, however, some truly noteworthy exceptions.

One of those exceptions was a man I refer to as one of Heaven's Warriors: former Mexico Federal Police Commander Omar Ramirez Aguilar, who was tragically assassinated in 2007 by the leader of Mexico's Zetas cartel named Miguel Trevino-Morales, more commonly known as "40." After taking a rare, noble stand,

and refusing a $1,000,000 bribe (in exchange for two things: for him to halt any pending enforcement actions against Trevino's cartel, and for the exchange of any and all DEA intel already gathered on the Zetas), Ramirez was brutally gunned down as he waited, unsuspecting and unaware, in Mexico City traffic. As the chief of narcotics and the supervisor of the DEA-supported SIU (Sensitive Investigations Unit), he'd been singled out by the Zetas, and given a choice many of his colleagues had already faced: be corrupted, or be killed. The saying was, and still is, infamous in Mexico: "Quiere plata, or quiere plomo?" ("Do you want the money, or do you want the bullet?") Sadly, many men choose the former, when in reality neither choice works out well in the end. But Ramirez chose the honorable path, and it wasn't long before the bullet came for him. Literally.

That evening, Commander Ramirez left his office around nine thirty. It had been a typically long, fourteen-hour work day for Ramirez—and also a productive one, with the completion of a lengthy investigative report on several cartels including the Zetas. But his day's work wasn't officially done: he still had to drive to the office of his supervisor, Ramon Pequeño, where he'd conduct his usual debriefing before finally, at long last, heading home to his family.

It was during this routine, familiar drive to Pequeño's office that Ramirez was brutally murdered, when two men sent by Trevino drove their motorcycles up alongside Ramirez's unarmored vehicle and opened fire, striking him three times. The final shot—which hit him square in the chest—ultimately proved fatal. Still, Ramirez clung to life for three agonizing hours before dying in an area hospital.

Ramirez wasn't just a career law enforcement officer, a PhD candidate, and a hero whose commitment to his own morals never wavered, he was also a devoted family man and father of three young children. His burial was the following day in Mexico City, and when I attended the funeral, I was shocked and saddened to see that the only others in attendance were his family members, a few of my fellow DEA agents, and our vetted officers of the SIU. Not one person from the Mexican Preventative Police bothered to pay their respects, with the sole exception of Pequeño, and even that visit seemed perfunctory. Even Pequeño—Ramirez's own supervisor—chose to skip the service entirely, opting instead to arrive shortly after, shake the hands of a select few DEA agents, then make a hasty exit. But even then, I knew in my heart that it was nothing more than a reflection of just how far the overall morale of the Mexican federal police had fallen. The majority viewpoint was that whenever a cop was killed, it *might* have been as a result of a justified, legal action made in the line of duty, but it's equally as likely (if not more likely) the result of accepting a bribe. And even if any morally-compromised, bribe-accepting colleagues *did* want to express their sympathy at a service, very few would ever take that chance. The cartels were and are always watching, and if you're in league with any of them, you'd better not make a public display of respect to those who aren't. No matter how much you may have admired them, or even how closely you worked together, no one would dare risk putting themselves next in the line of fire.

More often than not, examples of cartel vengeance are almost too shocking to share, and it's hard to believe—even for me—that anyone could do things that are so evil, and so dark. When a DEA-supported, successful operation led to the arrest of Mexican cartel kingpin trafficker Arturo Beltran Leyva, it also led to the untimely death of a young, Mexican marine soldier. Another unsung hero, he was swiftly buried in his hometown in the Gulf State of Veracruz. During his funeral, Beltran's hitmen (or sicarios, as they are more commonly known), opened fire on the marine's family, in an all too typical public act of retribution. In front of a group of distraught mourners, they massacred the marine's mother, even as she knelt and shook with terror, literally hiding behind her own son's casket. This was how the cartels responded to so many attempts at regulation or enforcement: you hit us, and we'll just hit you harder—and for added measure, we'll go ahead and destroy your family, too. Taking one life is not enough for them; they always have one goal in mind and they stick to it: destroy as many lives as it takes to get the point across. Because in their twisted, heartless minds, the end always justified their means, no matter how horrific.

In one dark chapter from my time in Mexico City, an entire Mexican SIU team—nine police investigators, all of whom were trained at the DEA Academy—were gunned down during an ambush in Michoacan (immediately after the order had been given by cartel leaders). The lone female agent was reportedly raped, multiple times, before her own brutal execution. All of this happened not more than seven months after I had personally presented each of them with their SIU diplomas at the DEA Academy.

These cartels don't just wreak havoc in the form of deadly violence, they have also infiltrated (and dominated) the government at the federal, state, and, most especially, local levels. They continue to diversify and grow their stronghold in licit sectors (including the oil and gas, mass transportation, mining, agriculture, and financial industries), turning them into licit-illicit ones in the process. They control the majority airports and seaports, and steadily destabilize national security, any sense of law and order, and entire government entities. Mexico's collective security—not to mention that of the United States—is at risk due to their tactics. And it continues to make no sense that even after forty years of US and DEA support, it remains obvious that Mexico's leaders are far from committed to helping overcome their problems. A sensible person might take that a step further and think, well, if Mexico is forever resisting change, why doesn't the US just take charge, beginning with doing something about our *own* insatiable appetite for consuming drugs? Believe me, I wish I had the answer. And those who are doing their best to effect change, whether in Mexico or the US, are often seen as just another enemy.

Where is a thankful nation? For that matter, where is *our* thankful nation? Truthfully, it often feels that while the public chooses to turn a blind eye, the DEA (along with our international partners) are entirely alone when it comes to the fight against the growing plague of addiction, not to mention the social, "casual" drug use that also contributes to the corruption and weakening of our society. The reality is that every single time someone indulges in the use of a drug either manufactured or smuggled through a foreign country, they have blood on their hands. Maybe they choose to remain in denial, or maybe they truly don't realize it, but the use of prohibited and scheduled drugs is a leading, growing cause of death and adds to societal destruction not just in the US, but on a global scale. And dodging blame isn't just for the public: on any given week, the Mexican police and military would brief me on a plethora of corruption allegations, always separately, and always pointing the blame at the other.

Toward the end of my assignment in Mexico City, I and my second-in-command, Assistant Regional Director Carlos Mitchem, were called by Mexico Federal Police Director Victor Garay and asked about several significant arrests they'd made the night before. Both Carlos and I considered Garay to be not just a colleague, but also a close friend: for Christmas the year before he'd even gifted us each a macuahuitl, a hand weapon once used by the ancient Aztecan warriors. It's a striking and intimidating weapon, studded with fragile yet incredibly sharp obsidian blades lining a sleek, sturdy wooden handle. Immediately upon opening my gift I laughed to myself, because my first thought was how I'd never want to be in fight with Garay if he was wielding that macuahuitl. I'd be a goner in less than three seconds.

After our debriefing, the Director asked us if we'd like to see the compound they'd just raided (which was described as an incredible sight to behold and that was saying something, considering the absurdly decadent cartel compounds we'd seen in years past). But it wasn't just a home tour, they were also offering to allow the DEA to document the exact location of one of our principal defendants, Mauricio Poveda Ortega. Poveda, a Colombian trafficker, was then of serious interest to the DEA. In fact, we'd been closely following his organization for some time, watching as they successfully smuggled over 150 metric tons of cocaine to Mexico (for further distribution to the US) since 1998. Carlos and I, of course, immediately accepted, and the Federal Police served as our escorts. The compound itself was in the well-known area and park referred to as the Desert of the Lions, a spot with which I was already familiar, having ridden my mountain bike many a time on their immensely challenging yet equally glorious trails on Sunday mornings.

Garay was a hulk of a man, with thinning hair and expensive-looking eye glasses, a combination which made him look like a college professor from the neck up, but Hulk Hogan from the neck down. It was Garay who'd led the recent raid—replete with Blackhawk helicopters and ATVs—on Poveda's compound, tucked just outside Mexico City. Like so many traffickers, Poveda came with an established nickname: in his case, "Conejo" ("The Rabbit"), a title deemed appropriate because Poveda wasn't just a well-known trafficker, but a sex addict, to boot.

Rumor had it (and the rumor was accepted as fact) that he had intercourse "tum alia" with as many as twenty women a day. The women, almost always prostitutes his staff would procure expressly for their boss, would first be "invited" to the ranch, then picked up in Mexico City by a member of the staff. These women, all of whom were likely desperate for money and willing to do whatever they needed to be able to survive, were treated just the same as anyone else "invited" to the compound—namely, that is, with major suspicion. Each of them would be tucked away in a windowless passenger van, which also came replete with a divider wall separating them from the front cabin so that they'd be blocked from potentially seeing through the windshield. Even after their drive through the Desert of the Lions and upon arrival to their final destination, they were still kept locked in that van until they were literally within the great walls of Conejo's vast compound.

The compound itself was undeniably garish, but also breathtaking to behold, both absurdly decadent and extravagant by anyone's outsized standards. In addition to a helicopter pad, it had at least ten independent cabins, each of them equipped with their own refrigerator, cable, and televisions (all of which were always set to a porn channel and/or CCTV cameras). The grand master cabin was perched atop the highest hill on the property and was significantly larger than the rest, with a wraparound porch crafted from imported, beautiful wood from Asia, and hand-carved pillars imported from Thailand. The porch carvings mainly consisted of exotic, intimidating animals (tigers, lions, bears, jaguars, etc.), intricately designed to look as if they were intending to make meals out of fleeing humans, mostly women. And there were live animals, too: the cabins encircled an actual zoo, made up of rows of cages bearing a white tiger, a stunning striped tiger, a lion, three lionesses, and one spectacularly grouchy baboon, among others. But while all of the wild animals were still there, the prostitutes were long gone. According to Garay, they had been thoroughly interviewed, then released.

Nonetheless, there was still more to see, and the more time we spent exploring, the more our jaws dropped. Hidden under the cages in the zoo was a man-made, elaborate cavern that was accessible only through a small tunnel, the sort of which one might see built for a gold, silver, or salt mine. The tunnel itself wasn't long—perhaps thirty yards, at most—but it curved unexpectedly before leading into a vast room, dominated by an enormous swimming pool. Lining each side of the pool were tall bleachers, both of which looked straight down into the pool's center, where there was an island-styled stage with a dance pole connected to the ceiling. There was so much going on, and all of it was so surreal, that we struggled to take it all in. At one point I focused in on a heap of curious-looking beach balls and floating noodles, but they weren't like any pool toy I'd ever seen before. It took me a minute, but I soon realized they were, in fact, a very different kind of toy. This was clearly not a G-rated family pool, not by a long shot.

What this all was, Garay explained to Carlos and I, was Conejo's beloved "play den", his preferred spot to which he brought the prostitutes on a daily basis to "perform" for him and his guests. Things got much more sinister than that on the property, though: one of Conejo's staff confessed that they'd often used the bigger wild animals to devour some of the traffickers

Conejo had murdered, all in the name of his drug business. What purpose the cranky baboon served, however, remained a mystery. On my way out I threw him a banana, and the bastard threw it right back at me, almost nailing me in the head.

Soon after that surreal day at the compound, I was called to Attorney General Medina Mora's office for an impromptu meeting. When I arrived, he was atypically hyperactive—nervous, even—and clearly troubled. As it turned out, he had good reason to be, as he'd just heard a serious allegation directed at Garay, offered up by one of the other Federal police officers present at the Conejo raid. The officer—Edgar—had claimed that he'd joined Garay's team and stolen money alongside the rest of the group, justifying the theft as the rightful taking of the "spoils of war." After taking the money, apparently, the entire police team celebrated their newfound bounty with an orgy in Conejo's precious play den pool with the prostitutes who hadn't yet left the compound. Needless to say, Garay hadn't said one word to me or Carlos about any stolen money, let alone any prostitutes or post-raid after-party orgies.

The Attorney General knew that if he could corroborate Edgar's statement about the theft, he'd have to indict and arrest Garay. Clearly torn, he asked me if I thought it was worth the inevitable blowback from Secretary of Federal Police Genaro Garcia-Luna. All I could offer was my own description of my time with Garay at the compound the day following the raid and alleged post-raid crimes. Of course, Medina-Mora was momentarily entertained by all of the lurid details, but we both agreed that there would have to be an immediate investigation. Taking it a step further, I told Medina-Mora that whenever something like this happened in the US, we'd run it right down to the ground in order to determine if the allegations were, in fact, corroborated in any way. Medina-Mora paused, then asked: "Would five more witnesses be enough for the DEA?" Floored by this revelation, I told him that yes, of course, if they really had five additional police witnesses, that would be more than enough to convince any jury to convict. This fueled his confidence, and after thanking me he rushed out to brief President Calderon.

(One quick culinary sidenote: in addition to his strength of character and admirable work ethic, Medina-Mora also had damn good taste in Swiss chocolate. I'm not ashamed to admit that one of the things I always looked forward to at our meetings was my tradition of swiping a few of the little dark chocolate confections he kept in a large bowl on his desk. His personal assistant, to her credit, always made sure that the bowl was filled to the very top whenever I was due to visit, making her a permanent candidate for employee of the year, as far as I'm concerned.)

Eventually Garay and a handful others—including Edgar—were indicted by Mexico's Attorney General's office, and every single one of them (with the sole exception of Edgar) went directly to prison. Instead of prison, Edgar was admitted into a SIEDO (special crimes prosecutor's office) as a protected witness, and kept at the local SIEDO compound. Once protected, it was, of all things, his craving for caffeine that did him in: after convincing (or bribing) one of the witness guards to allow him a half hour furlough so he could walk the half block to Starbucks, his newfound stint as a protected witness came to an untimely end, as did Edgar himself. As he walked back to the compound with an overpriced super venti flat white latte in his hand, a sicario came up behind him and put two bullets in his head before casually walking away, slipping anonymously into the ever-crowded Reforma Avenue.

Shortly thereafter, Garay was released for lack of evidence. I later heard from Mexican Federal Director Ramon Pequeño that the day after Garay's arrest, then-Secretary General Genaro Garcia Luna called a directors' meeting at nine p.m. All of the Directors were present with the obvious exception of Garay, but Secretary Garcia-Luna kept Garay's place at the table, even placing a pad, pencil, and glass of water in front of his empty seat. Garcia-Luna then gave a speech to his directors, making a point of explaining that the seat was empty because Garay had let his guard down. Pequeño couldn't be certain of the actual, intended meaning of "letting his guard down," but he made it clear that Garcia-Luna certainly thought he couldn't trust the DEA, let alone the Federal Attorney General's office in Mexico City. Garcia-Luna was livid, no doubt about it.

About a week later, Pequeño called me and said that Garcia-Luna would like to speak with me in his office on Constituyentes Boulevard, which took about two hours to get to from my office in the Embassy, due to Mexico City's ridiculously heavy traffic. Scrambling, I wasn't sure I'd actually have enough time to get there and have the meeting, then return in time for all the other commitments I had scheduled for later that day. I told Pequeño that I could spare just about three hours and no more than that, and he told me to go to a close by spot where a police helicopter would be waiting for me. This actually calmed me down and not just because of the time factor, but because I realized that if they wanted me dead, they'd have to trash an expensive helicopter in the process (unless they simply threw me out of it along the way. Trust me, those things crossed your mind, and with good reason.) Nonetheless, I followed Pequeño's directions, and walked the fifteen minutes to the SSP (Secretaria de Seguridad Publica) lot, where I boarded a Bell 212 helicopter and flew for ten incredibly stressful but blissfully murder-free minutes to Garcia-Luna's Constituyentes office at the Secretary of Public Security Headquarters.

Once there, contentious words were immediately exchanged: he accused the DEA of setting up Garay and the Federal Police, and I deflected his accusations by challenging him on the witnesses' details surrounding the theft, along with the highly questionable ethics of the police choosing to spend the rest of that day having sex with Conejo's prostitutes. At one point our voices were getting loud enough that his assistant appeared in the doorway, looked at both of us with a stern expression, and raised an eyebrow. We both knew full well what that meant: take it down a notch. She then left, closing the door loudly behind her. (While Medina-Mora's assistant had a way with fine chocolates, Garcia-Luna's had a way with dramatic exits.)

As soon as the door closed, Garcia-Luna told me, "Dave, estas cosas si son la cultura Mexicana." ("This is a Mexico thing.") In all honesty, I can't say for certain if he was really implying that stealing a trafficker's drug money is part of Mexican police culture, rather, the justified "spoils of war," or if he was saying that it was—in their minds—acceptable to be with the prostitutes, not least because they had already been paid. Either way, we kept it civil by agreeing to disagree, and I didn't see him again until just before my time in Mexico City was coming to an end, when he invited me to a farewell dinner. That final night and conversation proved to be cordial and devoid of any Garay or American agent mentions: we ended things on a good note, and with mutual respect.

Now, over a decade later, the US Department of Justice has indicted Garcia-Luna for conspiracy to commit drug trafficking in conjunction with the Sinaloa Cartel, accused of taking bribes from the Joaquin 'Chapo' Guzman-Loera crime organization. I was alerted to the case via the US Attorney's Office in New York, with whom I shared everything I possibly could. At the time of this writing, Garcia-Luna sits in a New York jail, awaiting his federal trial.

Not long ago, Mexico's former Secretary of Defense, Salvador Cienfuegos Zepeda, was arrested while in the US, also accused of colluding with the Sinaloa Cartel, and charged accordingly by the Department of Justice. However, after Mexico's current President, Andres Manuel Lopez Obrador (more commonly known as "AMLO"), threatened to kick every last DEA agent out of his country if Cienfuegos was not released to Mexico, our government essentially rolled over and repatriated the (allegedly) corrupt General. Mexico vehemently insisted Cienfuegos would be prosecuted once back in Mexico, yet once he was back on his native ground, he was immediately freed. Upon being awarded his freedom, AMLO wasted no time in arranging the release of all of the DEA's evidence to the open press in Mexico, thereby exposing our methods, techniques, and even a number of our informants' identities. Is this what we're calling bilateral cooperation?

As it turns out, I was well-versed in the duplicitous nature of AMLO long before this happened. When I first arrived in Mexico as DEA Regional Director in August 2006, President Calderon-Hinojosa had just narrowly defeated AMLO in the national election. AMLO's large political supporter groups actively protested the election, and set up tent cities directly in front of the American Embassy on Avenida Reforma. These protests went on for nearly a year, and in every single Country Team meeting there would be the inevitable discussion about just who AMLO really was and how so many Mexican voters could possibly have supported him. I was always confident that the American Embassy suspected AMLO and his inner circle of being financially supported by a number of cartels (even prior to the 2006 election), so I'm not surprised that—over a decade and a half later—he's essentially in the same boat, allegedly in league with the career criminals who so blatantly aid and abet today's drug trafficking organizations in Mexico. But for me to elaborate—or even to speculate any further—would just be asking for trouble. And, God knows, I've already seen more than enough of that in my lifetime.

In 2007, then-US Ambassador to Mexico Antonio Garza and I traveled to Washington, DC in order to solicit congressional support for Mexican security forces. Ambassador Garza, a political appointee and close friend of President George W. Bush and the entire Bush family, is a highly intelligent man, and a strategic genius when it comes to foreign policy. Garza oversaw US government affairs with Mexico with a hands-off approach, keeping a close eye on everything, but also allowing agency heads to work out any problems on their own and keep the ship moving forward without issue.

This particular style of management was a pleasant change for me, after so many years spent in Bogota, Colombia with career-appointed Ambassador Bill Wood, who had his hands in every last aspect of the Embassy affairs. However, for all his micromanaging, Ambassador Wood was an absolutely brilliant diplomat. Wise, acerbic, and affable, he was also one of the funniest men I've ever met. For every complaint directed his way, Bill always had the perfect retort at the ready. One afternoon, I was taking a breather from my small, basement office, and retreated to a second-floor balcony. I was reveling in the fresh air and privacy, and began to go over a presentation I'd been preparing to deliver to the CNP Director General and Colombia's Attorney General. Without even realizing it, at some point I apparently began actually saying some of the speech out loud, and was only knocked back into reality when I heard a booming voice coming from above: "Don't worry, Dave! It's not *that* bad!" Even from his own balcony perch two floors up—to which he would retreat whenever a nicotine craving hit him—Ambassador Wood had perfect comedic timing.

Ambassador Garza on the other hand, while not a natural born comedian like Wood, was an equally dedicated and driven leader. Together in DC, we were fully committed to getting as much support for the Mexican security forces as possible. Our proposal to the US Congress was entitled "The Merida Agreement," named as such because our respective Attorneys General had brainstormed the joint strategy during a series of meetings held in Merida, Yucatan. The main goal of the proposal was to further strengthen and reinforce bilateral efforts in combatting crime, with US taxpayer commitment starting at one billion dollars. Of course, when heavy-hitter bureaucrats come up with an idea, it's us—the far lower-ranked technocrats—not them, who inevitably do all of the work. Always mindful of this dynamic, Ambassador Garza and I had our noses to the grindstone in DC, stealthily working congress with more vigor than a vacuum salesman in a messy 1950s mansion foyer. Day after day, we tracked down dozens of congressmen, congresswomen, and senators, doing our damnedest to sell them on the Merida Agreement and get their support. Even without practice, Garza and I were a naturally great team and worked incredibly well together. Between our persistence and our charm, we made enormous strides, winning over many a politician and gaining more and more confidence in the process. At times our challenge was, in fact, that many more politicians than we'd anticipated had genuine concern over the rising federal deficit and the importance of supporting Mexico. Many of them also shared a common viewpoint: that Mexico had proven itself over and over again to be a weak and unrepentant facilitator or, at the very least, far too forgiving (and enabling) when it came to the powerful drug cartels destroying their own country.

I'm convinced that it was because of our joint efforts—and refusal to ever give up—that the Merida Initiative Program eventually became US law in June of 2008, credited with giving Mexico nearly a billion dollars in resources to combat crime. That initial one billion has since grown into a multi-billion US dollars campaign, all of it coming from the hands of hard-working American taxpayers. Does AMLO appreciate any of that today, or did he then? I doubt it, and I certainly don't expect to ever hear him say otherwise.

In 2007, Ambassador Garza and I joined forces once again to get Mexico the help needed to build their capacity initiatives, so that they could stop (or at least significantly reduce) illegal migration to the US (separately, I also worked on separate legislation designed to assist equally desperate Central American countries.) Despite our joint efforts this time, and even after billions of dollars have been spent toward supporting Mexico and Central America, at the time of this writing the conditions of immigration to our southwest border have only worsened, as wave upon wave of Central Americans and Mexicans continue to caravan to the US southern border in the hopes of gaining illegal entry. Nearly a decade and a half later, the citizens of the United States find themselves once again in the throes of a Mexico and Central America migration mess.

Recently, I listened to a Bloomberg interview with Ambassador Garza, during which he discussed what needs to take place in order to triage the short-term migration problem, with the longer-term goal/solution of having the US Congress truly facilitate immigration reform. The Ambassador referenced the endless, cyclical surge of illegal migrants, and how this continuing crisis has been going on for years (and I agree that this is indeed fact, not opinion). Current numbers in regards to the migration of Mexican males—along with Central American, unaccompanied minors—is alarming, and show no signs of slowing down. It's no secret that this conundrum is, largely, caused by the failure of both Mexico and Central American countries to put in the effort to defeat (or at least better control) the criminality that is so ubiquitous in their societies. Thus, I've concluded that our own efforts can only do so much if the efforts of both Central American and Mexican leaders are half-hearted and ineffective. All these years later, the current times find the DEA still arresting numerous relatives of Central American politicians, and they've even opened an investigation into the President of Honduras, who's been accused of colluding with a number of major drug cartels. Does any of that sound like a solid, mutually respectful, anti-drug partnership?

To face the truth is to acknowledge that although the DEA has succeeded in arresting and/or neutralizing many drug cartel kingpins, our capacity-building strategies with Central America and Mexico have been a complete and total failure for nearly forty years now. Worse, the last fifteen of those years have just seen things get even worse—something many didn't even think was possible. Thus far, anyway, the giving away of large sums of US taxpayers' money to Latin American countries has not done much for them, let alone anything to truly protect our interests.

It's important for me to note, however, that I have no regrets when it comes to all of our efforts and, on an even more personal note, I truly enjoyed every minute of my time spent working with both Ambassadors Gárza and Wood. While they couldn't have been more different in their management styles or personalities, I regard each as loyal, earnest men, and both of them incredibly effective US diplomats who served their country with honor, dignity, and respect. They showed me how to be a better leader, and for that I am eternally grateful.

CHAPTER 18

CHECKMATE

For many years now here in the United States, we've been facing several complicated and serious problems within our police system, issues that have become even more divisive in recent months. The competition that persists between law enforcement agencies (and federal law enforcement department heads themselves, even) is not only destructive, it actually adversely affects the success level of missions against organized crime both here and throughout the rest of the world. My good friend and fellow agent, Derek Maltz, speaks about this topic often. Derek served our nation in many DEA positions, but the most influential was his time spent as Special Agent in Charge of the DEA's Special Operations Division (SOD), located in Northern Virginia. Derek's command involved overseeing daily coordination with dozens of US agencies and departments, and he was—and still is—always the first to educate anyone on the complexities of interagency cooperation and coordination (or lack thereof). As President Lincoln once said: "A house divided will not stand."

But just how, exactly, did all of this negativity come to be? For the most part, it all started just before 1973, following the infamous cultural revolution of the sixties. At that critical point in our history, the country was facing a juxtaposed path and had to make a decision: allow the blossoming drug culture to continue to explode throughout American society, or nip it in the bud once and for all. With continuing confusion over which part of the government would possibly take the lead in handling our country's anti-drug policy, President Nixon took action and decided that indeed, drug use (back then, mostly heroin, marijuana and acid), and addictions were destroying America's youth. In order to remedy this growing disaster, he firmly believed, we needed one sole, singularly-focused law enforcement agency to tackle and defeat the problem. In July of '73, he signed an executive order and created the Drug Enforcement Administration—the DEA— that would from then on lead the nation in the fight against the illicit drug supply, trafficking, and abuse.

Once established, the DEA soon realized that in order to accomplish Nixon's monumental goal, they would need to greatly expand, and bring a physical presence to the countries supplying those illegal drugs to the US. In other words, the DEA recognized that we needed more than just a localized effort: we needed a defense in foreign environments, or a "Defense in Depth." Soon thereafter, DEA agents were assigned to myriad locations abroad, and living in exotic places like Turkey, Afghanistan, Burma, Thailand, Mexico, and Colombia, among others. The structure and practice of the international counter-drug liaison was built, and quickly evolved into a multi-faceted system, one that soon yielded massive drug seizures, arrests of major traffickers and, eventually, mass forfeitures of assets and valuables held by those equally wealthy and illicit enterprises. With this focused mission—a mission heavily backed with bipartisan support—came success, and with success came envy. Other law enforcement agencies quickly expressed frustrations, and one of those agencies actually evolved into a formidable DEA adversary: the US Customs Service.

My very first month as a DEA agent was spent at our Miami office, and that's really where I began to learn the trade in earnest. My first tasks were, as expected, mostly menial chores (maintaining the government vehicles, running evidence packages back and forth to the prosecutor's office and the drug warehouse, etc.—everything short of fetching coffee), but once I got past that mind-numbing phase my first *real* task was thrilling: I was to join a senior DEA investigator on a day trip to Key Largo to meet an informant. This would only take a matter of hours, but if everything worked according to plan, we knew that the informant could get us in undercover with a major Colombian/Cuban cocaine trafficking cartel. This cartel was enormously powerful, had been successfully shipping literal tons of drugs to South Florida every month, and could ultimately provide us with untold amount of the critical intelligence we so needed in order to expand our work and presence throughout the United States and elsewhere.

When Senior Agent Bruce Washington (not his real name) and I arrived at the preselected hotel on one of the Florida Cays (and I use the word "hotel" loosely, as in reality it wasn't much more than a strip of lousy rooms in the distorted shape of an L), Bruce saw and recognized a customs agent from the Miami Customs Service office speaking with the informant in front of his room's front door. Bruce immediately got out of the car and confronted the customs agent, who proceeded to aggressively inform Bruce that this informant "belonged" to US Customs, and not the DEA. That was all it took: the fight was on. So, as it turned out, my first day on the job was indeed filled with drama, but not the kind I'd expected: instead of gathering intel and cultivating informants, that day's drama was personal and soap opera-level riveting, and I just stood back and watched as two equally headstrong agents—one DEA and one Customs—duke it out (and I do mean actual hand-to-hand combat) in the crappy hotel parking lot. The only thing missing was my tub of popcorn and box of Junior Mints. Ultimately, the DEA won that particular battle. But the war was far from over.

Eventually, the coveted informant in question led us to the acquisition of a full load of coke in Key Largo, dismantling fifteen or so traffickers in the process. But on that day, like me, he was a spectator: watching the proverbial peacocks battle it out over his loyalties from the comfort of his hotel room, safely tucked behind his bedroom curtains. And as I watched *him* watching *them*, I couldn't help but wonder: how would we ever win an actual war against drugs, when the enemies were rarely entirely identifiable, if at all?

I had no idea that day what this one minor fistfight in a hotel parking lot actually represented, or exactly just what a place in line in the war on drugs would mean or lead to. To me on that one surreal day as a rookie agent, my enemy was the drug dealer, and potentially the informant we were meeting, as well. But then a wrench got thrown into the mix, and I was left thinking: perhaps the Customs Agent himself was also the enemy—after all, he was robbing us of our opportunity to build a good case (which, admittedly, was the most important thing to me in my life at that time, for better or worse). That was probably the first time—but certainly not the last—that I felt such confusion about who, exactly, was really on my team. From that one tussle in 1986 all the way up to my retirement in 2011, I watched US agencies fight over who had the control and supreme power in America's drug war—and I participated, too, no doubt about that. And all the while I heard Lincoln's words, and learned over and over again: a House divided cannot stand.

In August of 2001, I was transferred from DEA headquarters (where I worked as the Deputy Chief of International Operations) to North Carolina, where I'd be serving as their new DEA Chief. Since I was born in North Carolina and my parents still lived there, I was thrilled. There was also an additional sense of excitement over the move and new environment, too, as I'd never actually lived in Charlotte itself. I couldn't wait.

My timing arrival, however, turned out to be inauspicious: I set foot in Charlotte less than three weeks before September 11, 2001. On that horrific day, I was in the office just getting started when my colleague Dave Dongilli ran into my office, frantic, to tell me that one of the Twin Towers had just been hit by an airplane. We immediately set up a television in the conference room, plugged in the cable, and no sooner than we had things working, we just sat there frozen, collectively in shock watching the second plane smash into the South Tower. Soon, with the entire office gathered all together, we watched the unforgettable replay of both towers, one after the other, collapse. We watched the US being attacked and knew it was forever changed. Over and over again we watched.

Less than twenty-four hours later, every single house in my South Charlotte neighborhood had an American flag flying high. US citizens of every color, race, and religion suddenly had one very important thing in common: being proud to be American. We were now a house united. It seemed that for all of us, every day thereafter was a day devoted to working together as one unit in order to keep our country strong. Everyone, that is, except the Federal drug enforcement agencies.

As the de facto chief for the DEA in the state, I was tasked with approving investigations focused on targeting the highest-level traffickers in our region. Nine out of ten of those investigations were ones directly connected to drug cartels in Mexico: methamphetamine smuggled in from Michoacan, cocaine smuggled in from Sinaloa, heroin smuggled in from Durango, etc. We knew all this thanks to our increasing Title III (wiretap) cases that plugged us directly into the communications of the traffickers in both countries.

However, as our criminal investigations advanced even further, we found that we were routinely discovering that the Department of Homeland Security's Immigration and Customs Enforcement (ICE) offices in Charlotte (and other cities) were also working on a number of our international cases and suspects. Those of us in the DEA constantly attempted to deconflict our tangled investigations with ICE, but always to no avail. Not only did ICE refuse to cooperate, it actually got to a point where it seemed as if a literal policy of non-cooperation was coming directly from their own Ronald Reagan building in Washington, DC.

And I'm only being slightly hyperbolic: all throughout my subsequent three years in North Carolina, I spent more time wrangling ICE agents and surrogates (including one Assistant US Attorney) than I spent fighting the drug traffickers who were leading us directly to the Mexican cartels. Local and state police departments both noticed the growing discord between ICE and DEA, and were justifiably discouraged by the federal tug-of-war over mutual defendants.

I have countless examples of the ongoing strife. One of our cases involved wiretap evidence indicating where and when our top defendant was crossing the Mexico/US border after negotiating a multi-ton cocaine deal set to be sent to North Carolina. The Assistant US Attorney at the time had a special relationship with an IRS Criminal Investigator, and an equally strong one with an ICE supervisor. After the DEA case information was somehow relayed to the ICE San Ysidro, California office, they proceeded to incarcerate the suspect as he crossed into the US, all the while knowingly and willingly sabotaging the DEA Charlotte investigation (an investigation that had already spent $80,000 of hard-earned US taxpayer money). These kinds of incidents occurred so often that the DEA Administrator was eventually forced to establish field reporting mechanisms just to keep ICE in check, which was virtually impossible.

Another example of the DEA/ICE struggle involved a DEA Charlotte deputized Task Force Officer (TFO) who'd identified a powerful Mexican heroin trafficker, one who held direct ties to a supplier in Hidalgo, Mexico. The trafficker and his supplier were on their phones all day long and being observed on surveillance, so the TFO knew that a wiretap would blow open the investigation and take him to the "source of supply." After preparing a forty-two-page affidavit and submitting it to the US Attorneys Office in Charlotte, he learned that it was immediately turned away by an Assistant Attorney, an attorney who very clearly only wanted to work with his friends in IRS and ICE.

A TFO is essentially considered to be a sworn DEA Agent—one of us—and DEA treats them as such. Because they typically have local roots—whether in Reno, Nevada, Long Island, or, in this case, Kings Mountain, North Carolina, TFOs always have the best connections, and always know just what's happening in their home cities and towns. I'd go so far as to estimate that nearly seventy percent of DEA success within the US domestic theatre derives directly from their work, and we respect, value, and appreciate them all. So, when I found out the Assistant Attorney had intercepted my TFO's affidavit (effectively sabotaging our investigation as a consequence), I immediately made an appointment to meet with the Assistant.

Not long into that meeting, and in an unabashedly sanctimonious tone, the Assistant advised me that it was the general policy of the US Attorneys Office to *not* use TFOs in federal wiretap affidavits, even though federal law had established the precedent to do exactly that. It became clear to me that I'd have to bring our complaint directly to then-US Attorney Bill Constantine (not his real name). Constantine, a former Clemson basketball star and overall nice guy, was overseeing the US Attorneys Office with his brand of affable, genteel, old-fashioned Southern charm, replete with enough hearty handshakes and back-slapping to keep the local police chiefs and sheriffs happy about their roles with the Feds. Still, it took me several weeks to get my sit down with Constantine, because his ass-kissing Assistant Attorney was bent on keeping us from doing so, busily poisoning the well prior to what he had to know was a conversation he couldn't get his boss to avoid. When we finally sat down together in the same office, Constantine calmly explained that he was simply supporting his Assistant Attorney, and didn't want to knock over the apple cart and then have to clean up any coordination or deconfliction messes. During our discussion I then explained to *him*—the only one of us who was an actual US Attorney—what the law *really* allows, but he quickly responded with a trite, "There is much law to cite on whether you can do it or not do it." This was a clear indication that Constantine, the chief prosecutor, and his sycophant sidekick had already decided to stick with their argument in favor of keeping a deputized, sworn-in TFO from fulfilling their DEA investigation-related responsibilities. I told Constantine — respectfully—that he was making a huge mistake, because the local police agencies with officers deputized by the DEA all already knew that they do, in fact, have the right to be affiants for federal cases. Nonetheless, Constantine blew me off (as graciously as possible), and that was the end of it. Or so he thought.

When I returned to my office, the TFO asked to see me. During our chat, he informed me that a year or so ago he and that IRS agent and ICE agent had a case "run-in," and that they went to their mutual pal (the Assistant Attorney) to complain, instead of handling the conflict directly, like adults. From that day on, those three attacked the hardworking, fair-minded TFO every chance they could get, making every effort to hold him back in his career. Hardly exemplary behavior from three men who should have been busy setting examples in civility and support, not in how to seek vengeance over misguided, petty grievances. As with so many other power struggles, this one was clearly driven by ego: three very large ones, to be exact.

It took less than a week for the news of the TFO incident to get to the Charlotte Chief of Police. Chief Stevens, with a refreshingly direct, no-nonsense approach, called Constantine (as I was later informed by the man himself) to relay one simple message: "Let me tell you this, Bill: if you aren't going to treat *all* of my officers with equality, dignity, and respect, and as fully-deputized and sworn DEA Task Force Officers, then I suppose I'll just have to pull every single one of them out of ALL of your federal task forces!" I wasn't there, but I'm fairly sure that when Constantine heard that, his genteel Southern manners aside, he likely hit the roof. He certainly wasted no time expressing his displeasure to me, as he called me the minute he got off the phone with Chief Stevens. After I sat back and let him rant a bit and ask the absurd question of why I'd filled Stevens in on what had happened, and tell me how I had a lot of nerve, disturbing that apple cart, I reminded him that in all fairness, I'd warned him (Constantine) of the repercussions during our talk and he'd chosen to ignore them. "How convenient!", was all he said, then ending the call.

Months later, Constantine called and asked me to meet him for breakfast at the renowned Anderson's Restaurant, near downtown Charlotte. Comfort food does have a way of bringing people together—well, at least momentarily, anyway. As we sat and savored our southern grits, fried liver mush, and piping-hot, fresh biscuits, Constantine confessed that I may, in fact, have been right all along: right about TFO authorities, right about precedent law, and right about pissing off local law enforcement leadership with his decision. But—and this was a pretty big caveat—he made it clear that in the end, the US Attorneys Office is in charge of federal law enforcement in Charlotte, and what they say goes. And that was really the only important message he wanted to tell me. So much for a completely harmonious meal.

Not long after that, the Charlotte US Attorneys Office began to come after the DEA hard, which didn't surprise me. So hard, in fact, that Agent Dongilli was told by the Michelin Man lookalike assistant that from then on, they planned on going full-on nuclear (the Assistant Attorney's words, not mine) against DEA Charlotte, and wouldn't be supporting DEA at all. It was obvious that I needed a plan B—knowing that when one door closed, we'd better find the next one to open—and I came up with one soon thereafter. OK, I thought, if that's their stance, then it's time for me to go to the State Bureau of Investigation (SBI), and work together with them in order to create new North Carolina State law for T-III wiretaps. If we could pull that off, DEA and SBI could work together against violent drug cartels.

Driven by the need to find a resolution and finally move forward, in that spring of 2002 I orchestrated a trip to New York City with the SBI Director, Assistant Director, and their Chief Attorney in order for us to tour the city's Drug Investigations Division, also known as the Drug Courts, where they routinely used state wiretaps to investigate drug traffickers. The North Carolina SBI didn't yet have such a program, but were very interested in establishing one, especially after seeing how things worked at the Manhattan Drug Investigations Division. I then went a step further, and arranged to have two of our top DEA intelligence Collection Agents from the Special Operations Division (SOD) come and join us in the city, so they could brief the SBI on how SOD could assist them as well, and work together to link North Carolina T-III cases with other cases around the world. It was a great group, and the trip was off to a great start.

We managed to spend time on meaningful things aside from our work while there, as well. The NYPD very graciously made plans to take our entire group down into the cavernous hole at Ground Zero one afternoon, and it was a sobering, special day for all of us. After an atypically slow drive downtown, we spent a long time observing the construction site, where thousands of workers were using enormous machines and equipment to remove the remaining earth and debris left behind from the worst terrorist attack in our country's history. Watching them work and silently reflecting on the horror that had unfolded on that very site, at some point I thought to myself: as a result of this attack our entire country and so many of our partner nations around the world have come together, but I can't manage to get one small group of ICE agents and US attorneys to work with us?

The SBI and DEA returned from New York with a plan in

place. We were driven and determined to create something entirely new, and it would be an historical development in North Carolina law enforcement. On our flight back home, sitting in the cabin of the SBI KingAir 350, we collectively strategized and developed an outline for what was to be North Carolina's first Title-III wiretap program.

One week later, the SBI Director called me with some unexpected, bad news: the wiretap program was going to have to wait, at least for now. "But why, Director?", I asked. "Why, when we already have the program design organized, we've coordinated with the DEA Special Operations Division, and we're all set to go?" She informed me that it had taken one week for our Chief Attorney (who had been with us on the trip to New York) to receive a call from the US Attorneys Office in Charlotte, who very definitely didn't want us to proceed, and went so far as to say that to do so would quite possibly be counterproductive to federal law enforcement standards and policy. She finished our call with the promise that they were, however, trying to work it out. But what I was left with was the harsh reality that we had a US Attorneys Office in Charlotte patently refusing to work with the DEA, and actively doing everything in its power to block the DEA from succeeding with other State agencies. A House divided, indeed, and a situation that still saddens me when I think back on that era. It was a depressing situation, and hardly very encouraging for the future of interagency cooperation. However, I am thrilled and proud to report that, eventually, the state of North Carolina succeeded in establishing their own statewide wire-tapping program, and I can only hope that the US Attorneys Office in Charlotte has since abandoned its toxic mix of old Southern Charm and sabotage.

These kinds of issues were ones we certainly weren't told

about while in the training academy in Quantico, Virginia, or the Atlanta, Georgia DEA Southeast Headquarters. I can't imagine that similar problems were nonexistent then, or that the instructors hadn't faced plenty of communication issues already themselves. Clearly the topic of interagency conflict was the elephant in the room, and nobody wanted to talk about or even acknowledge it. On that one day in Key Largo, I witnessed a rivalry, one I never could have expected would grow into *such* a high level of competitiveness amongst agencies and departments that they'd succeed in both upsetting and disappointing even the most optimistic of DEA Agents (or, for that matter, the most optimistic of US citizens). In the final days of my career, I was observing rivalries on a daily basis and on an unimaginable scale. During the time I was with the DEA (1986-2011), it seemed as if interagency envy, jealousy, and negative competitiveness (of course, there can be a positive side of competition, as well) only grew, and never waned—much to the detriment of drug enforcement efficiency around the world. Worse still, the men and women behind those law enforcement rivalries included top agency and department heads, many of whom were answering directly to the President of the United States.

For the sake of our nation, I can only hope that any internal antagonism has become far less common since my retirement, because I found then—and still believe now—that when elephants fight, only the grass dies. And tragically, in this case, that grass is US drug law enforcement effectiveness.

CHAPTER 19

MY ENEMY IS MY FRIEND

ack in 1996, I was serving as the Resident Agent-in-Charge
of the Hermosillo Resident Office in Sonora, Mexico. During
my tenure there, I supervised five special agents, all of
whom trusted me to watch their backs. And they, in turn, repaid
the favor with consistently hard work, discipline, and undying
loyalty.

Their efforts were equally matched by several of my Mexican
colleagues. Enrique Ibarra-Santes, who was one of my most-
admired Mexican law enforcement counterparts, truly set the
standard for what it took to fight the drug wars in earnest. A
successful orthopedic surgeon who'd been inspired to leave
the medical field and segue into law enforcement, he made the
drastic change in order to rally against the political corruption,
murder, and borderline chaos that had been wreaking havoc in
his beloved country. This man was not just a true pro, but a true
hero as well.

Enrique often called on to join him in his valiant (but extremely
challenging) efforts to thwart the ubiquitous successes of the
Baja-based Tijuana Arellano-Felix drug cartel. The AFO cartel,
as they were commonly referred to, was a family-run group led
by a literal band of brothers, primarily Benjamin and Ramon.

245

Together, they and the cartel smuggled millions of kilograms of Colombian cocaine from the northwest border of Mexico over to Southern California, Nevada, and Arizona. They also utilized hundreds of young enforcers—referred to as the "Juniors"—who were universally feared for their constant use of extreme violence (even by cartel standards), stopping at absolutely nothing to silence and shut down any threats, critics, or opponents. The Juniors were led by a vicious, heartless monster named David Baron, who acted as the devil's son over the course of many years, personally murdering hundreds of competitors, law enforcement officials, and even journalists.

On one occasion, Baron suspected someone connected to the Juniors of being an informant, so he did what came so naturally to him: ordered that he be killed. The supposed informant (who was, in fact, *not* an informant at that time, and also barely a man, at just twenty) was driving down Highway 5 in San Diego, California, when Baron's hitmen of choice drove up alongside him. The assassins yelled "Hey!", the boy turned his head, and was promptly shot several times right through his neck, instantly severing his spine. Incredibly, he survived (but, tragically, lay paralyzed and in shock for many months), giving DEA San Diego the opportunity to both keep an eye on him and debrief him on all of the unsavory inner workings of the Tijuana Cartel. As fate would have it, he did eventually become an informant—a favorite of the San Diego office, in fact—with copious amounts of helpful information to share. He also had a sense of humor, happily welcoming his new nickname, the "Talking Head." Over the following years, this young man helped us indict dozens of AFO cartel members, including the brothers themselves. And, eventually, Baron was the fatal victim of his own intended crime, after he unintentionally invited his own demise in Tijuana after setting up an ambush to kill a journalist. His own death was as grisly as any he'd engineered, with him being shot through the eye (and losing half of his brain matter) via crossfire from one of his own men. He died where he stood, and the ensuing rumors were rampant: his death was, *maybe,* an accident. Or not.

Over time, Dr. Ibarra-Santes had collected an enormous amount of intelligence against the AFO, and was preparing to launch a major assault against the cartel, in partnership with the region's military service. A week before the intended start of the operation, I flew to Tijuana. At midnight, and quite unexpectedly, Dr. Ibarra arrived unannounced at my hotel room door, accompanied by six burly, imposing bodyguards. He also came equipped with audio tapes of Benjamin and Ramon Arellano, filled with lengthy discussions about their plans to assassinate several local politicians they believed were potentially uncooperative. I asked the doctor if he had any copies that I might be able to take with me, and he calmly told me that no, that would be unwise. He explained that having the tapes would place my life at extreme and immediate risk, and for my own well-being he thought it best to instead deliver them to me in Mexico City the following week. While I was frustrated to be left without the tapes in my possession, I was also genuinely grateful, and agreed.

Just a few days later, Enrique flew to Mexico City in order to brief the Attorney General on the operation and then, per our plan, to pass those tapes along to me. Unbeknownst to him, several hitmen from the AFO were on the same flight, and covertly followed him out of the Mexico City airport. They then kept him and his small entourage under close watch as they made haste to the Federal Attorneys' General office, in the heart of the enormous capital city. Enrique and the rest of the group were just about to step out of their car when the stealth sicarios fired en masse, blanketing them in hundreds of rounds of bullets. Not content to just leave them for dead, they also disabled the car as one final precaution, then left their bloodied bodies behind for all the terrified and shocked natives and tourists to see. The body of my colleague and dear friend Ernesto *alone* received over 180 hits from the favored tool of AFO's trade (the infamous "Cuerno de Chivo" AK-47 submachine rifle)—every last one of them a result of that deadly weapon's 7.62 bullet.

Tragically, that hit was just one of many reminders that when it comes to the reach of Mexico's cartels, no one – no matter their title, no matter their power, no matter their wealth – *no one* is safe. It was soon discovered that a handful of corrupt Federal Police officers had assisted the Arellanos with the planning and execution of the murders. Indeed, this was another "inside job." Worse, a briefcase was found in Dr. Ibarra's vehicle containing $60,000 US dollars, and all of the Mexican media that had been loyal to the AFO (and dependent upon the money they got for that loyalty) immediately printed stories flatly stating that Ibarra himself had been the corrupt official.

The reality is that I can't say definitively if he was corrupt or not, but DEA intelligence did, ultimately, determine that the hitmen had planted the cash after the assassination, knowing that its presence would be all the "evidence" needed to categorize Enrique as a dangerous and duplicitous man, one who needed to be killed. The sad truth is that in Mexico, law enforcement corruption is so pervasive that most people already assume that all cops are on the take, so even one small, unproven, potentially disreputable act is all that the cartels—and their paid journalists—need in order to paint the picture that the dirty cop deserved what he or she got.

At that point I'd spent a good deal of time with Enrique, even hosting him in my own home for dinner with my family. I thought highly of him, always: he was clearly well-educated, a wonderful conversationalist, a gentleman, and (in my impression) a highly moral and professional man who always came across as earnest, and never sanctimonious. I always believed that he was sincere in his desire for Mexico to become a safer, better place for everyone. The news of his death was devastating to me, and I still consider him the furthest thing from a zero. In my eyes, he was Mexico's hero.

My work, and the inner workings of any government-related law enforcement business, is enormously complicated. *People* are enormously complicated. Without question, one of the most discouraging parts of my job was not what you'd expect (dealing on a daily basis with dishonest, disloyal informants, violent and amoral drug traffickers, and cold-blooded killer hitmen). Rather, it was the people I would never have guessed would disappoint me, the people who, in theory, were on *our* side, that proved to be the most disheartening. One would think that, with such a closely-shared mission, everyone (regardless of department or organization) would work together and support one another. Unfortunately, that wasn't always the case. Countless times before, I'd been shocked by my dealings involving other US law agencies and officers, ones who wanted to work drug enforcement cases with our primary foreign partner police contacts, but for all the wrong reasons. Nothing is more embarrassing and shameful in the eyes of our partners than when a "gringo" cop sabotages the efforts of another, all for the sake of advancing their own, singular agenda.

In Mexico, drug-trafficking cartels have some of the most sophisticated, complex, and advanced models for organized crime to ever exist. The system permeates nearly every aspect of Mexican society, including every imaginable financial sector, the oil, gas, and mineral business industries, and even the retail industry. Billions upon billions of dollars flow through Mexico every year as a direct result of narcotrafficking, and that money isn't all just being spent on the criminals' lavish lifestyles, or adding to the inordinate amounts of corruption on all levels. Rather, this much-needed cash supports the improvement of their infrastructures, firearms, munitions, and explosives businesses, and the production and sales of countless ships, planes, and automobiles. And as the story of Pablo Escobar so perfectly showed, sometimes these criminals can come to actually be viewed as heroes, even as they're also widely acknowledged to be villains. The Mexican *corridos*—local ballads, often made up of pro-cartel narratives and lyrics—are a perfect example of how common it is for drug traffickers to become idolized, local folk heroes. I'm still amazed, even after forty years of bearing witness to this complex, corrupt system, of just how resilient drug traffickers and their organizations are when it comes to thinking of new, enterprising methods to promote both their illicit businesses and their own reputations at the same time.

But again, people are complicated, and so is bureaucracy. But as complex as these men were, and are (not to mention their illicit enterprises), it often seemed as if our own, internal efforts to combat them were even more muddled. Time and again, wires got crossed and investigations got bungled, all because people were simply not on the same page, often deliberately so.

One of the most popular smuggling methods to come about as a result of both technology and ingenuity involves the use of both small and large aircraft as the ideal mode of transportation. Smuggling via aircraft is the obvious preference because, of course, aircraft can smuggle drugs in mere hours as opposed to the days, weeks, or even months it would take trucks or ships to make the journey from South America to Mexico. Knowing this, in the 1990s the DEA identified a slew of G-2 and G-3 jets, all of which were being actively used by the Mexican cartels to smuggle drugs and overseen by a transportation specialist and Colombian pilot named Pedro Bermudez Suaza, also known as "El Arquitecto" ("The Architect"). Pedro, a savvy operator and longtime staple in the drug world, offered up transportation to any and all cartels (if and only if they could afford him, of course). With a fleet of jets each capable of smuggling up to five tons of cocaine at a time, productivity was quickly ramped up, and the routine was simple: first, the cocaine was smuggled over the Colombian and Venezuelan borders, where it was then packed and processed as cargo. After loading the drugs onto one of the jets, the delivery was a breeze, with the flight from Venezuela to Mexico lasting less than three hours long. So, in less time than it might take for the average citizen to pass through airport security and even *board* a flight, five full tons of cocaine could be in the hands of any one of the six major cartels throughout the United States, ready to be distributed.

In September of 2007, one of those jets crash-landed, a direct result of the pilot not receiving the necessary clearance to land at the Cancun International Airport. The crash-landing, like the circumstances that led up to it, was a huge, avoidable mess. Worse still, it was a mess of our own government's making.

Eventually, the details trickled out: apparently, the landing clearance had been blocked that day due to an unscheduled Mexican Army unit's arrival at the Cancun Airport. Their arrival had, of course, sparked immediate fear amongst the traffickers responsible for paying bribes to airport police officials, so as

Pedro's pilot approached the airport, he was informed by his ground contact (and fellow Pedro employee) to *not* land in Cancun, but to instead wait for an entirely new airport assignment to be provided. That assignment never came, and as the pilot was frantically circling the zone waiting, the plane ran out of fuel and went down. The pilot survived (and was immediately captured), and a staggering four tons of cocaine was quickly seized from the crash site. Crash aside, it was business as usual, but what the DEA didn't know was that our Homeland Security "sister" agency—ICE—had coordinated the entire smuggling operation with the use of a Miami-based pilot/informant. Of course, once the facts were entirely laid out, the US government was both mortified and livid that while the DEA was busy working *their* investigation against Pedro Bermudez Suaza alongside Mexican counter drug officials, an entirely different US agency was busy conducting an investigation all their own, even using myriad traffickers for smuggling as well as Pedro's own assets and resources. Both agencies were fastidiously juggling countless contacts, informants, plans, promises, and meetings, and yet, none of it—no coordination of any sort—was happening between the two.

Fortunately, this mess didn't damage the prosecution's case against El Arquitecto, and in 2010 he was extradited to the US, where he currently sits in a prison cell waiting to answer for his crimes. Also, both Mexican and Colombian authorities have since seized tens of millions of dollars from El Arquitecto's financial troves of ill-gotten gains, all reaped from his cocaine-trafficking business. When the DEA asked ICE why they never bothered to even attempt to deconflict their investigation, they just cued up the same old song and dance routine they always did: finger-point, deflect, deny, repeat. This was far from the first time ICE had intentionally sabotaged a DEA investigation to stop a drug cartel operation, eschewing any possible regard for the big picture. It pained me to think of it then, and it still pains me now.

I couldn't help but to think of that day in Key Largo, Florida over twenty years prior when I first saw CUSTOMS usurp a DEA investigation. Just because two federal agents are using the same informant, why fight over him? The DEA agent and customs agent each report to their own, entirely unrelated superiors (and are each a part of two separate chains of command), thus each stood to receive full, individual credit for any and all successes related to the shared informant. So, then, why not work together, without any strife? Ego, arrogance, and jealousy, that's why. Simple as that.

The tensions between the two agencies always felt almost tangible, even in person. In 2009 I was in Mexico City to meet with officials from the Attorney's General Office between Mexico and the United States, known as the Bilateral Commission Meeting. I had been invited to speak alongside then-DEA Administrator Michele Leonhart, with the two of us leading a presentation on the countless joint problems and vulnerabilities between our two nations with regards to counter drug-trafficking and anti-money-laundering efforts. Michelle was a career administrator and former DEA Agent, and her fierce intellect, heightened natural instincts, and sincere, unparalleled compassion for people had taken her swiftly up the corporate ladder. A highly-professional speaker with a calming yet authoritative tone, Michelle never took on a job—let alone a presentation—she didn't want to. When she had something to say, whether it was to a fellow agent or to the President of the United States, she meant what she said.

And people listened.

After our presentation, then-ICE Commissioner John Morton was the first to approach me, and he wasn't exactly subtle in his delivery: "Well, the great DEA does it again. So, do tell, Dave, what's next?" Despite his obvious sarcasm I kept my cool, giving him my best faux-conspiratorial smile, and telling him he'd just have to wait and see. Not long after, I was once again chatting with Administrator Leonhart—who was always calm and consistently game-faced—and I mentioned the exchange. Ever mindful of the delicate politics involved, I referred to Morton not by his name, opting instead for "empty suit." And while I would never swear to it, in that moment I was positive I saw the distinct hint of a smile on her face. And while that one smile certainly brought some much-needed levity to that night, the sad fact remained that this overall dysfunction ran as deep and high among the most esteemed of supposed collaborators as it did anywhere else.

Again, my exposure to this kind of duplicity was far from rare. Not long after the presentation in Mexico, Larry, an ICE agent in Mexico City, wanted his investigative personnel (one Mexico-based and the other on temporary duty from the US), to participate in the debriefing of captured Zetas member Jaime Gonzales, nicknamed Hummer (the nickname being a result of his vast, expensive collection of Hummer jeeps). Hummer was one of the Gulf Cartel's most notoriously violent members—no easy feat, considering how vicious they were known to be. Aside from their reliance upon extreme violence, they also excelled at collecting high-caliber firearms and explosives, which the Zetas used throughout their reign of terror and torture all across Mexico. Thanks to DEA intelligence shared with their Mexicans counterparts, Hummer was captured in 2008. As a result, SIEDO (Mexico's own version of an Attorneys General division, with a focus on organized crime), permitted US agents to be present during Hummer's debriefing by Mexican prosecutors. Then-Deputy Attorney General Marisela Morales Ibañez and I agreed that as part of the process, we'd allow for the participation of one agent—and one agent only—from each relevant US agency.

Now, this was an absolutely understandable caveat to me, as the sudden presence of a gaggle of gringos in the debriefing room would come across as the reddest of flags, and attract some very unwanted attention. So, I offered spots to the usual suspects: ICE, ATF, DEA, and the FBI included. Not one of them had an issue, save for—of course—ICE, who not only turned down the offer, but also insisted I offer them *two* spots. I've always been a fairly good mediator (even when it comes to that kind of bureaucratic melodrama), but in this case I stood my ground. Fair, after all, is fair. But ICE didn't share that outlook, and Agent Larry, at this point a proverbial thorn in my side, took it a step further, complaining to Deputy Attorney General Morales that she'd essentially chosen us as teacher's pet, when it should be ICE. To be fair to Larry, perhaps he was being pressured by his own superiors and didn't have the power to push back. Still, it was childish behavior, and embarrassing for everyone involved. My subsequent discussions with Morales about our collective lack of teamwork only served to make things worse—but it was simply par for the course. I'd been let down not by the operation itself, or by any of the Mexican counterparts involved, but by my own government. Yet again, I'd seen the enemy (and the enemy's ego) firsthand, and yet again I'd only seen it from within.

Make no mistake: international and domestic drug trafficking is the United States' number one organized crime threat, as well as Mexico's number one national security threat, so it's not just our country's reputation at stake here. In order to have any real success in the fight against transnational organized crime, the ICE and DEA must remain committed not just to a shared goal, but to one another, as well.

CHAPTER 20

THE STEERING WHEEL

I n Washington, DC, these days, there are so many federal government agencies and departments that it's literally a near-impossible task to name them all. In addition to all of those, there exists an equally staggering number of smaller law enforcement agencies, most of which make their main hub of operations in DC, Maryland, and Northern Virginia. Regardless of location, however, they all share one thing in common: the majority of the meetings in all headquarters almost always revolve around the planning of *other* meetings, often ones aiming to simplify and streamline various overlapping, interagency efforts rife with conflicting jurisdictions. It's typically a lot of pomp and circumstance and talking in circles, made up of far too much admin and far too little substantive action or follow through. Obviously, it's a vicious cycle, one that hardly ever leads to quick, effective results. I call it "The Old Potomac Two Step."

In 1973, President Nixon recognized the need for a different, brand-new kind of agency, one with a sole mission: to manage all aspects of both drug trafficking and drug abuse. The legislative branch of government took things one step further, acknowledging that even broader, newer legal/law-based additions were warranted in order to effectively combat organized crime and drug trafficking. Along with these developments came new laws—ones that would change the entire landscape of the drug wars permanently—including anti-money laundering statutes, complex conspiracy laws, and two new, immensely powerful and influential statutes, the CCE (Continuing a Criminal Enterprise statute) and RICO (Racketeer Influence and Corruption Organizations statute). With these new, critical legal developments aiding the DEA's efforts, success came quickly, leading to the DEA's stronghold within federal drug law enforcement throughout the '80s and '90s. In fact, the DEA racked up so many massive asset seizures in rapid succession (including cash), they soon became known as "The Feds Working for Free." And this wasn't all that far from the truth—incredibly, they were, in fact, seizing double their own annual operating budget year after year.

Predictably, other agencies took notice, and then they took action. Agencies including the US Customs Service and the FBI, understandably, were increasingly wary of losing any of their political ground, and quickly went after use of those same statutes to support their own missions. In 1992, the FBI went so far as to propose a convoluted takeover plan to the Department of Justice that, ultimately, aimed to take the DEA and weave it into the FBI, transforming it into the FBI's own anti-drug division. The DEA's response was both decisive and swift. Spearheaded by Deputy Administrator Stephen Greene, the DEA's rebuttal was successful at first glance, but there was a downside: while the FBI lost that first battle, their overall strategy to gain ground in the drug enforcement world worked. As a consequence, the DEA began to be consistently challenged on deconfliction issues with other agencies at an increasing and alarming level. Again, although the Attorney General and National Security Staff had refused that one FBI proposal, attentions had been sharply refocused in the process, bringing about newfound expectations of the DEA. Suddenly, everyone seemed to consider themselves justified in their demand for the DEA to share both its mission and tactics. Up until that point, other agencies had essentially been getting away with doing whatever they wanted to get in the game, passive aggressively waiting for the DEA to raise hell and demand deconfliction. In simpler terms, whenever two or more agencies had conflicting cases, the DEA was then forced to intervene, challenge one or both, and/or bring a solution to the table. In the meantime, they also had to just live with the fact that the onus was always on them, and never the other way around.

This vicious cycle proved both exhausting and time-consuming for the DEA, not least because the DEA staff was *supposed* to be spending their time and efforts targeting drug traffickers and narcos, not resolving conflict amongst the other myriad "good guys" who were trying to help win the same war in theory, but were instead just getting in the way. The end result: while the DEA was, technically, officially steering the wheel of America's anti-drug policy, everyone else now had their hands in a firm grip on it, too. This messy new overload of power-hungry, aggressively battling, aspiring backseat law enforcement agency drivers ultimately rendered the entire machine ineffective.

This was no more apparent than in early 2011, when an ICE agent was shot and killed in Mexico. After the murder, the DEA demanded the Mexican government take immediate and aggressive action against the Zetas cartel traffickers who were so blatantly responsible for the crime. DEA intelligence was vital to the Mexican government, and universally recognized as a critical component needed by the Mexicans in order for them to successfully identify the locations of the various Zetas. Per equally recognized procedure, the DEA would then report its actions to their parent organization, a.k.a. The Justice Department. But when then-Department of Homeland Security Secretary Janet Napolitano heard of the imminent advances against the Zetas cartel, she had her staff immediately schedule multi-agency briefings. In the weeks that followed, the Justice Department (then headed by Attorney General Eric Holder) and Secretary Napolitano engaged in an endless debate on whether or not one single department's agencies should brief another department, with the DOJ remaining livid that the DEA—entirely their charge, technically—was "summoned" by Homeland Security. By the end of the month, Holder finally brought an end to the administrative circus, and informed Secretary Napolitano that the Justice Department (a.k.a. *his* people), would *not* be directly briefing the Secretary. Instead, Holder informed Napolitano, he and his staff would bring her and her people up to speed...when it was convenient for them to do so. This became the new established pattern and order of power, and it is how it would remain, with the Deputy Attorney General (or the acting Attorney General) always the one truly in control of the wheel, not the DEA itself. The DEA Administrator (in title and practice the actual head of the DEA), works directly for and reports to the Attorney General (through the Deputy AG), and as such lacks the sufficient political firepower (or nerve) to even attempt to try to regain control of the wheel from the Deputy AG. In fact, it's been decades since a DEA administrator had that kind of authority. You'd have to look all the way back to the 1980s, actually, to identify a DEA Administrator who held an uncontested firm grip while also maintaining total control: Ronald Reagan's personal choice and personal favorite, former DEA Administrator Jack Lawn. Since

Lawn, many administrators have made valiant efforts to win that power struggle and maintain control and some have gone so far as to pretend they did, but in truth none ever even came close.

Within a few weeks of arresting the Zetas cartel murderers responsible for the ICE agent's death, the Mexican government had seized their weapons, then matched them to the very same US weapons used in a failed, poorly-planned and executed undercover scheme known as Operation "Fast & Furious." In other words, at the same time as Napolitano and Holder were engaged in a useless political control tug-of-war for ownership of that proverbial steering wheel, the United States government was busy supplying Mexican drug cartels with the very weapons used to kill our own US agents.

Could the United States of America have learned some hard lessons from that experience, and taken actions to improve on its deconfliction policies and processes, leading us to far better efficiency against a common enemy? Of course. But we did not. And if history keeps repeating itself, and bureaucracy continues to take precedence over a shared, critical mission, we never will.

CHAPTER 21

BLOOD OF THE LAMB

I officially began my career in law enforcement nearly four decades ago, and I spent more than twenty-five of those years with the DEA. Half of that time was spent abroad, working and living in several different countries, and during that time the men and women with whom I worked came to mean just as much to me as any of my American colleagues. I shed tears with them, I bled with them, and I watched as they gave their lives over to a cause that almost always went unappreciated and overlooked. I was always even a bit in awe, as I witnessed firsthand hundreds of foreign police officers and military soldiers (many of whom were supporting, or supported by, long-struggling families) show up to their jobs every single day no matter how exhausted or overworked, all the while earning shockingly meager salaries. Despite the efforts of these men and women, their intentions, or even the danger they faced on a daily basis, their salaries were even lower than those of our *most* poverty-stricken in the US. I truly cannot express how much respect I have for them, and also for how they still continue to work the hardest for the least amount of money (and rare, if any, public recognition for their sacrifice). It's the kind of selflessness you don't often see in this country, all done in the name of keeping the citizens of their nations safer from both drugs and the powerful criminals and cartels who supply them.

One of these unsung heroes was a Colombian National Police Major named Leonardo Molina. Along with nine police officers then under his command, Molina was targeted and killed on the first of February 2005, by a corrupt Colombian Army patrol who was under the control of the North Valley drug cartel (NVC). That patrol, the Altas Montañas Army Unit, was led by a sinister military Lieutenant Colonel whose actual allegiance was to North Valley Cartel Kingpin trafficker Diego Montoya-Sanchez, for whom he worked as an enforcer. Their assassination of Molina and his men was an egregious, heinous crime, but it wasn't an uncommon one. However, it did have something in common with so many of the other crimes the NVC and its underlings committed: both the plan and the execution were brutal, premeditated, and merciless. The victims weren't just decent and honest men, they were also enormously successful: a result of their hard work, dedication, and diligence. It was this success, tragically, that ultimately cost them their lives.

The Major and his small unit of elite investigators had first worked for several months with a DEA team in Bogota, a collaboration focusing primarily on anti-corruption cases that targeted cocaine and heroin-smuggling in the air cargo section of the El Dorado International Airport. All the men had been vetted by both Colombian and US officials, passed all polygraphs, and been trained in advanced investigative techniques. They'd made a significant number of seizures and arrests of corrupt former (and active) duty CNP officers, in addition to myriad airport officials. Combined, these efforts had made a significant dent in the routine operations of the North Valley Cartel, who'd grown more and more complacent as they grew further accustomed to successfully smuggling their drugs through Colombia's major airports without disruption.

After Molina's elite unit had pulled off a particularly astounding airport cocaine seizure (weighing in the actual tons), immediately followed by a number of nearly equally formidable seizures from air cargo shipments at the Mexico City International Airport, Major Molina and his team had no time to pause and celebrate their achievements. Immediately, the Mayor and his men were deployed to an area outside of Calí where, they were told, they'd be searching for an elusive drug stash site.

At the time, the mission didn't really raise any red flags to the unit, focused and dutiful as they were. But, looking back, it's impossible not to ask: Just why, exactly, were these brave officers taken off their successful investigative assignment, and subsequently sent to Calí for something of far lesser importance? Without question, the Cartel had felt the impact of their work. And, with their added ammo of well-established, high-level connections within the CNP (and, most likely, the military), perhaps the NVC simply wanted them gone, and set about making that happen.

The sad fact is that the truth will never be fully revealed, but this much is certain: it was during this unexpected deployment that Diego Montoya's NVC infiltrated the CNP Major's unit and took the lives of ten honest men.

Using an informant as an additional pawn, and presenting the ruse that the elite team would just be conducting routine enforcement raids on a cocaine-filled warehouse, the NVC arranged for the men to be lured into a remote, desolate, area for what would become both an ambush and a massacre. Personally instructed by Montoya-Sanchez himself to sit and wait with his equally corrupt squad for the Major's unit to arrive, the Colonel was patient, even calm, as he kept watch. For him, the act of mass murder was just another day on the job.

And he made sure they got that job done. That afternoon, in a murky, heavily-wooded spot in Jamundi, Valle de Cauca, Molina's entire unsuspecting team was ambushed, murdered, and left for dead. According to statements taken later from a handful of incarcerated Army soldiers who'd been part of the ambush, when the team arrived, both the Colonel and his band of assassins were ready and armed with rocket-propelled grenades, frag grenades, and machine guns. In unison and without warning, the corrupt soldiers opened fire, first with 7.62 and M-60 rounds from automatic weapons, then with hand and rocket-propelled grenades, easily killing the most-exposed of the police officers. None of the terrified men—despite being dressed in full uniform and frantically identifying themselves as police officers—were spared: they were either instantly killed or subsequently executed. After the explosions finally stopped and the dust settled, a small handful of men were still alive, gasping for air, and trying to make sense of what had just happened. As they lay there in their own blood, begging the Army soldiers to spare their lives if only for the sake of their parents, wives, and children, the Colonel gave his soldiers an unmistakable order: execute them all with a single shot to the head. This, of course, was done to ensure that here would be no witnesses left to recount the deadly ambush—including the sacrificial informant who'd been used to set up the slaughter.

The following week, in a surprising and incredible act of unity, all of Colombia's leading magazines ran the exact same cover page: a jarring, ghastly image of the Major's bloody police cap, replete with a bullet hole front and center in his forehead.

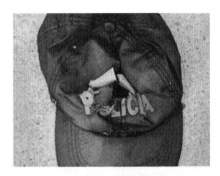

Colombian National Police Major and DEA Sensitive Investigations Unit (SIU) Commander Major Molina's duty cap shot through the forehead. The murderers were a corrupt Colombian Army unit hired to protect the North Valley Cartel.

These men deserve our undying respect and gratitude. Major Molina and his team sacrificed their lives at the hands of crooked officials, all while doing what they'd made a pact to do: serve and protect all Colombians, as well as citizens of consumer nations such as the USA, from the scourge of narco-trafficking. Actually, in retrospect, I'd prefer to call it narco-terrorism.

The day immediately after the tragedy, I traveled to Calí to attend the officers' funerals. Once there, I met with Special Agent Terry Cole, a relentless tracker of cartel members and their surrogates. Terry's work had always been nonstop, and he'd managed to make an exceptional number of impressive contacts within the National Police, including Molina himself. With Terry at the ceremony was National Police Commander 'Colonel Camacho,' who was, along with everyone else in attendance, completely devastated by what had happened. During our car ride to the church, Camacho was visibly distraught—so much so, in fact, that he was unable to bring himself to say anything at all. He'd just lost men he clearly thought of as brothers, and I know for a fact that Camacho still thinks of them often, even after all these years have passed, and even with the incessant daily distractions he faces while serving as the #3 General Officer of the Colombian National Police.

At that point in my life, I had certainly already witnessed loss. In fact, I had witnessed more than my share of loss, along with shock, grief, rage, even denial. But on that day, as I looked around at the faces of the mothers, fathers, wives, friends, and children left behind, I felt something unwelcome and unfamiliar along with my sorrow: emptiness. I felt a void, a space that had once been filled with what I thought was an unwavering pride for my country. All I could think about at that moment was how America's incessant, insatiable lust for drugs had brought us here. To mourn.

A few weeks after the funeral, I invited Major Molina's young wife and five-year-old son to our DEA office in Bogotá, Colombia. After showing them around, I did something that helped start to fill that void back up again, a gesture made possible by my colleagues and superiors. Working and giving together, all of us had raised a significant amount of money (money we knew they badly needed) and, knowing the money could never replace what they had lost, we handed it over. Later, when I at last began to speak to the crowd that had assembled, I was thrown by the sight of the Major's little son crying, clinging to his mother as he tried to grasp the scene unfolding around him. Suddenly, that facade of toughness I'd built up over so many years, which I had thought was impenetrable, disappeared. Looking at the boy, all I could think about were my own children. Trust me, if you think there's no crying in baseball, I can tell you this: there's *far* less crying in a DEA office. But on that day, we all caved, and simply gave in to our emotions. I cried for that little boy, I cried for his mother, I cried over the very thought that my own daughters might ever experience such grief, and, finally, I cried for my country, and how its obsession with drugs had brought this kind of suffering not just to us, but to people all around the world.

.

CHAPTER 22

LA LIMPIEZA

When I was reassigned from Bogotá, Colombia, to Mexico City, my directive from DEA Administrator Karen Tandy was crystal clear: "Clean up Mexico!" Okay, I'm going to clean up a country that, starting in the 1920s, had been built on corrupt beams and fraudulent walls. Even native Mexicans, including more than a few government employees I have known, acknowledge this reality, frequently joking about how corruption is the glue that keeps their country together. I thought to myself, "How did you go from the frying pan into the fire?!"

I had served as DEA Chief in Bogotá for about three years when Administrator Tandy asked me to help her in replacing the current Regional Director of DEA in Mexico. This unexpected request popped up a few weeks before the International Drug Enforcement Conference in Montreal, Canada, where the Administrator and I had planned to discuss findings and recommendations based on a review of DEA Mexico's operations. A results-oriented executive known as the "Iron Lady," Tandy had not been satisfied with DEA Mexico's performance, to put it mildly. After reviewing an assessment report, the Administrator decided to take on the largest and most dangerous drug cartels in the world with new field leadership. To be an investigative asset to the US State Department's mission of shaping Mexico's law enforcement into a more productive body, DEA Mexico had to develop both a formidable strategy and a practical game plan to operate in the "Lion's Den" of global drug trafficking. As in all of my assignments, I took this job seriously; besides, as the Regional Director in Colombia, I knew that if DEA Mexico was successful, my own agents in South America would be beneficiaries of an effective and reliable working partner in the Mexico and Central America theatre. So, I energetically agreed to travel to Mexico and survey the ground to see what was going on.

Little did I realize at the time of my review in Mexico that the Administrator was actually positioning me to be transferred there from Colombia and develop new strategies and tactics to fight the cartels. While at the annual IDEC Madrid, I struck up a conversation during happy hour with our Chief of Operations, Mike. I started briefing him on my findings in Mexico and let him know I had a name to recommend for the top job: a distinguished, aggressive, and committed agent named Joe Evans. The Chief looked at me with a dead scope stare and said, "Damn Dave, you're gonna be that guy." "Bullshit," I shot back. "She asked me to find someone, and I found him." Mike replied, "Okay, but remember: I told ya so."

Later in Montreal, I briefed Karen on my Mexico assessment and made my recommendations. She never mentioned the possibility of my being reassigned to Mexico, so I assumed I was free and clear to remain in Colombia. I loved Colombia with every fiber of my being and was behind the US government's mission 100 percent. I worked well with the Ambassador, Charge de Affairs, and local intelligence and law enforcement teams. I also had an extraordinary team of agents, analysts, admin assistants, and program managers.

The week after my Montreal trip, guess who called me? Yes, it was the Iron Lady. I immediately closed my office door so no one could hear me beg for my Bogotá job. She started her pitch. "Dave, I want you to be my Grant. Can you do that?" I knew exactly what she was referring to—throughout DEA, it was common knowledge that the Administrator was a big fan of our sixteenth President, Abraham Lincoln. She studied Lincoln and his leadership tactics and at times, even cited those tactics with precise knowledge of every detail in history. President Lincoln had gone through several Union Generals who were losing battles in the war against the Confederacy. In fact, Lincoln was losing more battles than winning—until he picked General Ulysses S. Grant. According to the Administrator, she needed me to go to Mexico and succeed where others had failed. I knew her expectation was nearly impossible to meet; after all, for years many highly capable Directors worked in Mexico with little to show for it. DEA Mexico was an island of promise surrounded by an ocean of corruption and inefficiency. I didn't want to leave Colombia, but in the end, I had no choice. DEA is a para-military organization, so when your commander says go, you go. Within a month, I and my family were living in Mexico City.

After a few months on the job in Mexico, I realized that, as lucky I was in Colombia with President Alvaro Uribe, I had found another "wave of energy" in Mexico with President-elect Felipe Calderón Hinojosa. President Calderón had two things going for him. First, he was a seasoned economist who took in the facts of daily occurrences, public interactions, and activities, then analyzed them to revert with a plan of action. And second, he had the "cojones" to enforce his decisions and empower results. In other words, he served the Republic of Mexico admirably. In fact, early in his six-year term, I was told that the Mexican

President considered allowing US forces to secretly conduct "neutralization" operations of the kingpin traffickers from every Mexican drug cartel, much in the way US forces took out drug traffickers in the popular movie *Sicario*. Obviously, this proposal never came to fruition. Admittedly, I cannot say for certain that Calderón wanted the Mexican drug kingpins killed. I was not present during any such conversation.

In fact, I never met President Calderón. To a Mexican President, meeting a DEA Chief is the political kiss of death, particularly if the Mexican media finds out about such a meeting, and Calderón was astute in not taking that chance. Not only do the Mexican people see DEA as the overbearing "Dutch Uncle"—or as former US Ambassador to Mexico Jeffrey Davidow described it, "the Great Bear squeezing down on the Porcupine"—but they also know that what we are doing in their country stretches the limits of any diplomatic accord and agreements. In Mexico we can't kick in the doors, officially speaking, but we sure as hell find the right doors to kick in and in doing so, oftentimes must independently investigate using exclusive DEA sources, methods, and techniques. I'll say no more about that.

Mexico's suspicion of DEA. and frankly, their anti-DEA sentiment, stems back to the 1980s when DEA Special Agent Enrique 'Kiki' Camarena exposed the entire Mexico political system as corrupt and complicit in international drug trafficking. I have met with many Presidents of various countries— Nicaragua's Daniel Ortega, Costa Rica's Miguel Angel Rodriguez, Colombia's Alvaro Uribe and Manuel Santos, and of course, our USA Commanders-in-Chief George H.W. Bush, George W. Bush, and (twice) Barack Obama. I can tell you that based on my conversations with dozens of Mexican officials, President Calderón is a man of honor and action, which is precisely what

Mexico needed in 2006. What he did for Mexico is nothing short of miraculous–he reminded all Mexicans that corruption and evil do not define their country. Mexico is instead defined by its people's determination to fight these forces and reflect what the Mexican spirit is about: independence, success, and the right to be recognized as a free and responsible human being, made in the image of God. Arriving in Mexico, all of this President's "promise" meant one thing to me: I will have to work my ass off!

I moved my family into a house in a suburb of Mexico City called Interlomas (meaning "Between the Hills") and began my work. My commute from home to work, and vice-versa, routinely took close to two hours, but living in Interlomas afforded my children to safely travel to the British Green Gates School in about fifteen minutes and that was far more important to me. As I descended from the neighborhood where we lived, I would always pass a mega mansion sitting on a hillside looking over majestic cliffs. This mansion had a helicopter pad (with its helicopter usually parked there), an Olympic-size swimming pool, and the most expensive cars imaginable... Bentleys, Lamborginis, Maseratis. I frequently thought, "Wouldn't it be nice to be on that side of the tracks?"

I often imagined the owner as being the telephone corporate giant Carlos Slim or perhaps a shipping magnate or even the CEO of Mexico's state-run oil and gas company, PEMEX. Yet, as I soon discovered, the owner of this palatial estate was none other than Hector Beltran Leyva, one of the Mexican cartel kingpins that I would be tracking and pursuing. What a surreal experience to know that I'd be hunting the very man who lived in my neighborhood in a mansion on the hill that daily harnessed my envy as I drove past. I kept strategizing ways to cripple his empire and his life. But I could never get my hands on him. At the end of my assignment in the fall of 2009, the federal police raided his mansion and eventually, in November 2018, then fugitive Beltran Leyva was tracked down and killed, thanks to the hard work of our DEA office under effective, hard-working management. Well, you know what they say, "All's well that ends well!"

Here's a quick example of how I had to bring new synergy into the Mexico office. In March 2007 I was notified that FBI and DEA intelligence had identified a mainland Chinese pseudoephedrine trafficker, Zhenli Ye Gon, in Mexico City. With a knowledge that I construed as support from the Chinese government, Ye Gon was illegally importing hundreds of tons of "pseudo" into Mexico for the sole purpose of supplying the cartels with the most important precursor to manufacture pure deadly methamphetamine, most of which would be smuggled into the United States. When US Ambassador Antonio Garza convinced the Mexican government of the toxicity of methamphetamine to Mexican and US citizens alike, Mexico passed regulatory laws prohibiting the import and sales of pseudoephedrine. Facing these new obstacles, Ye Gon simply spent a few million dollars of his ill-gotten gains and built his own pseudo manufacturing plant in Toluca, State of Mexico. For Ye Gon, it was business as usual to continue supplying the cartels.

When news of Ye Gon's money stash house came to light, one of our top agents in the office and his FBI agent partner coordinated with our contacts in the Federal Attorney General's office in Mexico City to target this Chinese surrogate cartel member. Within a couple of days, I received a call around 10 at night from one of the supervisors, with news that was "music to my ears": the Mexicans had seized one million dollars from the Chinese trafficker's house in Bosques de Las Lomas, a suburb of

Mexico City, based on our intelligence. I was happy to know that DEA information led the Mexican officials to make a significant cash seizure. However, when I walked in my office at 7a.m. the following day, I quickly found that it wasn't one million, but over $207,000,000 in cash! The supervisor lacked a direct liaison and simply took the word of someone who was told by someone else that a million bucks was seized. This clearly reflected that the case had little or no DEA management oversight and I had the wrong supervisor.

A committed and responsible action-oriented boss would apply hands-on management of such a case by meeting their agents and Mexican counterparts at the site to ensure that, first and foremost, DEA had accurate information about the outcome of the raid and seizures, and then, in coordination with our Mexican counterparts, collect all of the valuable evidence and intelligence that Ye Gon possessed in his Bosque de los Lomas mansion. This intelligence could be shared with our DEA colleagues in the US for criminal indictments against both the pseudo traffickers and their partner Mexican methamphetamine traffickers. Once we have those criminal indictments and US arrest warrants, more pressure is applied against the Mexican government to take enforcement action against them. Additionally, we would place those targets on the INTERPOL Watch List, referred to as the Red Notice, and get them snagged when they travel anywhere around the world and eventually extradited to the US. Since none of this was done, and had not been done for years in DEA Mexico, things were about to change.

I immediately removed that supervisor and installed a replacement: an action-minded, results-oriented performer. This top-to-down management model was how I started the office's cleansing or "La Limpieza." The following day, I heard back channel from Mexico's Attorney General Eduardo Medina Mora that my local nickname, both at the Attorney General's office and DEA Mexico, was "Genghis Gaddis," because of my no-play attitude with a direct and sincere approach. Apparently, the Attorney General was pleased to hear that DEA Mexico had that kind of boss and had been waiting for a more proactive and assertive DEA in Mexico. An example of how this new approach changed the paradigm of DEA in Mexico-Mexican law enforcement relations occurred in a discussion I had with Jose Luis Santiago Vasconcelos, the Deputy Attorney General at the start of my assignment in Mexico.

As soon as I arrived in Mexico City from Colombia, Santiago Vasconcelos asked US Ambassador Antonio Garza if he could meet with the Ambassador and myself in the American Embassy. Ambassador Garza, being the proactive and helpful manager of US drug policy in Mexico, promptly agreed. We sat in the Ambassador's office and spoke with Santiago Vasconcelos for about an hour, covering many priorities of both governments, and all of us left that meeting with smiles. I agreed to a follow-up meeting with Vasconcelos the next day. Upon arriving at his office, I, in direct and mediocre Spanish, told the Deputy Attorney General, "Look, Jose Luis, yesterday we had a nice and constructive conversation with the Ambassador, but now you and I need to push away the bullshit and talk about how we can work outside of corruption and get a few things accomplished." Santiago Vasconcelos preferred to joke about women, talk about tequila, and nice things to do while living in Mexico City, but I'd have none of it. Ghengis Gaddis was on the hunt for drug traffickers and so were the DEA personnel in Mexico. I swore to myself that I'd not let down those brave DEA men and women in Mexico.

I'd like to take a quick detour to highlight China's influence in international drug trafficking and direct participation in attempts to weaken the power of the United States of America. Ye Gon was not the first Chinese national to work directly with the Mexican drug cartels. In the 1980s, Chinese shipping brokers were illegally shipping pseudoephedrine throughout the Pan-American "tunnel" in Central America and into Mexico to supply the methamphetamine manufacturing in our Southern neighbor's country that was all destined to poison citizens of the United States. By 2000, the traditional "mom & pop" methamphetamine labs, where amounts of an ounce or two had been manufactured, were replaced by mega meth labs in Mexico that were producing 500+ kilograms, or more than 1,000 pounds, of high-grade meth in any single production cycle. Then the "meth" was smuggled into the US to markets intended to "hook" a consumer population that turned into an army of addicts.

Meth addiction is unlike any other drug in that it sparks violence at the personal level. Sure, crack cocaine and heroin are commonly associated with community violence, but an absolute fact is that addiction to meth reduces the user from human to beast, resulting in the complete mental breakdown of basic empathy, giving way to barbaric emotions and maniacal acts of violence. Addiction to meth has victimized thousands in our society, from the addict to everyone who comes into contact with him or her. Furthermore, the physical manifestations of chronic meth use are an obvious curse upon the human body, as apparent from "meth mouth" and the physical changes captured in the mug shots on "Faces of Meth." (Do a Google search and prepare to be horrified.)

When I served as Chief of Global Enforcement, China relied on excuses such as lacking a national database to monitor and regulate the production and flows of pseudoephedrine, which challenges any level of credulity. China, a Communist country and highly regulated society, easily controls the actions of its people; enforcing drug laws in China today is far easier than in free Democratic nations. In truth, China did not want to regulate the illegal flow of pseudoephedrine for two major reasons. Firstly, their government received mass amounts of revenue from this illegal international enterprise, and secondly, they know where the poison we call methamphetamine will end up: in the United States of America, weakening our society coast-to-coast from the inside out.

If we fast-forward twenty years, we see that China continues to execute this same strategy, only using fentanyl instead of pseudoephedrine. Fentanyl, a highly addictive and extremely dangerous drug, is equally being funneled into Mexico from China and mixed with Mexico's heroin, then tableted into pills that appear to be legitimate pharmaceutical medications. The intent and, frankly, success of this Chinese "war space" strategy is to defeat the United States as their primary government foe. China will not attack the US head-on, but instead effectively attacks us with the cancer that our citizens keep spreading by inadvertently consuming Fentanyl embedded in other illegal substances. How ironic!

I speak highly of Attorney General Medina Mora. Well, upon my arrival in Mexico in 2006, Medina Mora was actually the current Secretary for Public Security, later becoming the Attorney General, Mexico's Ambassador to the United States, then eventually a Mexico Supreme Court Justice. Medina Mora and I discussed how DEA and the federal police could work together for a successful bilateral outcome against the dark evil of drug cartels in Mexico and their poisonous tentacles extending into the United States. Unfortunately, in our first meeting, Secretary Medina Mora was dealing with a major social and political disturbance in Oaxaca, Mexico, not to mention the protests of the 2006 presidential election outcome. Oaxaca was the center of Mexican Nationalistic sentiment that demanded absolute freedom and independence from ANY foreign nation or association, especially regarding the "Great Bear" USA. In fact, an American journalist named Brad Will was covering the riots in Oaxaca when he was shot and killed by a local mob. It was not the greatest time for me to occupy the Secretary's time, and I knew it. However, even though under substantial pressure and stress, the Secretary displayed diplomatic grace and professionalism that established a relationship that I value to this day. A year or so later, President Calderón selected Medina Mora as the Attorney General, and I worked even closer with him throughout my assignment.

The Attorney General, much like his President, took on tough issues and made difficult decisions for a better country. While we worked together, he had decided to act on hard evidence and arrest his own Deputy Attorney General as well as high level federal police commanders, all complicit with narco cartels. In other words, I'm a big fan of Eduardo Medina Mora, and when President Calderón nominated him from the position of Public Security to the Attorney General of the Republic, I knew instantly that I had a partner whom I could trust and rely on for bilateral efforts and successes. I was right; in combating international organized crime and drug trafficking together, we had many successes. I loved riding that wave!

That's not to say that all of our bilateral operations were successful; they were not. During my tenure as the Regional Director in Mexico, our office endured failed operations due to corruption, arrests of Mexican officials and assassinations of others, leaks to traffickers by a myriad of our host country counterparts, and of course, basic incompetence in the Mexican mechanics of government. But I can say with confidence that the DEA Mexico offices were operating on all cylinders—a fact I was proud of when I eventually handed off the Director's responsibilities and duties to Agent Joe Evans, the man I had pushed for my job in 2006, in September of 2009.

CHAPTER 23

AFTERLIFE

D EA employees often refer to their retirement as "The Afterlife." This phase of life is dramatically different than their active DEA life, and for obvious reasons: in rapid fashion, one's entire focus radically shifts from a life spent investigating, tracking, and capturing narcos—replete with all of the inherent drama and adventure that entails—to living a more (for lack of a better word) "normal" lifestyle. Whenever I try to describe The Afterlife, I think of the particle theory, in which there is nothing but a blank void in between the particles that make up matter, and all of those particles are in constant motion in all physical states. The DEA "life" is the equivalent of those particles in constant motion, while The Afterlife is more akin to the dull space between those particles. Needless to say, the very thought of this phase fills all agents with dread. By the way, agents also lose their beloved official government vehicle upon retirement, just to make matters worse. One more final kick in your tired, old ass on the way out the proverbial career door.

As enjoyable and fulfilling as a DEA agent's work is, though, make no mistake: it almost always consumes their life to the point where they're spending more time with their fellow agents than they are with their own immediate family. That's not to say that the Intelligence Research Specialists (analysts), Diversion

Investigators, and all other DEA employees aren't equally committed to their work, but an agent's life is dominated by it: their job *is* their life. And as with any major life change, when that ends, people react in a variety of different ways. Some agents read self-help books on how to cope with retirement, some take on new and unusual hobbies, some just can't sit still and immediately look for a new line of work, some start drinking too much (or stop drinking altogether), some quell their discomfort with travel, some wax poetic and begin to wallow in nostalgia, posting decades-old DEA photos on Facebook and waiting for others to comment, and some do a combination of the above. But whichever path one ultimately chooses, it's never an easy transition.

Another oft-used DEA nickname for The Afterlife is "Finding the Chute," which is just another way of saying that the Agent had better hurry up and find (and pull) his "chute" when jumping out of DEA, because if they're not mentally and emotionally prepared, their "landing" will be brutal. Leaving a job is one thing, but leaving a job *and* a cause is quite another. And when you spend so many years giving of your entire self to just one cause, one common mission, that passion consumes you. Everyone has to learn it the hard way: having a passion, then having to let that passion go—well, better to have loved and lost, etc., but some might argue that the loss of that passion is just too devastating to make it all worth it. Many people would probably be surprised by the fact that for far too many agents, that devastation is just too much for them to bear, and their Afterlife ends shockingly soon—despite the federal pension the DEA provides, or the opportunities they have to actually explore new paths. In the end, a lot of retired agents simply can't find the chute.

During my lengthy tenure with the DEA, I worked my ass off to make my way up the ladder. By the time I retired, I felt incredibly fortunate to have earned the coveted position of Chief of Global Enforcement Operations, DEA Headquarters. As Chief, I was tasked with serving as liaison between an enormous number of people, including all Senior Executive Service members of the agency, as well as the Regional Directors and Special Agents-in-Charge in the international and domestic theatres (the military term for a region of focus), and the DEA's numerous headquarters entities. The majority of my work necessitated a constant focus on classified projects, investigations, and international affairs—things I couldn't openly share or discuss then, or now—but one thing I can say without hesitation is just how much I adored this job, and every single thing that came along with it. This was my second assignment in Headquarters (or "tour," as we prefer to say in the DEA), and my first time in Washington as a Senior Executive Service (SES) member. I'd worked as an SES before, in the field, for six years: three in Bogota, and three in Mexico City. In those field positions as Regional Director, I was incredibly fortunate and often kept some impressive company, frequently meeting with US Congressmen and Congresswomen, Department of Defense, Justice, and Homeland Security Heads, and even two radically different but equally gracious US Presidents: George W. Bush and Barack Obama.

For a guy who'd thrived off of career operations it was a dream job, and to this day I miss walking through those lofty old doors at 700 Army Navy Drive. My office was on the eleventh floor of Arlington Virginia Headquarters, in the West Building, and faced one of the most famous landmarks in the world (not to mention the world's actual largest office building): The Pentagon. I still can't believe the view with which I was gifted:

all the walls were windowed, so I didn't just get to revel in the beauty of The Pentagon each day, but also the Washington Monument, the Capitol Building, and the expansive majority of all of Washington, DC, itself. People often forget that DC was literally built to impress visitors, and as far as I'm concerned, it still does. It never fails, especially when I'm driving by one of the monuments at night. Illuminated and blanketed in shadows, they all seem somehow even more grand.

But eventually, I knew I'd have to face "The Afterlife". Facebook posts and self-help books not being my thing, I went with the "finding new work immediately" option. I certainly had plenty of motivation: first and foremost, at forty-nine and still a relatively young man, I was hardly ready to settle into any kind of retirement at all. In my mind, it was a very slippery slope from embarking upon a more relaxed lifestyle to spending all day in an easy chair playing Pinochle and Backgammon. I'd also just barely come down from the constant adrenaline high that was my career, and thus was not exactly inclined to segue right into rest and relaxation mode. Most pressingly, though, I recognized that for years I'd been daydreaming about owning my own business. Many times over I'd already envisioned the details, the highs and the lows, the profits and the losses, and how I'd relish managing all of it, with no one to depend on but myself. Eventually I realized that this years-old fantasy should actually be my new reality, and that it was time to create and tackle the work I wanted. Myself.

My professional life wasn't the only thing undergoing dramatic changes. At the same time as my entire work world was upended, I found myself grappling with an equally jarring shift in my personal life: a second divorce. As I've said before, the DEA life is not easy on any marriage, and mine was no exception. Still, it was a total shock and surprise when, after what I had considered to be seventeen years of a strong, wonderful relationship, my then-wife decided to step out of our marriage and into the arms of another man. What I'd thought of as a seamless plan—working at DEA Headquarters in DC for the final eighteen months before the official start of The Afterlife (routinely returning to Carolina on weekends and special occasions), then starting our new chapter together in our lake house in beautiful Belmont, North Carolina in order to relax and watch our children grow from high schoolers into young adults—well, what's that quote from President Dwight Eisenhower? "A plan is necessary and effective until the time when you need to use it."

I was devastated. Without a doubt, this was the toughest period of my life, but as both a father and a survivor, I had to find my way through it. I also had to toughen up and face some sobering facts: first, that I wasn't infallible; in fact, I was far from perfect. My ego took a beating, but I came to understand that even "Genghis Gaddis" wasn't immune from experiencing an unexpectedly broken marriage. Second reason: now I *had* to work. Thanks to the divorce, my savings income was cut in half, and I still had two young daughters rapidly approaching college age. Although I'd long been diligent about saving for their college tuitions, the divorce complicated that. Again, my trusty plan had proved useless, and I realized that if I wanted to help prepare my children for the life they wanted (and that I wanted for them), I'd better start earning. I was ill-prepared, too, for the unexpected onslaught of expenses aside from tuition (the sum of which is terrifying enough), the ones that all parents face when their children head off to school: new clothes, work books, text books, computer-related materials, field trips, parking...every day, there seemed to be an expense I hadn't anticipated. It was time for a new plan of action, and I knew that in order to succeed I'd have to move fast. So that was that: I was going to become a self-employed, one-man road show and success in the security world, and my girls were going to start their own new chapters at the very same time.

And so, on March 31, 2011, it became official: After twenty-five years, one month, and thirteen days, I was no longer an active DEA Special Agent. Gone along with my title were all of the things that the title had entailed, all the rights, the authorities, the responsibilities, and, of course, all of the privileges. Who was I without all that, and what now, exactly, would be my new identity? Had I even chosen the right "chute," and would I nail the landing? And even if I did, could this new identity and life ever possibly compete with the life I had as a DEA Special Agent? After much soul-searching, it finally dawned on me: why was I wasting time competing with myself? Maybe nothing would ever hold a candle to the action-packed adventures of my (now) former existence. But really, who cared? Best thing or next best thing, it didn't matter to me anymore. I was now a Security Risk Management expert, founder of G-Global Protections Solutions, Inc., ready to use my knowledge and skills (not to mention my hard-earned, diverse and impressive network of connections) to serve others—and to reap an ample paycheck at the same time. Before I knew it, I was off and running.

My first project was the development of a corporate security plan for a golf community in Cabo San Lucas, Mexico, just the environment to complement my fresh start and fresh outlook on life. Between the festive environment and the frequent, much-welcomed visits from my daughters, I was in an ideal place for the nascent stage of this new phase of life, and I felt free enough to finally let go of the chute. Ten months quickly passed, and then ten years. True to form, I didn't exactly slow down. Throughout the past decade I've conducted corporate and legal asset recovery cases, testified in corporate federal civil cases, managed civil investigations in international property disputes, owned and operated executive protection details (EPDs) for corporate and high net worth clients, developed security risk management programs and crisis management portfolios for a plethora of Fortune 100 companies, and served as a hostage negotiator in kidnap for ransom and extortion cases in Yemen, Nigeria, Guatemala, Mexico, Brazil, and the US. I've even been fortunate enough to guest lecture at several colleges and universities on topics including transnational organized crime, the DEA Experience, policing in America, and opportunities in corporate security. I've loved all of it, and was floored when I realized that not only was I fulfilled and inspired, I was also making double what I had been as an agent. My original plan had gone awry, sure, but what took its place has turned out to be far better than anything I could have imagined.

Another brother in "Blue" Chris Feistl (right) and me (left) during a cocaine raid in Miami, 1989

No matter what obstacles we face in the future, or what obstacles I faced in the past, with my incredible family with me, I will always be a very Blessed man. My chute opened just fine. And I'm ready for the next jump.

CHAPTER 24

THE HERETIC

I n 1929, then-President Herbert Hoover said something that resonates with me still. In a publicly delivered speech, Hoover said that while the prohibition of alcohol had indeed been a noble experiment, it was also a failure with the majority will of the people. Soon after this very public acknowledgement of defeat, both liquor and other brew-based offerings became officially legal once again. Since then, our society has seen results both good and bad from the growth of the alcoholic beverage industry. But, just as that growth has allowed for more jobs and overall financial gain (in hindsight, actually, maybe I should have skipped law enforcement and opened up a beer distributorship, or ten), for many people (both then and now), the impact of alcohol in their lives has been a toxic one, wreaking havoc, misery, and self-destruction. And the preference for teetotaling is hardly obsolete. Even today, there remain a number of communities who still believe that alcohol should never be sold on a Sunday, or after midnight, or sold at all (rendering them a "dry" county). Rules vary from city to city but, despite the insatiable demand for alcohol, in more than a few places those outdated rules yet remain.

The alcohol industry is a vibrant one, encompassing a multitude of jobs and typically generating roughly ten billion dollars annually in tax revenue. To many people it routinely provides— in varying degrees—a plethora of joys: a bit of relaxation after a stressful day at work, a bit of a boost on a hard-earned weekend, or even just a complement to a simple (or, better, an extravagant) meal. It also plays a big part in social bonding and rituals: a beer at a baseball game, a glass of champagne at a celebration, a dangerously-stiff cocktail at an office party. The flip side, of course, is well-established. Addiction wreaks havoc in so many ways, and affects so many people, that it's become a destructive part of nearly everyone's lives in one way or another. Alcohol dependency has destroyed families, derailed careers, damaged friendships and loyalties, weakened the mind and body, and decimated the human body and psyche to the point where it is, time and time again, someone's actual cause of death. From a consumer standpoint, it's not difficult to estimate the financial effects on the population (admittedly, the statistic is nonetheless shocking, with alcohol use costing the American taxpayer roughly two hundred and twenty-four billion dollars per year[6]), but how to estimate the other cost? How do we possibly rate or rank the emotional cost of all the suffering, disappointments, heartbreak, and loss that we experience as a direct result of alcohol addiction?

Now, so many years after our failed attempt at prohibition, it feels as if we may be headed down a similar path with yet another substance: marijuana. To be very clear, I am not officially promoting the legalization of any "scheduled," controlled substance (including marijuana), rather, I am bringing the debate further into the light. My hope is that in doing so, we can try to evaluate the situation together, and do our best to ensure that we make as few mistakes as possible when it comes to making decisions about legality moving forward. Reflecting upon Hoover's "noble experiment" is, suddenly, prescient and potentially helpful. "Water finds its way" (another saying I think of often), and the fact that twenty-seven states (as well as Washington, DC) have already legalized both cannabis possession for medicinal and recreational use only reinforces my worry about history repeating itself.

Let's start with some basic facts concerning usage: At present, it's widely estimated that between twenty and forty million American citizens over the age of twelve (approximately 7.5- 15 percent of the population) already use marijuana in myriad forms for both medicinal and recreational purposes. With that great a number, there lies a potential resource for hugely informative studies on the medical development and possible health benefits (and/or adverse effects) of marijuana use. By now, most of us know someone who benefits, health-wise, from cannabis use. I know several, and all from very different walks of life: a former US Army soldier who uses it to relieve his crippling, post-war PTSD, a close friend who uses it to treat the severe pain that stems from her scoliosis, and another friend, an elderly man, who depends on it to alleviate his immense physical pain from cancer. The issue is a very personal one for every family and individual, but before I broach the topic of legalization as it pertains to one's morals (or its impact on the realities of day-to-day life), I want to address some of the issues around the impact of drug-trafficking not just in America, but in countries all around the world.

While drug use and dependency has remained a constant throughout the years (in the US and elsewhere), the current drug of choice has always consistently evolved: acid gets replaced with ecstasy, cocaine gets replaced by bath salts, heroin gets replaced with fentanyl, etc. In fact, fentanyl-related deaths are now the *leading* (!) cause of death in the 18-35 age bracket. Yet marijuana remains irreplaceable. And the other seemingly permanent factor, as the drugs themselves come in and out of fashion, has always been our nation's insatiable need for something, anything, to satiate the lust for (and ensuing addiction to) both illegal *and* pharmaceutical drugs. It's not an overly Rockwellian sentiment to point out that, not too many years ago, the citizens of the United States of America seemed far more focused on service to others, acts of self-sacrifice for the community, hard work, and commitment to family than they do today. Times change, and cultures change, and in many ways that's a good thing. Stagnancy would be the death of our society, and it's most ideal for everyone to progress and grow and learn from our past mistakes. But for all the leaps forward—social justices, voting rights, environmental awareness—we've also seen a steady decline, in many aspects of our lives, ethics, and disciplines.

On the heels of the casual drug use explosion in the '70s came a steady deterioration of not just a shared morality or respect for others, but humankind's overall priorities and approach to life in general. This is evident not just in our rampant drug use, but also in how we've come to approach our ethics, lives, and neighbors. I'm no saint, of course—far from it. But it's clear to me that as the years pass, more and more people give less, while taking more. I've seen people come together in the worst of times and help one another, but I've also seen people cheat, steal, and do whatever they can do in order to get ahead—or to simply get by. Nightly newscasts focus more and more not on community service or positives but on showing us our decaying city streets, littered with addicts and flagrant acts of crime and vandalism.

It seems as if we, as a society, have actually begun cheating ourselves in countless ways. We cheat ourselves by limiting our education; we cheat ourselves by opting to not assist others more; we cheat ourselves by choosing to escape our own reality through the use of both drugs and alcohol. Complacency and laziness are becoming the norm, as is the desire to avoid the often admittedly harsh circumstances and challenges of modern-day life, so is there anything even remotely surprising about the fact that there's such a rapidly rising momentum to legalize marijuana? Again, unlike almost all other drugs, widespread use of marijuana has been a constant: it's never been "replaced" with a newer, trendier drug (while we can admit that cannabis infused gummy bears and other assorted edibles are all the rage, that's just another way of ingesting the drug), and its popularity has only increased over the years. It also appeals to the widest demographic, with devoted users ranging from grandparent to grandchild. And as its popularity spreads, THC potency grows, as has the number of ways one can both purchase and ingest it. The industry has exploded within the past few years, and even though the now countless number of CBD-related products may seem both ubiquitous and innocuous, it's still all cannabis.

The government can't realistically say that marijuana was, is, or ever will be, replaced by another drug, so how is it still defined as a "gateway" drug? And regardless, the gateway drug argument doesn't impact the current trend involving all of the *other* drugs, does it? I believe that the anti-marijuana contingent has lost that particular battle. And while these may sound like the words of an unabashed heretic, as a DEA agent with over four decades of experience dealing with and witnessing the US marijuana-trafficking phenomenon, I can comfortably say that not only have we lost that battle: it wasn't even close. Marijuana and hemp aren't going away, and probably never will. Again, its popularity has only grown, and cannabis is far more popular today than it's ever been before. The fact that its appeal isn't limited to recreational use, and that newer, better medicinal uses are being developed every single day, only increases the role it now plays in our society. With its growing importance in the medical world, it's also earned a certain amount of previously unimaginable respect, in a sense. Doctors, scientists, and even consumers continue to develop more and more medicinal uses of cannabis and its critical THC component in both oils and plant material.

I may be going out on a limb here, but one possible option to consider (and here is where the heresy comes into play): what if we decriminalized marijuana at the federal level, leaving its legal status up to each US state and territory? By decriminalizing federal marijuana laws, the path would be cleared for more medical research initiatives, and researchers could more confidently promote the use of cannabis for treatment (and even as a possible cure, in some cases). Each US state could then figure out, independently, how exactly to manage the manufacturing and distribution of cannabis. Pot is a drug, like alcohol and tobacco; and it is also a drug that is commonly used in the United States by people from 12 to 92 and beyond.[7]

I've heard arguments from several colleagues that keeping cannabis as a Schedule 1 narcotic offers law enforcement the ability to lock up career criminals who are out on the streets, even after they've previously committed (and been arrested for) heinous violent and drug trafficking crimes. The "three strikes" law allows law enforcement to use a marijuana trafficking charge as that "third strike" against those criminals who weren't incarcerated for the appropriate amounts of time because of legal loopholes, incompetent or lazy prosecutors, or judges who might—like a lot of people sometimes do, no matter the profession—let their personal bias interfere with their jobs. With all due respect to prosecutors and judges alike, my rebuttal to that argument is that loopholes are *our* criminal (anti-) justice problem and should be fixed individually rather than covered up by using a cannabis charge. In other words, we should focus on doing correctly what should have been done correctly in the first place. I firmly believe it would be a mistake to conflate cannabis use with serious criminal activity, and if that stance makes me a heretic, so be it.

Other factors to consider:

• The public demand for medical treatments and recreational use is increasing exponentially and motivating more states to approve legislature to legalize marijuana use (with some states making eligibility dependent upon certain conditions).

• The financial costs related to law enforcement (on both a state and local level) when it comes to marijuana-based crimes is a constant drain on resources desperately needed elsewhere. Shifting some of that focus to far more dangerous drugs like fentanyl, methamphetamine, ecstasy, cocaine, and heroin would make an immediate, enormous shift in the paradigm. And if we decriminalize cannabis federally, then each state would still have the option to utilize private investigative firms and consultants to regulate and enforce cannabis control management programs.

• It may not seem like the most logical connection, but the legalization of cannabis could actually have a huge, lasting impact on our educational system, for starters. As a country, we have continually failed to pull together and find a way to direct tax money to where it is most sorely needed: to fund, build, and support our schools, mental hospitals, civil infrastructure, etc. If states legalized and taxed the sale of cannabis, the tax revenue would be staggering, and that money could be used to literally *improve* the health and well-being of our citizens, as well as the infrastructure of the country itself. In 2020, the tax revenue from cannabis sales in California and Colorado *alone* exceeded $1.4 billion dollars.

- Similar financial gains could follow as a result of legalization when it comes to our prison systems. By not imprisoning marijuana traffickers, dealers, and users (and often imprisoning those who have committed the smallest of "crimes" (busted on a college campus with a handful of joints, for instance) with sentences that are egregiously unfair, not least when compared to the many other, shorter prison sentences given out for far worse, *actual* crimes), just think of how much money the federal and state governments would save.

We face a real crisis (alongside our drug war crisis, of course) when it comes to the deterioration and condition of our prisons. The financial costs (and terrible human effects, and the failure to properly help, or rehabilitate, our prisoners) are endless: maintenance, prisoner supervision, housing, food, clothing, medical care, etc. Far too many of those imprisoned are there for minor infractions, and it's both a waste of our money, and a sometimes completely unwarranted blow that could negatively impact someone's life forever, potentially sending them into a spiral that just sends them right on back to the violent and unstable prison environment they'd finally left behind.

- On a larger federal scale, the truth is: currently, the federal effort toward combatting marijuana is essentially useless, because the effort itself is barely existent. It's certainly nowhere near the effort spent fighting the growing epidemic of addiction and crime related to other, more harmful drugs (and understandably so). In my own experience, I've certainly found that the feds have fatter fish to fry: perhaps they, too, realize that it's not only a losing battle, but one of very little significance compared to the battle being fought to combat the damage being done by newer, more addictive substances.

If we simply take the responsibility of marijuana enforcement off the federal plate, we clear a path for state authorities to dictate policy and enforcement, while the feds can then focus wholly on the heavier hitters. And believe me: those drugs, and the damage they have wrought, are more than enough of a challenge for them to tackle. And DEA is not the only influential force for "field discretion" in determining whether or not to prosecute a cannabis case.

During my career I have witnessed multiple instances of a Department of Justice (DOJ) US Attorneys Office simply refusing to prosecute a DEA-presented case that targeted only marijuana traffickers due to prosecutorial thresholds. A prosecutorial threshold is a minimum amount of drugs seized in a case that could be shown either in photographs, video or in person (or a combination of all), to the Court and jury. This is quite understandable in that federal cases and prosecutions should focus on more deadly drugs and the traffickers behind them. For example, during the 1980s I would have never been able to federally charge and prosecute only a marijuana case with less than a half-ton already seized and "on the table." This was due to the US Attorneys Office in the Southern District of Florida exercising a prosecutorial threshold of 1,000 pounds. This stark reality in which the DEA worked and lived was a fact of life in Miami during this troubled "cocaine cowboys" era and possibly remains a practice to this day

- Might it be possible that the decriminalization of cannabis at the federal level would have such an enormous impact that it puts an actual end to the seemingly boundless control both Mexican and Colombian drug cartels currently enjoy? Would they be able to rebound at all, and/or to sell any other drugs in the same way that they currently do with marijuana trafficking, which creates immense wealth that further corrupts governments? And is it not worth it, to legalize and see if that longtime fantasy can actually become a reality?

- If that reality did *not* come to fruition, would the cartels (both foreign and native to the US) still be able to earn enough revenue to maintain their control and continued corruption of their governments? Would they be able to afford the weapons that help give them that control? Would the narcos find that the revenue from cannabis is no longer a valid enterprise, and is instead a colossal waste of their time and energy, and thus stop? And, again, is the immeasurable progress and change that would result from that paradigm shift not something worth aiming for?

These are not uncommon questions, nor are they new ones, but they are, as of yet, still unanswered. If we are to move forward at all, we have to come together, have an earnest and frank discourse, make a plan, and then take definitive action. The actual outcome of our actions will remain uncertain until we really do, finally, find these answers. That's a requirement. And as always, I can only hope that our current—and future—leadership find that narrative path and take those next steps, because we truly have no time left to waste.

CHAPTER 25

NOBLE EXPERIMENT

In an earlier chapter, I told the story of an undercover case I worked very early in my career targeting a former Congressman from Colombia and his cocaine distribution empire, culminating in his arrest and effectively dismantling the organization. After I had received six hundred kilograms of the Congressman's merchandise from a Colombian supply source, I briefly considered a hypothetical scenario: If I were to inject cyanide into this particular load of pure cocaine, how many people would die in America consuming it? Who would these true victims be? And through one act of poisoning, how many addicts—and their families, friends, counselors, and employers—would be spared the pain attached to this six-hundred-kilogram haul of cocaine?

Of course, it's a preposterous idea. It only crossed my mind because we were not stopping the drug supply (and we never will). The fact that we were losing the drug "war" left me with an emptiness, intensified by knowing that the incessant American demand for drugs was the obvious and principal reason for it. Never would DEA truly contemplate such a nefarious and criminal act, yet as a drug warrior who'd sworn to defend the Constitution and protect law-abiding citizens of the United States, I couldn't help but to mull over this absolute crazy fantasy.

A cocaine seizure from the Congressman (Left-Right) DEA Special
Agents Alex Dominguez, AD Wright, Chris Feistl and me.

Indulge me for a moment. The cocaine we had seized from
the Congressman tested ninety-eight percent pure. Let's consider
what inevitably would have happened to that kilo if it were not
in the hands of DEA. Each kilogram of ninety-eight percent pure
cocaine would have been cut to multiply that kilo by ten. Ten
multiplied by six hundred is six thousand kilograms of standard
user-quality cocaine at about ten percent purity. There are one
thousand grams in a kilogram, so one thousand multiplied by six
thousand equals a staggering *six million grams* of ten percent
cocaine. A gram unit is the typical retail quantity a "recreational"
user or addict would buy at any given time—perhaps a few
grams more if a party or other memorable event were in their
schedule, but generally speaking for most users, a gram is all
that's needed to kick off a fun night on the town. Had that coke
been poisoned, say with cyanide, that's *six million* citizens that
could be murdered and dropped from our world as examples of
poor decision-making.

I used to think to myself, "I bet if that load of coke were poisoned
and passed to Jaime and Martin Ceballos for distribution, we
could damn near stop the demand for cocaine in the Eastern
United States within one month." Think about it. After six million

users—doctors, lawyers, members of Congress (remember *Charlie Wilson's War*?), business owners, realtors, engineers, construction workers, truck drivers, teachers, healthcare aides, childcare workers, stay-at-home moms, and even some kids under the age of eighteen among them—died from poisoned cocaine, most common users would just stop using. But maybe I'm being optimistic. For maximum impact, we'd have to do the whole thing again on the West Coast and in the Central US. Slip a little cyanide in eighteen million dosage units of cocaine and distribute the stuff throughout the remaining regions of our insatiable consumer markets. The result—*eighteen million deaths from cocaine use*—would definitely do the trick and end this nation's drug abuse problem. Or would it?

When I first had this ludicrous thought, little did I know that, years later, the Mexican cartels, supported by Chinese fentanyl suppliers (who, in this case, I would characterize as cartel subsidiaries) would actually profit from a similar scheme. At present, thousands of casual users and addicts are dying or being hospitalized every day across our country from fentanyl overdoses, after ingesting what they believe to be cocaine. No "body" of the US government, including the DEA, would ever commit such a horrid act, but the drug cartels have no hesitation or reluctance in having done so. You might be asking yourself a logical question, "Why would a drug supplier kill their own buyers? Wouldn't that hurt their bottom line?" The answer can be summed up in two words: *calculated risk*. By infusing their user-quality cocaine with deadly fentanyl hydrochloride, the chances of creating permanent addiction, and thus continued use for their products, outweigh the potential consequences of negative public opinion from overdose deaths. Drug cartels already have a bad reputation, so they scoff at the idea of more criticism—in fact, they far prefer an addictive population to supply drugs, even deadly drugs, for their enrichment. There is no honor among thieves!

Fentanyl and synthetic opioid overdose deaths have occurred at unprecedented levels in the past four years, yet it has not stopped that addiction or significantly changed the behavior of users. Compare that to the COVID pandemic, which altered human behavior—no family gatherings, no attended funerals, no public worship, no sports events, and forget about going out to eat!—practically overnight. Despite the well-known risks, drug addicts continue to ask for (and pay for) synthetic opioids like fentanyl-laced "killer" substances!

As a young agent, I was full of "piss and vinegar," wanting to take down the world responsible for drug abuse. Now, I realize that my mind worked in the macabre. In my wild fantasies, an effective and quick solution would only take a slight tweak (no pun intended) to Nancy Reagan's National Drug Control Policy: "Just Say No!...or you die!" Obviously, I was wrong—such horrendous tactics would not end addiction or the drug war.

After I let that scheme go, it occurred to me: I was in the DEA not to hurt drug users but rather to help them. If the actions of the DEA—and in particular, DEA Miami's Enforcement Group 4 and my teams in Central America, Mexico, Colombia, Atlanta, Georgia, North Carolina, and even at DEA headquarters in Arlington, Virginia—could help and not hurt one child of God from suffering at the hands of drug use, I would be sufficiently doing my job.

Our current drug control policy is not a war. Rather, it's like living with cancer and using an assortment of Band-Aids to cover the open wounds that metastasize throughout the body we currently call the United States of America. There is no cure for drug abuse; if there were, we would have already found it after a half century of spending billions of dollars and losing countless human lives.

Cocaine, like heroin, is a notorious killer. But does cannabis really hurt society in the same way other scheduled drugs do? I don't think so, and like the "noble experiment" as described by President Hoover in 1929, this scrutable topic can be adequately resolved through good faith and serious discussions, both inside our government and out, backed by a reasonable plan to sincerely determine our nation's path to resolve the inextricable cannabis policy with which we are currently living. Let me reiterate: I do not believe smoking marijuana is a good idea; it's simply not healthy. Regularly smoking marijuana does not promote optimal physical and mental performance on a sound productive body. But then again, neither does regularly drinking alcoholic beverages.

Speaking of drinking...US Treasury Special Agent Elliot Ness, the famous Prohibition agent of the 1920s and 1930s who brought down Chicago mobster Al Capone, actually spent sixteen years of his law enforcement career defending the country from the danger of alcohol abuse. Did Agent Ness make a difference? Before, during, and even after the official end of Prohibition, factions of society aggressively supported the Volstead Act, while others just as vehemently decried it. Two camps opposed one another on the issue—either *for* Prohibition or *against* Prohibition—much like the opposing camps on cannabis use today.

Although Prohibition was controversial, Agent Ness knew he had to enforce the law and that law protected lives, in one form or another. Elliot Ness thought he made a difference. However, Ness was a contradictory man and conflicted on the issue of alcohol. There's an interesting quote widely attributed to the former Prohibition agent. A newspaper reporter posed the question, "Agent Ness, what will you do after the Volstead Act is repealed?" His response was, "Well, I might just have a drink." A more sobering incident: in 1942, Ness was caught covering up his own hit-and-run accident and, it's been speculated, may have been driving drunk just before the crash happened.

There's another major consideration when strategizing the drug "war." How do we expect to defeat an enemy that travels lighter, is better equipped, funded, and armed, has equal or better intelligence, and a stronger personal motivation (money, power, control) than nearly any other criminal industry?

As drug demand continues at a high rate, we are never going to defeat the traffickers on their own turf, and with the prolific expansion of Mexican drug cartels in the USA, their turf now includes our country. So, we must think of new, progressive and innovative ideas for America to get its arms around our drug use and drug trafficking problem.

Keep in mind that the foreign-born drug traffickers we are trying to defeat have no *applicable* legal restrictions—meaning that corruption and government ineptitude allow traffickers to avoid accountability of the law. They have a total disregard for international borders and an unlimited supply of resources to complete their missions. Whereas our budgets are tight, we must respect foreign sovereignties, must follow the rule of law, and our inter-agencies infighting is a constant. Given all that, shouldn't we begin to consider focusing exclusively on what our top drug trafficking threat priorities are today and not fight on with the battles that we all know are already lost—cannabis, for example?

I know we think of ourselves as Ameri-*cans* not Ameri-*can'ts,* but when it comes to lawfully regulating and enforcing marijuana laws in this country, trust me: We can't. We have found ourselves at an impasse and can't negotiate our way around it.

Indeed, almost one hundred years after Prohibition, it appears our nation is again divided on a similar issue, and it is time for a holistic discussion about the true will and choices of our citizens. Enough of the hypocrisy in developing opposing narratives, which are largely politically motivated, to what is right about cannabis use in America. Our government, a body chosen by the People, should consider:

- Creating one, and only one, national drug enforcement intelligence center that uses US military, law enforcement, and intelligence services' capabilities. If information derives from outside of those resources, the center must absorb and process through it for investigation and casework. I realize that this entity would seem to have too much authority and power, but without it, there is no way to disentangle the confusion that already exists in our national drug enforcement policy programs.

- We constantly hear "Defund Police!" Who are the police but a microcosm of society? They exist to serve and protect. Is the law enforcement officer who enforces the laws of our country, even prohibition laws, a good or bad reflection of society? We, as a nation, need to get off of that "defund police" political stump and focus instead on supporting good policing and holding the extraordinarily low percentage of bad police officers accountable.

- Is cannabis good or bad for society? Allow science to dictate the need. If the cons outweigh the pros for recreational cannabis use, does it scientifically have positive medicinal use? If so, how can we engage in the process of regulatory administration? Can the US citizenry rely on our states to make cannabis Prohibition laws?

- Is there a form of cannabis, such as oil extracts, that can be effectively used for the betterment of people? An example is cannabis treatment for NFL players, active and former, who endure years of physical punishment to do their jobs. Many NFL players have expressed that cannabis helps them endure intense physical and mental pain and, in some circumstances, has prevented them from committing suicide.

- How would we manage cannabis usage with military personnel, law enforcement, or first responders? Would it be similar to addressing the alcoholic beverage use policy? We need to think "down the road" because the future is now. I do not suggest that the men and women in uniform—both military and civilian—be treated equally when it comes to drug use regulations in employment policy. We live in a country with an all-volunteer police and military system. If rules prohibit the consumption of any adulterating substance, then it is what it is, and volunteers don't have to be there if they choose. For example, can airline pilots drink alcohol within twelve hours of operating an aircraft? Hell, no! I believe we all agree that's a prudent workplace policy.

- Could tax revenue from cannabis sales, at least in part, be directed to law enforcement and drug and alcohol dependence programs that lessen the negative impact of substance abuse in our nation?

- Could the US government accept the People's will and a find place in society for cannabis in a similar way it accepted alcohol, and move forward? What a concept!

From the tender age of twenty, which was four decades ago, I wanted to serve my nation in a way that I could look back and say, "I made a difference." I believe most Americans, and most people around the globe, feel that way.

For more than twenty-five years, I worked in the Drug Enforcement Administration, and then just over ten more years in Security Risk Management Consulting, trying to help people and businesses build a safer world. My mission was to offer some light from the darkness of drug traffickers and other predators. During my career, I have had a few "close calls" and consider myself lucky to be writing this book. I am grateful to God.

Occasionally, someone will ask me if I thought I made a difference in this world. After all, illegal narcotics are still readily available on the streets of the US and suffering from the scourge of drug addiction remains. My answer is always the same: I did my best and I did what I could. And in the process, if I saved a single life from an overdose, spared one spouse from being battered by a "high" abusive partner, or eased the worry or heartbreak of a parent whose child didn't come home safe at night, I just might have accomplished something.

Yeah, I made a difference.

And what will I do after cannabis is federally decriminalized and, in some states, made legal for medical or recreational use? The answer is that I'd vote in my state over the cannabis legalization issue, one way or the other, based on proposed options to decriminalize cannabis possession, while developing steep regulations to keep cannabis products as safe as possible and only in the hands of lawful users. It is time for an honest, open discussion on America's drug control policy and whether or not cannabis should remain a scheduled narcotic.

Like Elliot Ness did with drinking alcohol, might I just give recreational smoking marijuana a try? No, I wouldn't need to. Cannabis is not for me, but I'm not everyone. Now, if I get sick and my doctor legally prescribes me a medicinal solution with cannabis? Well, that's a question open for discussion if and when that scenario arises.

About Dave Gaddis

Dave Gaddis was a Drug Enforcement Administration (DEA) Special Agent for more than 25 years, serving in some of the most dangerous drug enforcement regions around the world. From Miami to Mexico, Colombia to Nicaragua, he worked investigations against the Mexican and Colombian cartels responsible for supplying all of the cocaine and most of the heroin destined to the United States. Beginning as a criminal investigator in Miami's Cocaine Cowboys era in the 1980s, he finished his career in 2011 as the Chief of Global Enforcement Operations at his DEA Headquarters office overlooking the US Capitol and Washington, DC skyline. Dave is currently retired, and lives far off the beaten path in a quiet and peaceful setting. His profound experience in criminal investigations and US Drug Control Policy has enabled him to speak professionally around the world on both topics.

https://www.a-nobleexperiment.com/

Footnotes

[1] Alex Dominguez wrote a book about some of his DEA stories, which I highly recommend.

[2] Check out Chris Feistl on Netflix's *Narcos-Colombia*.

[3] Meredith, another Heaven's Warriors, was killed in the line of duty in 1994 when her surveillance plane crashed in Peru.

[4] While on another field operation in Mexico, I asked a Mexican police officer what he hoped to find inside his MRE, and he said "twenty pesos so I can go to McDonalds!"

[5] Chris Feistl was the chief consultant with Netflix's *Narcos: Colombia,* "Cali Cartel"

[6] www.cdc.gov

[7] Although the vast percentage of users are in their twenties and thirties, per the 2020 California report on marijuana abuse statistics.

Made in the USA
Columbia, SC
30 July 2022

64337980R00172